THE
WAKE
UP

THE
WAKE
UP

CLOSING THE GAP BETWEEN
GOOD INTENTIONS AND REAL CHANGE

MICHELLE MIJUNG KIM

hachette
BOOKS

New York

Hachette Go, an imprint of Hachette Books
Hachette Book Group
1290 Avenue of the Americas
New York, NY 10104
HachetteGo.com
Facebook.com/HachetteGo
Instagram.com/HachetteGo

First Edition: September 2021

Hachette Books is a division of Hachette Book Group, Inc.

The Hachette Go and Hachette Books name and logos are trademarks of Hachette Book Group, Inc. The publisher is not responsible for websites (or their content) that are not owned by the publisher.

Editorial production by Christine Marra, Marrathon Production Services. www.marrathoneditorial.org
Print book interior design by Jane Raese
Set in 11-point Minion

Library of Congress Control Number: 2021941863

ISBNs: 978-0-306-84720-2 (hardcover); 978-0-306-84721-9 (ebook)

Printed in the United States of America

LSC

Printing 1, 2021

To Grandpa.
We did it!
I love you. I miss you.

CONTENTS

AN INVITATION

A few years ago, I attended a training on convergent facilitation offered by Bay Area Nonviolent Communication. Despite my excitement, I was late. I could blame the ever-so-cautious Lyft driver, but really, I can only blame my social anxiety that desperately wanted to avoid casual networking before the session started. When I arrived, I found myself staring at a packed, quiet, and attentive room filled with fifty or so eager learners inside a church-turned-lecture-hall with fantastic acoustics. Why is it that when you want to be invisible, your presence becomes the loudest? All of a sudden, I was a scattered, clumsy Hulk destroying everything on my way to the last empty chair in the middle of the room, hitting people's faces with my oversized bag, dropping my phone, making way too much noise, and hoping nobody could see me. *Sorry. Oh, oops, gosh, are you OK? I'm so sorry.* I tried to act nonchalant, but my face was already burning with red-hot shame from the stares of the annoyed on-timers.

Just when I thought I was in the clear with my butt in the chair, the facilitator, as any excellent facilitator would, decided to name the awkwardness we were all trying to bypass. "What should we do with latecomers?" she asked the group. I smiled unnaturally while cursing myself in my head. "Glare!" someone shouted out. Others chuckled, and I sank deeper into my chair. The facilitator smiled gently and asked, softly but with weight, "And what does that achieve?" The room fell silent, and the energy shifted. No one was laughing anymore. "Uh . . . make them feel bad for being late," the person answered tentatively. "Right . . . what else can we do?" Other hands went up. Different, more compassionate answers started flowing in. "Pull them aside and catch them up on where we are." "Share notes with them during the break." I let out a silent sigh of relief and pulled out my notepad. The class had begun.

In 2017, I cofounded a diversity, equity, and inclusion (DEI) education company called Awaken out of frustration that so much of corporate diversity training is whitewashed and white-led, ahistorical yet outdated, and lacking ties to the broader movement toward social justice. As a team of majority queer people of color, we set out to deliver experiential DEI workshops more relevant to the times while creating compassionate space for critical dialogues with people across a wide spectrum of awareness and identities. To date, I've spent an estimated 2,500 hours on discovery calls with organizations across all industries—tech, media, nonprofit, government, education, health care—and countless more hours facilitating workshops and the conversations inside them. I've been face-to-face with thousands of people having what many call "uncomfortable conversations," learning where and why people get stuck and identifying the most common missing links that hinder us from moving together.

At one workshop, a middle-aged white man entered the room and said, "Well, this is going to be a giant waste of my time!" Most of our workshop participants aren't as honest or incensed as this man who wasn't afraid to let everyone know his true feelings about the mandated diversity training as part of the company's renewed commitment toward diversity. In fact, most people we meet tend to be outwardly eager and curious, indifferent (or checked out), or quietly skeptical: there are those who are keen to connect at a deeper level right away, sharing their raw emotions with an admirable level of vulnerability, while others quietly observe with a learned dose of cautiousness. Some express shock and exaggerated disgust at examples of overt forms of racism and sexism, while others share their lack of surprise given the sobering realities they've lived through. Some ask questions out of genuine curiosity, while others feel exhausted by the elementary level of awareness that has remained stagnant despite escalating violence. Some express hope and excitement for the future, while others roll their eyes in cynicism from the repeated pattern of broken promises and disappointment.

Over and over, I've watched diverse groups of people come together in search of solidarity only to find themselves on completely different pages. Many of us believe that denouncing the same evil puts us on the same team, but why doesn't it feel like it? When we gather, despite our shared condemnation of various social injustices, the subtle yet pronounced ways we are misaligned become quickly evident. As we speak over and around one another using similar words but with drastically different definitions and contexts, our disparate beliefs and survival reactions are inches away from crashing into one another. Marginalized people's anger, hurt, cynicism, and disappointment are palpable, as are feelings of fear, shame, confusion, and anxiety coming from well-intentioned people desperately wanting to catch up and be part of the solution. The temptation for people to throw their hands up and go about living their individual lives is substantial, not just for people with privileges to disengage but also for people who are exhausted by the continued cycles of harm and misalignment too. Our misalignment is costly, and our ability to connect with one another is in urgent need of inspection and serious repair.

So, if simply denouncing injustice is not enough to connect you and me, what holds us together?

BUILDING A CONNECTIVE TISSUE THROUGH SHARED PRINCIPLES

The speed at which multiple cycles of trauma are being refreshed every day calls for me to dive deeper into the waters, below the loudly crashing waves of reactive motion, into the quiet and steady place of groundedness. In that space of internal calm, I'm reminded to recall the principles that have guided me through the toughest of times since I first became politicized at the age of eighteen. These grounding principles—ones I've learned, shared, and practiced in my own life and with thousands of people to catalyze meaningful change—are what I'll unpack throughout this book. The language of social justice and the latest list of cultural faux pas will continue to evolve, but what I'm striving to share with you are the things that won't change with the latest news cycle: the fundamentals of the work that will help you create your own list of action items no matter the context, anchor you to be critical in your understanding and approaching of any situation, and enable us to move together to create social change.

In the chapters to follow, we will explore how to think about pressing issues, from the ongoing grappling over inclusive language to the debate around diverse representation, with discernment and criticality. We will pressure-test our proclaimed commitment to this work by asking ourselves what we are willing or unwilling to give up. We will learn about the difference between "cancel culture" and accountability and how to apologize and recover from mistakes. We will deep-dive into learning about white supremacy and its unrelenting manifestations in our society and within ourselves. We will challenge ourselves to go beyond intellectualizing this work to actually *doing* the work, and to actively participate in the disruption of toxic cycles of oppression that are killing all of us. We will grow our capacity to hold multiple truths at the same time and to stay in complexity and nuance rather than demanding simplicity or quick, self-congratulatory fixes that we have been taught to crave. We'll ditch the rigid "best practices" that only apply to a particular context with a preselected audience and replace them with frameworks and questions that can be applied to any situation. Finally, we will work to build resilient relationships to cultivate a community of values-aligned individuals with whom we can continue the work in solidarity, while allowing ourselves to experience joy, healing, and freedom along the way.

My ultimate goal is to make these foundational principles accessible and actionable for as many people as possible so that we can spend more time working toward our collective vision and less time trying to recover from the same cycles of misunderstanding and hurt that have us backtracking time after time.

TRANSFORMING OURSELVES TO TRANSFORM THE WORLD

As we march toward the ultimate vision of our collective liberation—a world where all of us, beginning with the most marginalized among us, can live free from oppression of all kinds and with uninhibited opportunities, respect, dignity, abundance, safety, and joy—we will experience many rude awakenings. They typically begin with our sudden realization of others' suffering that we've been snoozing on, followed by our becoming aware of the choices we have to make, now consciously, to either alleviate or exacerbate it. In other words, we wake up first to the external world, which offers us an opportunity to wake up to who we are in relation to it.

I write to you from a place of shared learning, as everything I've written for you applies squarely to me too. Each time I wake up to a different reality that many have been living and fighting in without my awareness, I feel an overwhelming sense of guilt for being late to the battleground. And though my personal reckoning makes me want to scream to awaken others, sometimes I hesitate, afraid of saying the wrong thing. I desperately want to do something to make a change *right now,* but quickly realize the answer isn't so simple. I am eager to learn and go deeper, but I don't want to be an added burden. I fumble, and each time I cause unintended harm, it hurts.

I imagine that this feeling of vulnerability, fear, discomfort, and inadequacy is quite common among people trekking through the social justice journey—and especially among those in the midst of their own waking up, activated and provoked by different alarms. Many of us want to do the right thing *so badly*, and yet sometimes it feels like we cannot predict the outcome of our well-intended efforts. So, some of us bottle up all of our good intentions and hold on to them, waiting for someone else to tell us exactly what to do, while others mistakenly end up burdening those already carrying more than their fair share in our rush to help. In these messy, uncomfortable struggles, however, we can awaken our capacity to do the deep work of transforming ourselves in order to change the world alongside others. And we learn that though mistakes and contradictions are inevitable, we also have the capacity to practice accountability and sharpen our discernment. As most of us already know, the work of living in alignment with our values rooted in equity and justice is an ongoing journey without a destination, and one that cannot be reduced to a checklist.

One of my favorite movement facilitators and thinkers of our time, adrienne maree brown, quotes Maurice Moe Mitchell in *We Will Not Cancel Us,* who said, "We have to have a low bar for entry and a high standard for conduct."[1] While everyone's bar will look different, my prerequisite for anyone wishing to be a part of the journey is their earnest desire to change themselves with honesty and accountability. If you've been outraged by the cruel reality of inequity and oppression but haven't quite figured out a way to turn your rage into action; if you are earnestly looking for answers as to why we sometimes don't seem to be on the same page despite our proclaimed shared values; if you are no longer satisfied with the empty promises of surface-level diversity programs; if you are frustrated by the ever-ubiquitous yet changing lists of "things you can or cannot say" that leave you feeling unsettled and more confused; if you are feeling overwhelmed while trying to process your own life, now freshly contextualized through your growing consciousness; and if you find yourself wanting to say, "I know I'm late. But I'm here now and ready to get caught up," not from a place of entitlement but from a place of genuine desire to connect without causing unintended harm, then, my friend, this book is for you.

While I believe this book will be beneficial to many on this same path, it's important for me to clarify that I did not write this book specifically *for* a white audience. Throughout my life, I've seen how centering whiteness can have damaging outcomes that replicate patterns of violence: diluted words, ahistorical analysis, co-opted movements, prioritization of comfort over truth telling, hyperintellectualization of human trauma—all in the name of pragmatism and meeting white people where they are, which ensures that we all remain in the status quo. Instead, I've committed myself to writing outside the white gaze, so that the words and lessons I share with you will have the sustainability and effectiveness we need to disrupt.

At the core of this book is the belief that we cannot transform the world without transforming ourselves and our relationships to one another first. So many visionary thinkers and leaders have repeated this mantra—among them, Audre Lorde, Grace Lee Boggs, Ericka Huggins, Mariame Kaba, Mia Mingus, and adrienne maree brown—and you'll see repeated validation of this truth from the universe of stories I share here. The poison of oppression doesn't just live in the systems; it lives within each of us and in the way we interact with one another and inside our spheres of influence, be it our workplace, school, family, or neighborhood. We must recognize our complicity in harmful systems as much as we see ourselves as part of the solution. Only from this place of honesty can we truly commit to living our lives in alignment with our proclaimed values.

Our waking up to others' suffering isn't enough; change requires that we wake up to *ourselves*—our complicity, our power, and our capacity to transform ourselves and the world around us.

Change means growth, and growth can be painful. But we sharpen self-definition by exposing the self in work and struggle together with those whom we define as different from ourselves, although sharing the same goals.
—Audre Lorde[2]

ABOUT ME AND MY WHY

I am a queer, Korean American, immigrant, abled, cisgender woman with class and education privilege. I grew up in Korea and moved to the United States when I was a teenager, where I grew up low income and became politicized as a queer youth activist. After college, I began my career in the corporate world with deep shame and guilt, believing it was the only way to make enough money to support my family and bring my mom to the United States from Korea. Over the years, I've had the honor of serving on and working with many incredible community organizations, from San Francisco Human Rights Commission's LGBT Advisory Committee to local nonprofit boards working on critical issues led by marginalized communities.

My entire life, I've straddled starkly different spaces, people, and cultures, whether as the bridge between my Korean immigrant parents and the English-speaking world or as an Asian person in America living in a hyphenated space sandwiched between neither-Black-nor-white. As a bisexual, queer woman, I've been told I'm not gay enough in queer spaces and not woman enough in straight spaces. As a grassroots youth activist turned management consultant, I've been called too radical in corporate spaces and pegged as a sellout in organizing spaces. I've been inside fancy boardrooms overlooking the New York skyline with some of the wealthiest people in this country, and I have stood face-to-face with riot cops ready to baton me down, my eyes watery from rage and air polluted with tear gas and pepper spray. What I have come to know is that the distance between these paradoxical spaces is always ocean wide and yet paper thin, and similar dynamics repeat inside them, albeit through different expressions. And though I often yearned to be embraced by and to fit into one home ground, it is in the in-between spaces that I am able to connect the dots, with my mixed-and-matched lessons serving as a bridge to possibilities rooted in compassion. My work over the last few years as an independent consultant has been focused on creating connection without distortion and understanding without dilution. My purpose has been to accelerate the mobilization of people earnestly wanting to join the movement and to share the lift of education and foundation building required for sustainable change.

For as long as I can remember, I have been living in a perpetually escalated state of being, experiencing extreme switches of emotions, ranging from shock to despair, numbness to rage in any given day or hour based on the latest crisis against humanity. One unmistakable feature of systemic oppression is the cumulative anguish and exhaustion endured by marginalized people as a result of the persistent and rapid onslaught of violence in society. *This can't be sustainable,* I often think to myself, and yet, in some twisted way, it signals that I am alive, alive and human enough to feel and care. Remarking at the unrelenting nature of this work, people often ask, "What motivates you to keep going?" My answer is simple, though crude. I do this work, and continue doing this work, because people are dying. People I love are dying. Our young and elderly people are dying. Too many Black and brown people; Indigenous people; Asian and Latine* people; women and femmes; queer, trans, and nonbinary people; poor people, disabled people, and many living at multiple intersections of marginalized identities are dead or are in the process of dying because our systems and cultures were built to dehumanize, violate, exploit, and ignore those who do not conform to the norms of white supremacy. I don't know if there is any other reason more compelling or urgent than not wanting to see people we love die. And I also know the forces that are killing the most marginalized among us are omnipresent in my life, their weight crushing me in subtle and overt ways. Against this backdrop there is undeniable desperation in my work, and knowing all of us are needed, I yearn for deep solidarity beyond the pretense of performative unity.

I didn't always believe that such solidarity was possible to achieve, not with privileged white people or with anyone I saw as being "colluders" in systems of oppression. At my first job out of college, a senior manager thought LGBT stood for Lesbian, Gay, Bisexual, *Together.* The same person, a cis straight white woman, once asked me, the only person of color on the team, to fish out a document from her trash can. When I formed a women's employee group at a men-dominated tech company, I was told by a C-level executive, a straight white man, to not bring politics into the workplace. "Don't create problems that we don't have," he said as we walked past a large

---

*I've gone back and forth between the terms *Latinx* and *Latine* and have decided to use *Latine* after studying the requests of a number of trans and nonbinary Latine people who acknowledge the importance of using a gender-neutral term (versus *Latino* or *Latina*) while also using a word that is more pronounceable and conjugation friendly for Spanish and Portuguese speakers.

glass boardroom filled with only men. I was once told by a woman of color executive that I should put my hair down more often, smile more, and wear heels. I was sexually harassed during my first week at a new company, and the pattern has continued at every workplace I've been a part of except my own.

As my rainbow bubble ripped, I became jaded. I found myself asking, "What's the point?" It got increasingly difficult for me to believe that a better, more just world was possible. I started losing my appetite for change, consumed by my growing disappointment toward the people and systems that were causing harm. And I thought that in order for me to stay critical, angry, and less complicit, I couldn't offer compassion, not to myself or others, because it felt like an excuse or a betrayal to the movement.

Years later, I realized that my cynicism about people's intentions and their ability to transform had made me a terrible agent for change. I realized that we can, and must, be critical, angry, and compassionate all at the same time to keep ourselves from getting stuck and to allow ourselves to hope, heal, and forgive—not just for others but for ourselves too. Today, I believe striking the right balance between compassion and criticality is imperative to creating sustainable change while inviting more people to be part of this important movement, and I've tried my best to model this in this book.

MY TEACHERS

As Audre Lorde, a self-described "Black, lesbian, mother, warrior, poet" and my greatest influence, said, "There are no new ideas, just new ways of giving those ideas we cherish breath and power in our own living."[3] None of the concepts that I share in this book are new: they are lessons I've learned and practiced over the years from and with mentors and visionaries who have dedicated their lives to this work. What I offer instead is my synthesis, interpretation, and practical application of these principles based on my lived experiences. I invite you into my personal journey of living them out, with both triumphs and shortcomings. While I cannot promise perfection, I have written with honesty.

I remind myself often of the countless teachers who have shaped my beliefs, approach, language, and experience, both consciously and subconsciously. My most profound lessons have come from those who have taught and lived in the world of grassroots organizing, philosophy, and poetry, and I'm excited to share what I've learned from them. To start with, I learned about my fear and fearlessness, queerness, and the power of language and discernment through the fiery words of Audre Lorde, whose book *Sister Outsider* shook my world upside down and rebuilt it when I was in high school. I learned about the importance of self-transformation and inter-racial coalition building from Grace Lee Boggs, whose legacy of visionary organizing I hold close to my heart as it reminds me of my dignified place in the solidarity movement as an Asian American woman. I am eternally grateful for the work of those who came before me, as well as those who are leading the continuously evolving journey of social justice, in particular queer and trans Black, Indigenous, and people of color (BIPOC) movement leaders from whom I continue to learn today. I have tried my best to trace my knowledge back to its sources and credit my teachers throughout the book—a small yet critical act of preserving legacy, especially important for historically marginalized and erased people.

I write this book with extreme care to do justice to the teachings of these great minds, and also because I know what a privilege it is to be able to historicize my own stories, when stories of so many marginalized people are too often told by those who did not live them. Writing this book is my act of reclaiming, healing, and honoring not only my life but also my an-cestral lineage and its intergenerational trauma and wisdom passed down without adequate institutional memory. Thank you for bearing witness, and for choosing to journey alongside me.

WELCOME, I'M SO GLAD YOU'RE HERE

In this precarious time, I write to you with audacious hope in my heart. While I am no stranger to the deeply challenging nature of this work, I have also seen so much goodness in it. I do this work because I have witnessed how transformative it can be for individuals, organizations, and our soci-ety and how a courageous act by one individual can quickly snowball into revolutionary change when we work in principled solidarity. I do this work because on the other side of this arduous, emotional, breathtaking labor is abundance, joy, and humanity that can withstand the opposing force. I do this work because I believe in *us*. And I believe we are capable of learning and growing beyond our wildest knowing if we allow ourselves to truly commit to the principles of the work.

I invite us to turn inward and get our foundations right before we rush outward, not because we have to be perfect but out of deep respect for those who have been on the front lines before us, and because we each deserve to tap into our expansive humanity, live it to its fullest extent, and use it to uphold others.

There is space for all of us here. You are needed in this work. So welcome, dear reader. Let's find your seat and let me share my notes with you.

> To make a revolution, people must not only struggle against existing institutions. They must make a philosophical/spiritual leap and become more "human" human beings. In order to change/transform the world, they must change/transform themselves.
> —Grace Lee Boggs[4]

Note on content warnings: To create a safer and more choiceful reading experience, I've provided content notes for sections containing detailed descriptions of topics that may be particularly distressing. Given the subject of this book, I did not provide content notes for when these topics are mentioned as part of a statistic or without a graphic description. Despite my best efforts, I realize I may have fallen short as my decisions are undoubtedly influenced by my own biases and experiences. Nonetheless, I hope to make clear that an absence of a warning note does not invalidate your own needs and their importance. While I'm unable to anticipate every reader's needs, I hope that some of these notes will help you to experience the book on your own terms.

PART 1

GROUNDING

CHAPTER 1

WHEN "GOOD PEOPLE" CAUSE HARM

In 2017, I began a private Google doc entitled "Shit I've Heard" for my own diversion. It's a bulleted list of, well, interesting things I've heard while working as an external DEI consultant and facilitator. Some still make me cackle (or want to take a nap), while others remind me of the urgent need for this work. Here are some that made the list:

- "I'm not white; I'm more, like, pink."
- "Privilege? Shouldn't people talk about that in therapy and not at work?"
- "We need to do something with white men first so they don't feel excluded."
- "Our current team? We have a diverse male."
- "Talking about microaggressions makes me *macroaggressive*."
- "Can we do an all-day workshop on all things diversity so we can learn everything there is to know about it? We want to be able to say we're diversity experts by the end of the day."
- "It's never enough, no matter how much we try. What's the point of even trying?"
- "Most of the men in our company are homosexuals [long pause] I think."

Sentences like "We care about diversity but we just don't want to lower the bar," "Can you not use the words *white supremacy*?" and "We don't want to talk about politics at work" didn't make the cut because their ubiquity made them feel less noteworthy. Some might assume these statements came from oblivious white men, but they'd only be about half right because some also came from people of color and women. But *all* of them were said by people currently leading high-profile organizations, and nearly all of these people are in positions of power as CEOs, CHROs (chief human resources officers), or even heads of diversity. And one hundred percent of them genuinely believe they are one of the "good ones" fighting against racism, sexual harassment, workplace discrimination, and the like.

Do *you* consider yourself a good person?

You try to keep up with the news, especially events and issues impacting marginalized communities.

You volunteer when you can and teach the children in your life to treat everyone with respect and kindness.

You always leave a tip—most of the time 20 percent, especially during the COVID-19 pandemic.

You choose not to shop on Amazon; you're not always successful, but you try.

You bring your own grocery bag to the market. You recycle *and* compost.

You've donated to Black Lives Matter and even have a sign on your window.

You've read *So You Want to Talk About Race* by Ijeoma Oluo, and Dr. Ibram X. Kendi's *How to Be an Antiracist* is placed prominently on your shelf.

You know you're not perfect, but the most important thing, you tell yourself, is that you *try* to be a good person. And most of the time, on a scale of saint to neo-Nazi, you feel pretty good about being above-average good—you know, disarmingly imperfect but all-around pleasant, benign, and sometimes even inspiring to those who aspire to be as good.

But the unappealing truth is that despite our desire to be good, we still cause harm, sometimes unknowingly and sometimes—perhaps more troublingly—knowingly. I don't know just how long my own list of harm is and whom I have hurt, but I suspect this list is as long as my "nice" list.

Many of us desire to be good people and to be *perceived* as being good by others. We are quick to jump in, wanting to know immediately how we can help, what we can do to spread our goodness. Ironically, this desire to identify, and be identified, as a good person can sometimes be the very barrier to our ability to actually create good impacts. These misleading concepts of a "good person" and what it means to "do good" are where we should begin to reorient ourselves and interrogate our impulses so that we can reflect on our larger role within the context of social justice work, while preemptively reconciling the tension that will undoubtedly arise when the way we see ourselves conflicts with our impacts.

Here are three lessons to get us started.

1. *GOOD* IS A TRANSIENT ADJECTIVE, NOT A PERMANENT IDENTITY

Social psychologists have long identified humans as "social animals"[1] whose need and desire to be accepted by others influence our behaviors. Our desire to conform to social norms intensifies if we belong to a specific cultural or social group, where we become concerned about our reputation and standing with other ingroup members.[2] For example, think of the self-professed feminist cis heterosexual men who wear T-shirts with the words "This is what a feminist looks like." They've read bell hooks and Audre Lorde, they are staunch supporters of the #MeToo movement, they believe in and practice consent, and they work diligently to ensure their partners orgasm. I used to be fascinated by them, like they were an endangered, exotic species that only a few with trained eyes could spot in the wild. During my romantic and professional time with these men, including activists and community leaders with social clout, however, I experienced some of the most disorienting forms of misogyny. Their misogyny came in different shapes and sizes, from gaslighting to patronization, and was difficult to detect under the cover of their public persona as "feminists" and "good men." Though I don't believe they were intentionally causing harm, without recognizing their complicity in the system they were too quick to denounce publicly, they failed to catch themselves when they ended up perpetrating harm in subtle and insidious ways that hurt the people they claimed to care for.

And many of us are guilty of this. We use all the right words, quoting our favorite social justice writers and boasting our academic understanding of social inequities—and yet in our most intimate relationships, we replicate the very harm we are trying to distance ourselves from without realizing it. White people do this with people of color, cis people do this with trans and nonbinary people, heterosexual people do this with queer people, abled people do this with disabled people. We are quick to declare that we are safe and that we "get it," but there is nothing safe or trustworthy about the ways we cause harm that multiply into macrolevel inequalities, all while we wear our "good person" name tags.

Being called an "-ist"—racist, sexist, ableist, and so on—can feel like a deadly attack on our character, causing us to either shrivel up and disappear into the abyss or fight tooth and nail to defend our goodness. The label *racist*, especially, which we often register as an identity rather than an adjective, is so abhorrent that we'll invest all our energies digging up receipts from that one time we donated to a racial justice cause; or quickly labeling distant acquaintances belonging to that particular racial group as our "friends"; or explaining away harm we caused by emphasizing how we never *intended* to be racist and demanding instant forgiveness or, worse, an *apology* for this incredulous misunderstanding about our character. But just like *good, racist* is an adjective that can be used to describe any of our actions, behaviors, thoughts, practices, systems, and narratives that uphold the false superiority of whiteness while maintaining unequal power dynamics—and we don't need to be wearing a white hood to perpetuate any of these everyday egregious acts of racism. Any action can be racist if it perpetuates the injustice rooted in white supremacy and racism. Any action can be transphobic if it perpetuates the injustice rooted in cisgender supremacy and transphobia. Any action can be sexist if it perpetuates the injustice rooted in patriarchy and sexism.

Part of our obsession with wanting to be seen as a good person is fueled by our binary thinking: if we are not good, then that must mean we are bad. And this good-bad binary leads us to expect moral perfection from those whom we've put on a pedestal while brutally punishing those we've crossed off as being bad. There is no room for mistake, growth, or transformation, and we do everything in our power to not cross over to the "bad" list because we've seen what happens to *those* people. This binary narrative hinders us from separating our actions from our identities, making it incredibly difficult to receive any critical feedback about our impacts, feedback that could in turn make our actions better aligned with our desire to do good. To be an absolutely "good person" is a near-impossible goal we cannot meet, and it puts our entire ecosystem at risk by setting all of us up to fail.

There are no good people because we don't always do good things. Rather, we are just *people,* engaging in different behaviors and actions, causing different impacts to different communities, making decisions that either benefit or deter the movement toward social justice. We are not, and cannot be, one-dimensionally absolutely good or bad. *Good* is an adjective, not an identity, that changes with our daily actions and impacts. So rather than asking, "Am I a good person?" ask yourself, "Do my actions have a good impact?"

2. GOOD INTENTIONS DON'T ALWAYS MAKE GOOD IMPACTS

The murder of George Floyd jolted America's heart and moved people to action like I had never seen before. As non-Black individuals and organizations contemplated their response to the horrific display of police violence against Black people, different calls to action began to emerge and lists upon lists were created to steer people in the right direction to show up for the Black community. In response to the delayed outcry, many of these lists encouraged people to proactively check in on their Black friends and colleagues while urging companies to make public statements about their stance on Black Lives Matter. And so people sent text messages to the Black people in their lives, and coworkers swarmed their Black colleagues' inboxes: "How are you doing?" "What can I do to support you?" While some appreciated what they felt were genuine messages of concern, others found these messages, sent by people whose care they had not felt before the global reckoning, hollow and too little, too late. The lack of preexisting relationships, coupled with a sudden, seemingly performative display of concern, left a bitter aftertaste of virtue signaling rather than a sign of genuine friendship that transcended the momentary attention.

Some messages, in addition to checking in, included an ask for guidance on how to show up and be a part of the antiracism movement. "How can I be an ally?" "What can I do?" "Can you share resources for me to check out?" Despite the good intention to be of support, these messages quickly became yet another source of pressure and burden to be shouldered by Black people. During this time, I heard from countless Black employees inside organizations who were tasked with finding an external consultant to help conduct antiracism trainings, most of whose daytime jobs had nothing to do with

DEI (diversity, equity, inclusion) or even HR (human resources). Not one of them told me they were being compensated for their additional labor. Instead, they recognized the impossible position they had been put in, both as a person suffering from the ongoing trauma and also as someone others wanted to listen to and be led by to address the issue that had received no prior investment or attention. "I guess it's better than nothing," some said, expressing their desire to take advantage of this opportunity to make a difference, even if it meant putting their live pain and exhaustion on pause so they could educate and bring others into the fold. In the face of non-Black people centering their need to be seen as "doing good" in these moments of deep trauma, Black people were expected to hold space *and* do the work to solve non-Black people's confusion, shock, and despair, rather than being given the space they needed to grieve in peace.

This intense period reminded me of a time when I was called in by a Black friend I had known for over a decade, who gently asked me to stop texting them every time there was a Black murder in the media because they were beginning to associate my outreach with such news. I was mortified, of course, and I had to sit and reflect for a while to really understand the hurt I had caused my friend, making them feel reduced to a news-cycle response rather than a multidimensional human being whom I cared about deeply beyond these moments of sadness and rage.

Our good intentions produce unwanted outcomes all the time. We can have good intentions calling for compassion and positivity, while inadvertently silencing justifiable criticisms and righteous rage. We can have good intentions about respecting the law, while mistakenly prioritizing the adherence to unjust laws over the need to defy and rewrite them. We can have good intentions focusing on commonalities rather than differences, while unwittingly trivializing the vastly different lived experiences of inequities. We can have good intentions striving for unity and belonging, while forgetting that the belonging of some can sometimes preclude others from accessing safety. We can have good intentions asking for the benefit of the doubt, while putting an additional burden of emotional labor on those already disproportionately doubted and disbelieved.

In spite of our good intentions, we can still cause harm. Good intentions don't make good people. Only good impacts make our contributions useful in the moment. And that's why our *intent* to do good is rarely a helpful measure of progress.

3. *GOOD* IS NOT DEFINED BY THE DO-GOODER

If beauty is in the eyes of the beholder, then similarly, a good action is defined by the people whom the action seeks to benefit.

In the context of DEI in corporate settings, the entity that has committed to "doing good" is most often the organization's leadership or HR and diversity departments, and the recipient of this good is, in theory, its historically marginalized employees. If my Awaken team and I measured the success of our workshops by the praises of well-intentioned white men in positions of power, we would not be in existence today. Instead, we measure the impact of our workshops by the sigh of relief and validation from the most marginalized people in the room. This way of measuring success sometimes poses risks to our existence because people in positions of power often demand that their requests be prioritized over the needs of the most marginalized. I've witnessed time and again companies analyzing their inclusion survey data and determining they are doing just fine by looking only at the fact that the *majority* of the organization feels they are safe, included, and treated fairly, and where the majority is comprised of mostly cisgender, heterosexual, white men. By failing to set accountability metrics that are driven by the very people such initiatives have been created to support, companies end up solving nothing and doing no good.

If the good we are seeking in this world is advancing social justice and equity for all oppressed people, then we must measure our goodness by the outcomes desired and impacts felt by those to whom justice and equity have not yet been granted. And only they get to decide when something—our efforts, our impact, our apology, our outcomes—is *good enough.* Just like my well-intentioned, heartfelt check-ins did not do good for my friend, we cannot call ourselves or our actions good when our impacts failed to do good. Instead, we must commit to continuous course correction based on the feedback we receive. Being good is not about indulging in our own self-aggrandizement; our ability to do good must be guided and determined by those we're trying to do good *for.*

We often like to imagine our good acts as something that is happening only in the present moment, without regard to our past. Our sudden awakening energizes us to do something immediately, quickly, and effectively; through our actions today, we hope to be a part of the solution tomorrow. But what we need to remember is the context—that different marginalized communities have been shouldering the pain and resisting systemic oppression for centuries, and while some of us may have just now become conscious of them for the first time, our excitement to do good should never come at the expense of those who have already been doing the work without us.

Here's the thing—our actions won't always count toward good if we don't make good with our past first. We need to spend time reflecting on our history, including when we weren't there for the people we want to show up for right now. We need to acknowledge that we may have even caused harm, regardless of our intentions or awareness, and that this harm may have never been addressed. We need to measure the marbles in our trust jar with each person and each community, and refrain from asking for immediate recognition or appreciation the moment we decide to show up. Instead of jumping into the fray, let's get grounded and oriented so we can do the work in a thoughtful way and in right relationship with those who have been carrying our weight while we were asleep.

THE PRINCIPLES OF DOING GOOD: ALLYSHIP

Over the course of three years, my team and I researched dozens of different definitions of allyship and tested multiple versions during our workshops. We ultimately ended up iterating on the definition offered by the Anti-Oppression Network,* which we found to be most effective in driving clarity and practical understanding in our audience. We believe these points capture the most important aspects of thoughtful allyship, and this definition,

---

*The Anti-Oppression Network defines allyship as "an active, consistent, and arduous practice of unlearning and re-evaluating, in which a person in a position of privilege and power seeks to operate in solidarity with a marginalized group," and they cite PeerNetBC as their source. In our workshops, we found that most people required a clearer purpose for allyship (to what end?) and that the phrase "operate in solidarity" needed more direction. Some also got stuck on the fact that something needed to be "arduous" in order to be considered allyship.[3]

incidentally, is a useful summary of the lessons in this chapter and a great framework for how we can channel our desire to do good in a principled way.

Our working definition of allyship is *an active and consistent practice of using power and privilege to achieve equity, inclusion, and justice while holding ourselves accountable to marginalized people's needs.* The following breakdown of the definition clarifies what constitutes allyship and what does not:

Allyship is an active practice that requires consistency.

- It is a *practice*, not a permanent identity we get to claim.
- It is not passive. Believing in the values of diversity, inclusion, and equity is great, but it is not enough to just believe—we must actively live those values through concrete actions and behaviors.
- It is practiced consistently and over time.

Allyship requires self-awareness around power and privilege.

- It asks us to recognize our multidimensional identities that marginalize and privilege us in different ways.
- It is built on the foundational understanding that our society has not distributed power and privilege equally among different social groups.

Allyship's purpose is to achieve equity, inclusion, and justice.

- It is not to self-congratulate, promote, or validate one's virtue.
- It is not about "saving" anyone from a place of superiority; rather, it's about working toward equity, inclusion, and justice for all marginalized people.

Allyship requires us to practice accountability.

- It is about understanding the needs of marginalized people and aligning our actions to meet those needs.
- It is not allyship if we fail to prioritize or advance marginalized people's needs.
- It is practicing accountability when we make a mistake or cause harm by reflecting, apologizing, repairing, and course-correcting.

As you come to this book wanting to create good impacts and real change, the principles outlined here will serve as one of the core tools in your toolbox. Return here whenever you need, and as often as you need, to reground yourself when you feel your defense mechanisms kick in or when you feel the need to hold on to your "good person" label at someone else's expense. The fact that this work challenges us to center our impacts, rather than our intentions, is such a simple concept, yet whenever our goodwill is underappreciated and dismissed or criticized outright, it can stir up instinctive emotions of rejection and shame, leading us to be defensive or, worse, check out of the work entirely. I know how frustrating, discouraging, and exhausting it can be to hear that our actions have fallen short despite our genuine desire and effort to be helpful. I've struggled with my own sense of inadequacy and being misunderstood many times throughout this journey, and I am sure I haven't seen the end of it. But we must remember that though we may not be perfect, we have the capacity to learn and do better. And that, to me, is far more interesting than the "good person" name tag slapped on a uniform.

> *You have to get over the fear of facing the worst in yourself. You should instead fear unexamined racism. Fear the thought that right now, you could be contributing to the oppression of others and you don't know it. But do not fear those who bring that oppression to light. Do not fear the opportunity to do better.*
> —Ijeoma Oluo[4]

CHAPTER 2

KNOW YOUR WHY

CONTENT NOTE: *transphobia*

We live in a productivity-obsessed culture where we've been taught to prioritize *doing* over reflecting, to chase *quantity* over quality, and to solve for *efficiency* over relationships. So, it is no surprise that "What can I do?" is among the most commonly asked questions I get as a facilitator from people wanting to do good. Sometimes, this manifests as a more direct request: "Tell me what to do." The focus on the *what* is often reactive and urgent, and it reveals our intense craving for immediate relief. People often express their frustration when the relief doesn't come immediately or easily. One time, within the first fifteen minutes of a half-day workshop, a white man raised his hand and asked in an agitated voice, "Are we actually going to learn anything practical today?" Though we had spent the first fifteen minutes aligning on our session expectations, clarifying the participants' learning and accessibility needs, and setting group norms—all practical skills to build inclusive cultures—what I suspect he meant by "practical" was being given a list of to-dos to check off so that he could move on to another list.

Another time, my company was asked to facilitate a workshop for the C-suite executive team of a fast-growing autonomous vehicle company led by a young multimillionaire CEO. Despite my skepticism around the CEO's earnestness, we took the engagement in hopes of bringing critical and urgent awareness to the dangerous repercussions of artificial intelligence (AI) technology ladened with biased and racist algorithms that systematically, and at scale, harm already marginalized people. When I entered the highly guarded and covert office headquarters, I was asked to check in using an iPad, which prompted a handful of questions, including my name, company, reason for visit, and gender pronouns. A name tag was printed for me, but oddly, the pronouns I had provided were not printed. Scratching my head as to why the question had been asked in the first place, I proceeded to the workshop space. More than a handful of executives showed up late, and some people needed time to get fresh coffee. During my introduction in front of a team of mostly white men leaders in their thirties and forties, I threw out what I thought was an easy question to get them going: "I noticed that your registration process asks people for their gender pronouns. So, can someone share why this practice is important?" The room fell silent. I wasn't sure if people genuinely didn't know the answer, or if they were too shy, or if they just couldn't care less about being in this session during their precious workday. The CEO broke the silence, leaning back on a black leather couch and looking at me with utter disinterest. "Why don't you just tell us."

Somehow my cofacilitator and I managed to get through the entire workshop without losing our cool, and we even received positive feedback from some of the executives who implored their peers to apply what they had learned about combating algorithmic bias. A few days later, while discussing a broader rollout of the program to the rest of the company, the head of diversity asked me to shorten the half-day workshop to ninety minutes and to drop any mentions of algorithmic bias causing harm to people of color and disabled people—a direct order from the CEO. We halted the partnership altogether, and I vowed to use a much stricter criteria to screen future clients. This company continued to employ other consultants to conduct diversity trainings and recruited hundreds of people each month with a promise to create a diverse and inclusive workplace where everyone would belong.

When it comes to social justice work, we often default to asking for the *what* first (e.g., "What can I do?") because we've been trained to crave immediately actionable solutions that bring immediate results. Companies that pump out public statements explaining their newfound commitment to diversity and inclusion and racial justice are a great example of how we are quick to declare the *what* before we've even figured out the *how* or *why*, without first examining the reasons behind our actions, commitments, or desired impacts. But what many fail to understand is that the *what* without the *why* can bring about shallow and misguided outcomes that become stale, or worse, harmful.

Asking for gender pronouns is one of many inclusion trends that organizations have begun adopting without doing a holistic review or much education around its significance. People are now quick to add gender pronouns to their email signatures, conferences supply pronoun pins that attendees can wear, and companies ask visitors for their pronouns during the registration process. These implementations give people the temporary relief they're looking for while striving to create a culture that is more inclusive for trans, nonbinary, and gender-expansive people. And yet, I've been inside companies where most managers do not realize such a practice is even in place at the reception desk, and I've been to events where attendees and volunteers have no idea what the pronoun pins mean. Once, a check-in volunteer pointed at them and said, "I have no idea what they are, but aren't they so cute?" and at the same conference, a fellow speaker was misgendered by the staff multiple times with no apology. The same people who specify their pronouns in email signatures are quick to ask, "Is it a boy or a girl?" when their coworker is pregnant, and the same workplace that asks for pronouns at the reception desk does not have trans-inclusive health-care policies or access to gender-neutral restrooms and is ill-equipped to support someone's transitioning at either interpersonal or procedural levels.

The practice of sharing gender pronouns without interrogating the deeper why can end up being yet another surface-level change that *signals* inclusivity without meaningful change. These well-intentioned but incomplete rollouts become performative gestures that cause harm when trans and nonbinary people are extended invitations to join a company under the pretense of inclusion, but where there haven't been any real shifts to treat them with the promised dignity. Consider these other whys that make establishing safety for trans and nonbinary people so urgent:

- Nearly 80 percent of trans and nonbinary people report having taken steps to avoid being mistreated in the workplace by hiding or delaying transitioning or quitting.[1]
- 43 percent of transgender youth have been bullied at school compared to 18 percent of cisgender youth.[2]
- 29 percent of transgender youth have attempted suicide compared to 7 percent of cisgender youth;[3] however, when a transgender youth's chosen name and pronouns are used consistently in various contexts (at home, school, or work or with friends), their risk of suicidal behavior can be reduced by more than half.[4]

The verbal and physical violence committed against trans people, especially Black trans women, is an ongoing epidemic that robs trans people of their safety and lives every single day.[5] In this hostile reality, getting someone's pronouns right is just one small (and important) step toward creating a more equitable and just culture for trans people, but it is also not the end-all or final objective. If we can grasp the deeper why with contextualized understanding, then maybe the practice of asking for pronouns wouldn't be so haphazardly implemented without additional considerations.

The what is important, but without first understanding the why, the what and even the how eventually fall short of achieving sustainable change. Before jumping into the what with frantic and reactive energy, practice understanding the why behind every move from a grounded and steady state. This will help anchor us to ensure that the implementation of the what is fully extended to meet the wide-ranging needs of marginalized communities, while guiding us to be in alignment with our deeper purpose throughout the journey.

"THE BUSINESS CASE": THE WHY THAT WON'T GET US THERE

When asked, "Why is creating a diverse, equitable, and inclusive company important for you?" most executives are eager to provide their tried-and-true HR- and marketing-approved answers, such as: "Diversity makes us more innovative." "Diverse companies are more profitable." "We want our team to represent the diverse customer base we have." While all of these—the business case for diversity—are compelling statements that have been researched and proven to be true, building upon the business case as the foundation for DEI efforts has led countless organizations to execute surface-level diversity initiatives that fail to stick and create lasting, meaningful change. Passionate diversity advocates have been refining, rephrasing, and retelling the business case for DEI for decades, but the reality is this "good for business" reason has not moved enough companies to take action beyond slapping on a feel-good marketing slogan. The business case for diversity is simply not precise enough to elicit the kind of urgency or long-term commitment that real change requires.

The limitations of the business case illustrate the significance of having a more compelling why for doing this work. Let's play it out. If the answer to "why diversity" is to increase profitability, organization leaders are going to be deeply disappointed by the upfront and long-term investment required for creating a truly diverse, equitable, and inclusive company. For example, to create a work environment that is inclusive for caregivers, organizations will need to provide alternative and destandardized ways of working, from flexible work arrangements to benefit plans that are much more comprehensive to meet everyone's needs. To make the workplace accessible for all employees, employers will need to consider the wide-ranging accessibility needs of each employee, from designing accessible office spaces and social events to doing away with arbitrary performance requirements that are biased against disabled or neurodivergent people. To address the inevitable tension and conflict arising from having different groups of people work together, the organization will need to invest money and time to upskill their managers and conduct team trainings, taking away precious hours that could've been dedicated to securing additional revenue. Despite the investment, there may still be conflicts or even lawsuits, and the company will spend additional hours and dollars to resolve them while wondering if it's any closer to reaping the financial benefits of diversity. What's easier is creating a homogeneous group of people who think similarly, enjoy similar things, work similar hours, and don't make each other feel uncomfortable. What's easier is providing standardized working conditions, streamlined benefits, and sticking to one default way of being. While homogeneity may not bring about the level of innovation that *Harvard Business Review* links to diverse teams,[6] it can lead to a well-oiled machine of like-minded people and an enjoyable working environment for those in the homogeneous group. None of the tech giants—Google, Facebook, Apple, and the likes—have made significant progress in their Black and Latine employee representation.[7] But their bottom line? Well, I'd say their shareholders aren't complaining.

Maybe we needed the business case to get started. Maybe, at first, it was the most, if not the only, palatable and celebrated approach to discussing topics that people in positions of power did not otherwise care for beyond the minimum need to comply with the law. In fact, in the United States in the late eighties, a perceived shift in demographic—baby boomer retirements and a growing presence and availability of women, people of color, and immigrants in the workforce—made it such that diversifying the workforce was seen as a matter of economic survival beyond legal compliance for many companies, and the term *workforce diversity* was introduced into the business lexicon.[8] But the profit-motivated business case as our continuing why sets us up to betray outright the core of what we are trying to achieve in the context of social justice. When profit is the motive, then the efforts stop making sense when there is no clear threat of sustained financial loss or a major gain in the short term. A 2013 McKinsey & Company report noted that the companies that are most successful at creating gender diversity have CEOs who are committed to the cause at a much more personal level, with a passion that "goes well beyond logic and economics. . . . Numbers matter, but *belief* makes the case powerful."[9] The economic justification for diversity has outrun its usefulness, and we need to shift our underlying motivations to create and sustain real change beyond diversity theater.

Most importantly, the profitability business case, guided by its accompanying how and what, leads us to replicate harmful patterns of commodifying people ("diversity hires"), prioritizing legal compliance over doing the right thing ("Don't get sued!"), demanding quick returns on investment, and choosing profit over people, every time. It pulls us further away from asserting the need for *corrective* action to account for centuries of systemic oppression on the basis of repair and equity, and achieving *justice* in the most basic sense of the word. Put simply, we cannot expect social justice outcomes using a why rooted in capitalism.

"IT'S THE RIGHT THING TO DO": THE UNSUSTAINABLE WHY

To Learn more

Turning now to you: Why did *you* pick up this book? My guess would be that these words are not your first exposure to social justice, DEI issues, or being antiracist. So, what makes you want to be on this journey? Why do you care?

"I believe everyone should be treated equally regardless of their social identities."

"I want my children to grow up in a better world."

"It's just the right thing to do."

These are some of the common answers I get whenever I ask about people's why. There is nothing wrong with them—in fact, they are much better than most answers I've heard inside corporate boardrooms. However, from my personal and professional experience, in order for us to stay tethered to the movement, we need a why that includes *ourselves* in it, one that recognizes *our* role and culpability, not a why that is only about others. When we frame our desire to achieve social justice solely for the benefit of someone else ("I want to support others," "I want everyone else to have the opportunities I had"), it becomes too convenient for us to give up when the path gets difficult or worse, to confuse solidarity with saviorism.

This is a why that positions us as a helper, do-gooder, or even a "savior" who is motivated to help with *other people's problems,* and it has a shelf life dependent on our internal threshold for personal sacrifice. In other words, this why requires an incredible amount of self-discipline and willpower for us to stay the course and is conditional on what we're willing to give up: we're only willing to pursue justice for other marginalized people until a costly personal sacrifice is demanded of us. This why relies on our good hearts, our desire to be seen as good people, and our fluctuating emotional, intellectual, and material capacities. For most, this works until it becomes too self-detrimental ("That's going to cost me too much"), or our goodness is challenged too frequently or without acknowledgment ("I'm just trying to help!"), or the goodness isn't returned to us and our own community ("They didn't show up for *me*"). Too many still approach social justice work like community service, as if we're doing a favor for marginalized communities, as if we're spending our time and resources to be selfless and as if we're deserving of grace because "at least we're trying." This attitude is problematic as it centers us as martyrs while mischaracterizing the necessary work of addressing centuries of systemic oppression as charity work.

One year, I was asked to speak at an intimate gathering of women on the topic of interracial solidarity and intersectional feminism. There was a diverse lineup of women speakers, and the white woman organizer asked me to speak about my experience of being fetishized in the workplace from the perspective of an Asian woman and why anti-Asian bias seemed more "acceptable" compared to other types of racism. *Interesting questions,* I thought. I gave a brief speech about my experience navigating the world of tech and the importance of building trust through accountability, especially in the realm of interracial interpersonal relationships. What happened next, however, was what made the event so memorable. The white woman host, an incredibly vocal diversity consultant focused on educating other white women, spoke about her passion for interracial sisterhood and how the first step to building solidarity was to diversify our social networks and foster genuine relationships with diverse groups of people (none of which I disagreed with). She then implored that white women take more interest in learning about their people of color neighbors and colleagues and befriending them so that white people could begin to understand their pain and needs while building trust.

Launching into an activity, she instructed the audience to pair up with another person of a different race to get to know each other through a number of prompts. I proceeded to introduce myself to my partner, a middle-aged Black woman. As she glanced over at the projector screen to read the first prompt, I realized what I really wanted to say, or rather, ask. In my most sincere voice possible, I said, "I'm not trying to be sarcastic, but I'm wondering, do you actually want to be friends with white people?" She stared at me and then burst out laughing. "Um, that's a great question. No one has ever asked me that. Let me think about that for a sec . . . not really, no." We spent the time describing how we both were on the fence about the idea of making new white friends and yet how often we heard about white people's desire to diversify their social networks in order to be better allies. I mentioned how I had no interest in befriending white people for the benefit of their education, which often happened at my own expense, and that I found no joy or satisfaction in sharing my race-related traumas as their education tool. "Can't white people just do the work without needing us to be their *friends*?"

Though the event had noble intentions of bringing different groups of women together to build solidarity, its incomplete why ended up centering the interests and education of white women. These women, hungry to expand their circles, showed up, ready to listen and learn from women of color so they could be better allies. But had they paused to think about how this would benefit these women of color in turn? What would these white women be offering in the relationship and had they thought about why women of color might hesitate to befriend them in the first place? Was it too much for me to want to see more white women willing to sacrifice their social standing within their preexisting circles—workplaces, schools, social circles, neighborhoods, and more—to call out other white women's racist behaviors *without* having a person of color BFF? I left the event feeling incomplete and a little bit frustrated.

When our why positions ourselves as do-gooders going out of our way to help others, it creates an imbalanced dynamic rooted in saviorism that causes harm despite our good intentions. And even if we position ourselves as the neutral party just wanting to help with someone else's situation, we create a false distance between us and our active participation in others' oppression, ultimately failing to recognize that there is no such thing as neutrality within unequal systems.

"OUR LIBERATION IS BOUND TOGETHER": THE MOST ENDURING WHY

If you have come to help me, you are wasting your time. But if you have come because your liberation is bound up with mine, then let us work together.
—Aboriginal Rights Group in Queensland*

The most sustaining why is one that directly involves ourselves. It is one rooted not in our desire to "help" others from a place of distance but in our understanding that we each play a critical role in upholding and dismantling systemic oppressions that ultimately impact *all of us*. This why reveals that our ignorance and inaction do not make us neutral bystanders to systemic oppression; instead, they make us complicit and also harm us in the long run.

As a person with multiple marginalized identities, I am often invited to share my stories piecemeal during designated time slots. For example, I am asked to speak about my experience being a woman working in tech during Women's History Month, and being an Asian person during AAPI Heritage Month, and being a queer person during Pride Month. Many expect me to discuss sexism at events themed "women's events" and anti-Asian racism at events themed "Asian events." But what most miss in this compartmentalized way of approaching social justice is that these issues, in reality, are rarely experienced by me in silos; rather, they overlap and happen simultaneously.† Asian issues also include sexism, homophobia, and other forms of

---

*Though this quote is often attributed to Lilla Watson, an Aboriginal activist, Watson attributes the quote to the collective effort of the Aboriginal rights group she'd been a part of in the seventies and does not feel comfortable being identified as the sole author, according to an interview in 2008.[10]

†I discuss this concept of intersectionality, coined by Dr. Kimberlé Crenshaw, in further detail in Chapter 4, Unlearning White Supremacy.

oppression, and queer issues also include racism, sexism, ableism, and so on. Solving sexism alone won't free me from racism, and solving racism alone won't free me from homophobia. As Audre Lorde said in her 1982 address "Learning from the 60s": "There is no such thing as a single-issue struggle because we do not live single-issue lives."[11] Discussing our issues in silos, as if they do not overlap and as if the forces that create such oppressions do not interact and reinforce each other, obscures the connected roots of our struggles. As we will unpack in depth in Chapter 4, Unlearning White Supremacy, anti-Asian racism and all other forms of racism connect at the root of white supremacy, which also underpins many other forms of oppression like homophobia, sexism, anti-Indigeneity, and ableism.

The deepest why comes from our intimate understanding of how all of our struggles are inextricably tied, and how there can be no true liberation without all of us being active participants in dismantling all forms of oppression. I want Asian people to want to fight against anti-Black racism not only because we don't want our Black friends to get hurt, but also because we understand that its remnants live on in our own communities through anti-Blackness, colorism, casteism, and neocolonialism. I want men to want to tear down the patriarchy not only because the women in their lives hurt from it, but also because they recognize it's the same force that forbids them from being emotionally vulnerable or staying at home with their kids without penalty. I want cisgender people to want to eradicate transphobia not only because their trans nephew is getting bullied at school, but also because they understand it's the same force that confines them to outdated and restrictive gender roles within the limitations of the gender binary. I want white people to want to eradicate racism not only because their coworkers of color experience racial trauma but also because they know it's the same force that creates enduring *moral injury*, as author and trauma specialist Resmaa Menakem says, "which creates shame, and ever more trauma, in white bodies."[12] No human being gets off injury-free after inflicting, witnessing, or experiencing violence. Oppression harms *everyone,* albeit to different degrees, regardless of the role we play. Commit to realizing that systems of oppression that seemingly do not hurt us actually do, even when we benefit from them simultaneously. My dearest friend Kenny Gong sums it up succinctly: "You do the work not because it's the moral imperative, but because it's *your* moral imperative."

PRACTICE COMING BACK TO THE WHY

So, what are we to do the next time we engage in an action for justice, and how do we get beyond the what to interrogate our why? The why serves as an important implementation tool to guide both the how and the what while helping us assess the usefulness of our actions. For instance, before putting out a declarative statement on social media about how you're committed to becoming an antiracist (or feminist, or anti-ableist, or LGBTQ+ ally, etc.), ask yourself, "Why am I announcing that I am antiracist? To let my friends know that I'm in solidarity with them? To let everyone know where my business stands so we don't lose customers? To apologize for my lack of engagement until now and to invite public accountability?" And as you reflect on your why, your next questions should be: "Who benefits from this action? Am I centering myself? How might I shift my actions to better align with my deeper why? How can my actions prove useful to our shared, communal mission?" If you belong to a team in the workplace, you might ask, "Why do we want to hire more underrepresented people of color, trans people, or disabled people? To diversify our team webpage? To make more money as a result of more innovative thinking? To provide equitable opportunities to historically marginalized people because we recognize that we've been given our own opportunities under an unfair system?"

Who does our why actually serve? How might we ensure our why is being achieved through the what we have proposed? How might we shift our why, how, and what to stay in alignment with our values and to minimize harm? Consistently interrogating our why helps unearth our true motivations and goals, guides our what and how to be more holistic and precise, and grounds us for the long haul. The most enduring why is rooted in our clarity around who we want to be in this world, and our relentless pursuit of living in alignment with our values day after day.

CHAPTER 3

WAKE UP TO YOUR
HIDDEN STORIES

"Come on, let's cross!"

I grabbed my partner's hand and hurried him across the road before the light turned green. I have a bad habit of jaywalking, something I learned to do well during my college days in Berkeley while rushing to class from my off-campus apartment.

My partner was fuming. "Don't. Ever. Do. That!"

"Why? There weren't any cars coming," I replied nonchalantly.

"There's a cop car right there."

What he said next sobered me right up. "They could literally deport me for something as stupid as this. *Don't you get that?*"

My partner moved to the states in 2016 with an ambitious dream of co-founding a tech company. Though he dislikes talking about it and sounding like another Silicon Valley cliché, I think his story is remarkable. He and his family are Sikh Indians, and both of his parents immigrated to the UK from Punjab, India, before he was born. He grew up in East London, in a predominantly Muslim and Sikh neighborhood, where according to him the majority of his school was comprised of poor and low-income students of color whose families had immigrated from countries such as Pakistan, Bangladesh, India, and Somalia (his one white friend's number is still saved as "Stuey White Boy"). My partner has been a serial entrepreneur his whole life, not in the Stanford-dropout-who-builds-stuff-in-his-parents'-garage type of way but in the most traditional sense—he sold SIM cards off the street, ran a hair salon with his brother, and started a printing business that sucked all the joy out of his life. When his old friend, an Indian immigrant who arrived in London with twenty pounds in his pocket (true story), invited him to cofound a company in the United States, he decided to leave his hometown for the first time to start a new adventure. After the initial rejection and a series of appeals, he was able to obtain a business visa, but with it expiring every few years, he has been living and working in a perpetual state of anxiety ever since he arrived. Even with a valid visa, each time he entered the country, he was handpicked by the airport customs agent and held for secondary questioning, something he blames on his brown skin and Sikh name.

I hadn't realized just how vulnerable he had been feeling about his uncertain status. His entire career and the new life he had finally started settling into, which included me, all depended on a piece of paper approving of his existence in this country. Given my experience of how the world often sees Asians, particularly East Asians, as the "model minority" (a problematic and stereotypical portrayal of Asians as a monolithic group of polite, hardworking, apolitical, and well-assimilated immigrants, created in the sixties to deliberately position Asians in contrast to the Black civil rights movement),[1] it didn't even cross my mind that he would harbor such an intense degree of fear around the police. With the political climate then under the forty-fifth administration and his brown Asian identity, he believed anything—jaywalking, speeding, getting arrested during a protest, or a scathing social media post about the president—could jeopardize his chances of being able to continue living his life here.

My chest clenched, sensing the panic in his voice, and I stood there, wide-eyed, not knowing how to make him feel safe again. Maybe he had never actually felt safe here. I wondered why we had never talked about the impact of policing in our own personal lives despite having engaged in multiple conversations about the ongoing police brutality against Black people—why we had never thought of framing it as our issues, too, albeit differently. I felt bad that I had put him in danger and made him feel under threat because of my useless impatience, causing unnecessary stress and activating his fear, reminding him of his precarious status. I felt like I had failed him as a partner for not understanding just how shallow his fear lives in his body and how he has to exist with an acute alertness I don't share. I felt ashamed of my ignorance and sad that there was nothing I could do to make him feel safer. I couldn't protect him, not even with my own privilege.

The term *privilege* is often thought of as this big, heavy word that triggers a lot of uncomfortable emotions in people. But really, to me, privilege feels light and airy. Kind of like the way I felt ice-skating in fourth grade when I was still living in Korea, after my skates were freshly sharpened and the ice cleaned. I would glide, feeling the crisp air on my face and focusing on making my turns as smoothly as possible. I didn't notice the conversation that was happening in the background between my coach and my mom about the dues, or how many late nights she had to work to be able to afford the lessons. And I definitely wasn't thinking about who was *not* in the rink, or who might never be in the rink. After the session, I felt pride for practicing hard despite the soreness in my body. *Hey, you worked hard today.*

I feel this same ease of movement and lightness as I navigate society as a cisgender woman. With my stereotypically feminine gender expression, I don't even think about misgendering as a possible consequence I need to brace for; it is so far from my reality that it is as if it doesn't exist. But the same cannot be said for others. Many trans and nonbinary people share the hypervigilance and anxiety they feel every time they enter a new space, go through the invasive airport TSA screening process,[2] or even in something as simple as ordering food at a restaurant ("And what would you like, *sir*?"). Our world puts extra bags of weight on the shoulders of people who do not conform to the rigid, predefined norms of society, bags of weight others often don't notice. Sometimes, we don't even notice our own skates.

UNCOVER YOUR HIDDEN STORIES

CONTENT NOTE: *stories about homophobia, racism, police violence*

As Kimi Mojica, my dear friend and one of the most skilled facilitators I know, says often, we all have a universe of stories that makes us who we are. When asked, "Tell me about yourself," we often launch into describing our lives in a series of milestones and achievements. We focus on things we've learned, overcome, and accomplished—the defining experiences that have shaped us. They position us as the protagonist, the overcomer, the challenger, the resilient survivor. For me, growing up in a divorced household, being raised by my grandparents, being an immigrant and a daughter of a once-undocumented parent, growing up low income and without health insurance in the United States, being a queer woman of color, owning a small business, and gaining financial stability despite various challenges— these are the struggles and triumphs that define me as a person, and I carry them as visceral memories everywhere I go, scars and all.

But what I often don't think about are my *hidden stories*—the experiences that are often missed or forgotten, the stories we may not even be aware of or may even believe we haven't lived but that are also part of our narrative. Despite our unknowing, these stories—marked by the absence of certain struggles or the absence of our awareness of having benefited from special and often imperceptible benefits not available to all—are being written into our storybook right alongside our hero's journey.

When I think about my life as a queer person, my dad's "don't come home" still rings in my ear, and I recall my high school friend who was kicked out of their house upon being "found out" that they were gay. I have been called a dyke on the street; I have endured awkward stares when hold- ing another girl's hand and have felt extra self-conscious when making out with her in public. What I don't remember, though, is ever having to worry about getting pulled over by a cop while driving to my date, fearing I might never make it.

When I think about my life as an Asian American woman, I recall the faces of white kids now blurry in my memory, with their teenage fingers pull- ing their eyes sideways, jeering, "Ching chang chong, ching chang chong!" as well as the times I was called "exotic" by people for the same features so often demeaned and exploited for their entertainment. I have endured fe- tishization and sexual harassment as an Asian woman working as a waitress at a Japanese restaurant and as an employee in corporate spaces. But I don't remember ever having to worry about not being able to get a job because of my documentation or incarceration status or being discriminated against on the basis of my physical or mental ability.

These "I don't remember" stories—my hidden stories—shaped my life just as viscerally and prominently as the ones I consciously remember. We cannot tell one-dimensional stories that deny the existence of our privileges because an absence of hardship *is* a story, just as the absence of privilege is part of our identity. To know who we are, how we came to be, and how we can show up, we need to understand the ways in which we are either harmed by or are benefiting from different systems of oppression. Once we understand and learn to hold these multiple truths that live within us, then we get to choose with greater clarity how we show up in the movement toward social justice.

I am often asked, "How do I know what privileges I have?" A quick internet search of various types of privileges will bring up a collection of lists categorized by different identities and systemic oppressions (e.g., male privilege, able-bodied privilege, cisgender privilege, white privilege, etc.), which are good places to begin our consciousness expansion. But what needs to become a regular practice is our ongoing, intentional efforts to uncover our unknowns, our willingness to understand the *whole story,** and our commitment to honest and contextual interrogations even in the face of discomfort. In discovering our privileges, we must also challenge ourselves to learn about the conditions that allowed for such disparities to be born, tracing their roots back to untold histories, unjust policies, and evolving legacies.

> *If you have questions, it's alright. Questions are sometimes more revealing than answers.*
> —Ericka Huggins[3]

Though I have studied these lists and have even written a few, in that instance of jaywalking with my partner, I was obliviously wielding my privilege as a documented person with US citizenship and as a light-skinned East Asian woman who is often perceived as nonthreatening and submissive, without regard to my partner who did not have a permanent status and who, as a dark-skinned South Asian Sikh man, is often perceived as a threat. My blissful ignorance led me to exercising my privilege, albeit unintentionally, which was quickly weaponized to pose a material threat to my partner whom I love dearly. Once the seed was planted, I sought out information on jaywalking to learn more about this hidden story buried in my privilege. Through quick research, I discovered that jaywalking laws were the outcome of aggressive lobbying by the automobile industry in the twenties that sought to put the blame of car accidents on pedestrians rather than drivers,[4] and that these laws, unsurprisingly, disproportionately target

---

*This is a concept I learned from my dearest friend and sister from another belly, Michelle "Mush" Lee, an Oakland-based poet, narrative strategist, and founder of Whole Story Group.

people of color, specifically Black and Latine people. In 2019, the New York Police Department issued 90 percent of its illegal walking tickets to Black and Latine people, though they comprise about 55 percent of the city population. Over 53 percent of the tickets were issued to young people aged twenty-five and under, who only make up 7 percent of the total population.[5] On June 4, 2020, in Tulsa, Oklahoma, two police officers violently tackled two Black teenage boys to the ground and handcuffed them for alleged jaywalking, leading to the arrest of one of the boys on multiple charges.[6] I have never personally experienced these stories, and yet I also *live* them in my own way, with my privilege as my shield, which enables me to jaywalk with impunity on a daily basis.

THE RESPONSIBILITIES OF PRIVILEGE

We often repeat the phrase *check your privilege*, but we also need to understand and remind ourselves of the deeper why behind this important call to action. Doing our own homework and learning deeply about our particular privileges is one way to take responsibility for our own hidden stories that we were not taught to investigate. We weren't supposed to find out about these hidden stories because our waking up to them threatens the widely held and proselytized belief that our society is a meritocracy in which people are given equal opportunities to succeed, and everyone's success is determined solely by their merit and hard work. This myth of meritocracy guards the same homogenous group of people (cis, heterosexual, abled, wealthy white men) who have held the majority of power, access, and resources for centuries, while invisibilizing systemic barriers marginalized people face by incorrectly blaming their "inability to pull themselves up by their bootstraps." These stories are hidden for a reason, and sometimes we may even want them to remain hidden because of our own fear, shame, guilt, and insecurities. However, they are our key to understanding the ways systems of oppression operate *through* us—and taking control of our privileges and their manifestations is a critical part of staying in alignment with our goals for equity and justice.

We have an obligation to understand our privileges because we have a responsibility to understand the repercussions of our ignorance; at the same time, we also have an obligation to understand that the opportunities we have, come from our having particular keys to unlock certain doors. Privileges can be weaponized in ways that cause destructive harm, even in our unknowing, but they can also be a strategic tool used to advance equity and justice. If I'm a documented person with US citizenship and am aware that most people, including law enforcement, do not register me, a cisgender Asian woman, as an immediate threat, I can use that privilege in ways that can be useful to those without access to it. For example, when I see the police stopping people on the street, I can approach them and stand by, sometimes asking what is going on to see if I can be a useful witness or de-escalator. When I attend large public gatherings where security is provided by local law enforcement, such as the annual Pride parade, I can march nearest to the police and security, becoming a physical buffer between them and others more often targeted—Black and brown people, LGBTQ+ people of color, disabled people, and undocumented people who bear the brunt of police brutality and criminalization. Knowing what privileges we have enables us to be strategic in how we show up and contribute in meaningful ways while minimizing harm.   "Do-Gooder"?

The clarity of our whole story may scare us because it can feel like our stories need to be rewritten completely, or we fear that our accomplishments and stories of overcoming are being discounted. But acknowledging that our privileges have played a part in, and in some cases allowed for, our successes doesn't erase or trivialize our efforts, hard work, or surviving different struggles. It just means that each of our struggles is different, and that our marginalized and privileged identities can coexist to create a unique set of experiences. We have the capacity to hold these multiple truths at the same time, and we must exercise it constantly to make room for honesty, complexity, and nuance.

ASK FOR THE BLACK NAPKIN

When I decided to pursue a corporate career after graduating from college, I was not quite prepared for the culture shock. No one in my immediate family had ever held a big corporate job in America, let alone a conventional salaried desk job. I didn't know the rules, especially the unspoken ones that you're just supposed to know, like the one that says you shouldn't reveal your real age in front of clients or that you should call PowerPoint presentations a "deck" and not a "presentation." For the first couple of years of my transition into the "real world," I suffered from massive cognitive dissonance between what I knew to be true and what was being presented to me as the more important truth in *this* world. The sudden sense of not belonging anywhere—I was a naïve idealist and "radical" in the workplace but a corporate sympathizer in the social justice space—took a toll on my mental health; I had never felt so alone. Nonetheless, I was laser-focused on not sinking in these uncharted waters, faking my way through it one imposter-syndrome-filled day at a time. I reminded myself that "I can make changes from within" and "I am just as good as everyone else here." Despite these daily affirmations, I often woke up crying in the middle of the night and suffered serious Sunday scaries.

One evening, a senior partner at the firm hosted a team dinner. Despite the fact that she looked nothing like me—a tall, thin, blond, and extremely elegant middle-aged white woman—I wanted to be like her. Actually, I just wanted her to like me. I craved her validation. She seemed to have everything together, from her neat, voluminous haircut to her perfectly tailored suit, to her warm smiles, which she would occasionally send my way when she caught me looking at her in awe. The dinner was at an upscale steakhouse—white tablecloths, dimmed lighting, uniformed servers, and all.

As we were shown to our table, the partner casually asked the waiter, "Do you have black napkins?" and pointed to her perfectly tailored black trousers.

Black . . . napkins? Was that a joke?

The waiter didn't think it was a joke, however, and regretfully informed her that they did not have any black napkins at this time. The partner was in disbelief. For an upscale restaurant like this, how dare they only have white napkins? She skipped putting the white napkin on her lap, taking her chances with food scraps rather than the inevitable white lint gracing her pants.

The entire time I was at dinner, I kept thinking about the black napkins. *Black napkins!? Is this something everyone else knows to ask for?*

How many more "black napkins" are out there? How could I have a chance at winning the game if I didn't even know how to play it?

This is a silly and trivial example of how access to certain information works through different networks. In my life, learning about the privileges

I did not have often came with the realization that information hoarding is insidious and pervasive and that gatekeeping knowledge is crucial to maintaining the status quo of inequity: from knowing what types of jobs and opportunities exist in the world to knowing how to negotiate contracts, pricing, and salaries; to investing money to lowering tax obligations; to understanding our legal rights and workarounds. The fact that myriad types of important knowledge remain within the exclusive purview of a privileged minority while elusive and obscure to the rest should alarm all of us.

It's not that we don't know what we don't know; instead, we *can't* know what we are barred access to. Access to spaces, resources, knowledge, and networks is one of the most powerful tools privilege affords some and not others. As we uncover our hidden stories and the privileges fueling those stories, we can begin to kick open the doors gating valuable information and resources, while critically examining the legacy of widening access disparity that has been compounding over the years.

In 2015, Erica Joy Baker, a seasoned engineering leader and advocate for DEI in tech, created an internal spreadsheet while at Google for employees to share their salary information. The spreadsheet quickly gained traction and exposed the wide gender pay gaps that existed among Google's employees. The information shared on the spreadsheet served to empower employees to better negotiate pay raises and correct unfair disparities that were revealed, while helping push the conversation on pay equity forward for the entire tech industry. Baker eventually left Google and noted that the "higher-up people weren't happy" about the spreadsheet and that they had denied her multiple peer bonuses, which her peers had awarded to her as a token of gratitude for creating the database.[7]

Make no mistake, knowledge hoarding exists to uphold existing power differentials between institutions and their members, between the mega rich and the working class, between white people and people of color, between men and marginalized genders. Information is gated for a reason, and it is our job to question why and how and proactively share knowledge and access granted to us via our privilege. Our ability to use our privilege in strategic ways to provide opportunities to others outside of the gate is another crucial reason why we must understand and claim our hidden stories.

Our blissful ignorance doesn't absolve us of our responsibility to become more conscious about our hidden stories and to constantly take stock of how they impact our lives and others'. While they may have been written without our control or conscious choice, choosing to interrogate them to get a truthful view of our whole story *is* within our control, as is using our mapped privileges in strategic ways to advance the movement.

PART 2

ORIENTING

CHAPTER 4

UNLEARNING
WHITE SUPREMACY

CONTENT NOTE: *white supremacist violence, antisemitism*

"We own this house! We own *you!*"

When a violent mob of Trump supporters and white supremacists besieged the Capitol building on January 6, 2021, demanding the 2020 presidential election results be overturned, the world watched in horror at the brazen attack on America's multiracial democracy. Just that morning, I had woken up with a glimmer of hope about the historic runoff election wins in Georgia. My heart was filled with gratitude toward Stacey Abrams and Black, Latine, and Asian organizers who had spent countless hours mobilizing votes in Georgia against all the odds of voter suppression and intimidation. But by the afternoon, white supremacy was unraveling in plain sight. White rage. White fear. White power. Burning anger born out of a sense of loss, a loss of what whiteness is inherently entitled to. Fear fueled by the slightest *potentiality* of losing power. They paraded their unobstructed immunity to remind the entire nation, *No, this is ours. You will not replace us.* The antisemitic chant, "Jews will not replace us!" rang in my memory from the white supremacist Unite the Right rally in Charlottesville, Virginia, in 2017. We've seen this before.

We spend so much time talking about how harmful racism is, how to be antiracist, and the manifestations of racism in schools, the workplace, policing, the judicial system, and society at large. Over and over, we are inundated with such conversations around racism, sexism, homophobia, ableism, anti-Indigeneity, and other forms of oppression in the quest to combat hate, violence, and discrimination. But in many spaces I've been a part of, these conversations rarely go far enough to interrogate what undergirds racism in the first place, and we spend a disproportionate amount of time explaining the symptoms of racism without tending to the root of the problem.

When people hear the term *white supremacy*, the trained brain conjures up images of Nazis, the KKK in white hoods, and a violent mob storming the Capitol brandishing Confederate flags. White supremacy has done a great job of concealing itself by creating an overt imagery from which we can distance ourselves, allowing its inconspicuous tentacles to reach into every crevice of our society without setting off the alarm for most well-intentioned people. A part of white supremacy's function is to disguise its ubiquitous manifestations and to make them difficult to name, thereby existing in the shadow but also the light all at the same time. It has been my professional and personal mission to make white supremacy more plainly available to name, discuss, and dismantle—and it all begins by defining it in the most basic sense. An uncomplicated definition enables us to always come back to it whenever we need clarity and discernment and helps ground us in our analysis and approach.

White supremacy is a set of systems, policies, and beliefs that reinforce the *myth* that:

1. Whiteness is inherently **superior** to other races, and therefore
2. White people should have **dominance** over people of other races.[1]

Author, educator, and activist Sonya Renee Taylor is deliberate in using the term *white supremacist delusion* to point to the inherent distortion of truth that is white supremacy.[2] Despite this false notion that whiteness and white people are inherently superior to other races and therefore should have dominance over people of color, white supremacist delusion still forms the foundation of racism we've seen throughout history and the present day. Historically, this toxic and fictitious belief in white superiority and dominance was used to birth and justify violent atrocities across the globe, from the Holocaust to the genocide of Indigenous peoples to chattel slavery to global imperialism and colonization. The legacy of these heinous acts still lives on today, and the impacts of white supremacy continue to cycle through our lives in both old and new forms.

WHITE SUPREMACY IS EVERYWHERE

CONTENT NOTE: *descriptions of how white supremacy manifests, including examples of racism, anti-Blackness, and mentions of murders and massacres*

White supremacist delusion is embedded in every aspect of our society. Legal scholar Frances Lee Ansley, when explaining white supremacy, expands the definition to implicate the *systems* that perpetuate white supremacy: "By 'white supremacy' I do not mean to allude only to the self-conscious racism of white supremacist hate groups. I refer instead to a political, economic, and cultural system in which whites overwhelmingly control power and material resources, conscious and unconscious ideas of white superiority and entitlement are widespread, and relations of white dominance and non-white subordination are daily reenacted across a broad array of institutions and social settings."[3] Let's unpack how white supremacy shows up in various systems.

White supremacy is in our health-care system, which prioritizes the health and well-being of white people over people of color. Black women are 3 to 4 times and Native women 2.3 times more likely to die of pregnancy-related causes than white women in the United States due to a number of factors that trail back to systemic racism, from inequitable access to quality care and insurance to racially biased medical professionals.[4] Emergency department doctors are less likely to order blood tests, CT scans, or X-rays for Black, Latine, or Asian children compared to white children. Black and Latine patients also experience significantly longer wait times, which means that their visits to a doctor, overall, are longer compared to white patients.[5]

White supremacy is in the American legal system, or *criminal punishment system* as abolitionist, organizer, and educator Mariame Kaba more precisely calls it,[6] which grants a presumption of innocence to white people while doling out disproportionately punitive outcomes to people of color. Black people are 3.7 times more likely to be arrested for marijuana possession than white people, despite the comparable marijuana usage across racial groups,[7] and Black adults are 5.9 times as likely to be incarcerated than white people, while Latine people are 3.1 times as likely.[8] As of 2001, one out of every three Black boys born in that year could expect to go to prison in his lifetime, as could one out of every six Latinos—compared to one out of every seventeen white boys—as a result of a legal system that advantages wealthy and white people over poor people and people of color.[9] Southeast Asians and Pacific Islanders are deported at a rate three times more than that of immigrants as a whole,[10] and state courts are twice as likely to incarcerate Native teens for minor crimes, such as truancy and alcohol use, than any other racial and ethnic group.[11]

White supremacy is in the education system, which teaches white-centered and white-dominant narratives while erasing the histories of the oppressed and centuries of white violence. Southern Poverty Law Center's 2017 research showed that two-thirds of high school seniors surveyed did not know that it took a constitutional amendment to formally end slavery, and of the fifteen sets of state standards analyzed, none addresses how the ideology of white supremacy rose to justify the institution of slavery.[12] The vast majority of Americans are not taught about the monstrous acts of state-backed white mobs that repeatedly destroyed Black neighborhoods and killed innocent lives, like the Tulsa Race Massacre of 1921 or the Rosewood Massacre of 1923, or their terrorizing of Asian communities, like the mass lynching of Chinese people during the Chinese Massacre of 1871 in Los Angeles or the destruction of the Filipino farm worker community during the Watsonville Riots of 1930. Most remain ignorant to the atrocities caused by the US military overseas, like the Mỹ Lai Massacre of 1968, during which US troops shot and killed four hundred women, children, and elders in a South Vietnamese village during the Vietnam War, or the No Gun Ri Massacre of 1950 in South Korea, in which a US air attack killed an estimated three hundred innocent Korean refugees, mostly women and children. To our dismay, most children are still not taught about the racist and genocidal history of America's founding and the mass killings and displacement of Indigenous peoples, whose battle to reclaim and steward the land continues today outside most Americans' awareness.

White supremacy is in product designs that cater to white consumers while leaving people of color as an afterthought. Groundbreaking research conducted by Black scholars Joy Buolamwini and Timnit Gebru in 2018 showed that facial analysis algorithms misclassified Black women nearly 35 percent of the time, while boasting nearly perfect accuracy rates for white men.[13] Despite the humorous online coverage (a 2017 *New York Post* headline read: "Chinese users claim iPhone X face recognition can't tell them apart"[14]), iPhone X's Face ID failure among Asians continued to exacerbate the dehumanizing trope that all Asians look alike. According to a ProPublica investigative report, crime risk assessment software used by the legal system in assessing recidivism potential and in sentencing considerations has been found to use biased algorithms that result in racist outcomes. The report revealed that Black defendants are 77 percent more likely to be pegged as being at a higher risk of committing a future violent crime and 45 percent more likely to be predicted to commit a future crime of any kind compared to white defendants, while holding other factors such as prior crimes, types of crimes, age, and gender constant, with an accuracy rate practically equivalent to a coin toss.[15] *Cupertino - all Asian ↓ neighborhood + schools*

White supremacy is on the map, literally, with lines drawn that separate our neighborhoods into "desirable" (predominantly white, wealthy, and well resourced) versus "undesirable" (predominantly Black and brown, working class, and disinvested) areas, school districts, and voting districts, which end up impacting lifetimes of opportunities, access, wealth generation, and home ownership. The legacy of redlining, a discriminatory practice that was used by the housing industry and banks to suppress home ownership and development in communities of color, still lives on even after the passage of the 1968 Fair Housing Act, which prohibited this practice. A 2020 research study found that racial inequality in home values is greater today than it was forty years ago, with homes in white neighborhoods appreciating almost two hundred thousand dollars more since 1980 than comparable homes in similar communities of color.[16] Between 1776 and 1887, white settlers and the US government seized over 1.5 billion acres of land from Indigenous people[17] and created reservations as a way to isolate and exert control over them, while withholding public funding and investments. The legacy of settler colonialism continues today, with 27 percent of all Native Americans living in poverty and many more with limited access to adequate health care due to government policies that prohibited wealth-building opportunities through forced removal of lands and resources.[18]

White supremacy and, more specifically, white *male* supremacy are in the overwhelming, hegemonic power white men have over decisions that impact *everyone*. Virtually every industry is dominated by white men in executive leadership positions. In 2020, 92.6 percent of Fortune 500 CEOs were white and only 7.4 percent were women, while only 1 percent were Black, 2.4 percent were East Asians or South Asians, and 3.4 percent were Latine.[19]

A striking report by the *New York Times* in September 2020 revealed in a review of more than nine hundred officials and executives in prominent positions that 80 percent of them were white, while 20 percent identified as Black, Hispanic, Asian, Native American, multiracial, or otherwise a person of color, pointing to the disproportionate representation of white people in positions of power in a country where they make up only 60 percent of the population.[20] The reviewed positions included military officials, police chiefs, Supreme Court justices, entertainment and media industry executives, publishing CEOs, major news organizations, principal owners of sports teams, elected government officials, and more, who get to decide and have lasting influence over the fundamental shaping of our society.*

> *When God looks like the ruling class, you know you're fucked,*
> *basically.*
> —Gloria Steinem[21]

As many in the criminal punishment system reform and abolition movement have been saying, our systems are not broken. They are working exactly as designed, upholding white supremacy and rapidly reproducing it to penetrate our minds, relationships, organizations, and institutions so it can continue its delusional and destructive legacy.

White supremacy is deliberate and relentless. It is insidious and omnipresent. It is everywhere. And because it's everywhere, because it is the air we breathe and the water we swim in, it also feels like it's nowhere, deeply ingrained in our psyche as the default way of being. For example, because whiteness is thought of as the norm and the point of departure, white people are often described simply as "people" or "an individual," rather than "white people" or a "white person." (So when we are told that the police protect *people*, does this mean *all* people or just white people?) Toni Morrison said it best: "In this country American means white. Everybody else

---

*If reading the list of examples of white supremacy above has exhausted you, you're not alone. I thought long and hard about how to present these harsh realities and statistics, before realizing there actually isn't a way to make any of this palatable or less overwhelming. There is nothing light or easy about living inside the reality of white supremacy. The only way to dismantle white supremacy is to face it as bluntly and as honestly as possible. That said, I encourage you to move your body, stretch, and take a few deep breaths before continuing on.

has to hyphenate."[22] To live in alignment with our values, then, we ough. learn how to recognize the toxicity we are breathing in every day and discern whether it's poison that we've been taught to appreciate. Unless we take the time to understand, acknowledge, and actively unlearn white supremacy, we will continue to perpetuate it—just like how we can unwittingly weaponize our unclaimed hidden stories.

> We have to constantly critique imperialist white supremacist patriarchal culture because it is normalized by mass media and rendered unproblematic.
> —bell hooks[23]

WHITE SUPREMACY CULTURE IS *WITHIN* US

CONTENT NOTE: *descriptions about chattel slavery and racial capitalism*

Because white supremacy is found in every facet of our lives, from the systems we are part of to the policies we abide by and the stories we ingest, it is only natural that it also lives *within* us as we carry on the work of white supremacy through our beliefs, values, norms, and behaviors. Tema Okun's writing on white supremacy culture, which builds on the work of many racial justice activists and scholars, including Kenneth Jones, Beverly Daniel Tatum, Daniel Buford, and more,* seeks to highlight a list of characteristics of white supremacy culture widely observed inside organizations. These characteristics work to both overtly and covertly advantage whiteness and Western norms while devaluing, often with penalty, traits that deviate from them. According to Okun's article, the list of characteristics include, but are not limited to:†

---

*Full credit found on Okun's website: "The original piece and therefore this website builds on the work of many people, including (but not limited to) Andrea Ayvazian, Bree Carlson, Beverly Daniel Tatum, Eli Dueker, Nancy Emond, Kenneth Jones, Jonn Lunsford, Joan Olsson, David Rogers, James Williams, Sally Yee, as well as the work of Grassroots Leadership, Equity Institute Inc, the People's Institute for Survival and Beyond, the Challenging White Supremacy workshop, the Lillie Allen Institute, the Western States Center, and the contributions of hundreds of participants in the DR process."[24]

†The descriptions provided below are a summary of Okun's work from 1999 and include my broader interpretation of the characteristics outside a strictly organizational context. Since I

sm: hyperfocus on inadequacy; "making a mistake is con-
)eing a mistake"; little to no appreciation for individuals or
orts; no allowances made for reflection or learning from

- **Sense of urgency:** prioritization of efficiency over relationships or thoughtful decision-making
- **Defensiveness:** focus on protecting power; "criticism of those with power is viewed as threatening and inappropriate"
- **Quantity over quality:** overvaluing of things that are measurable, while undervaluing immeasurable things like emotions, process, relationships, or conflict management
- **Worship of the written word:** obsession with documentation and credentialing; "if it's not in a memo, it doesn't exist"
- **Only one right way:** inability to accept multiple truths or solutions; achieving consensus through force
- **Paternalism:** decision-making rights reside with those with power; refusal to understand and center the needs of those without power
- **Either-or thinking:** oversimplification of complex things; binary thinking (e.g., good/bad, right/wrong, with us/against us) and never both-and thinking
- **Power hoarding:** scarcity mindset about power; fear of losing power
- **Fear of open conflict:** inability to receive constructive feedback or criticism; "emphasis on being polite"; punishment for those expressing conflict
- **Individualism:** discomfort working as a team; excessive desire for individual credit and recognition; valuing of competition over collaboration
- **I'm the only one:** superiority/savior complex; inability to trust others' capabilities; refusal to delegate and share responsibilities
- **Progress is bigger, more:** success is defined as bigger or more; undervaluing of quality or process

---

wrote this chapter, Okun released an updated article and added resources in June 2021, and I encourage everyone to visit www.whitesupremacyculture.info/ to access more detailed descriptions as well as antidotes for each characteristic.

- **Objectivity:** belief in the notion of neutrality; obsession over logic over emotions; invalidating emotions
- **Right to comfort:** entitlement of those in power to feel comfort and be comforted at others' expense; "scapegoating those who cause discomfort"

My team and I often experience intense defensiveness from workshop participants whenever we present these characteristics. The rush to dismiss is most palpable within for-profit companies, which is understandable given that, to a large extent, many of these characteristics (like perfectionism, sense of urgency, objectivity) are seen as positive cultural values that have consistently been promoted and rewarded inside organizations in order to run a profitable business. What we need to remind people of in these situations is the importance of contextual analysis, and to not use this list as yet another reductive rubric to create a good-bad binary devoid of nuance. For example, it is not that collecting quantitative data in and of itself is white supremacist regardless of context; rather, it is the weaponization of quantitative over the qualitative and consistent devaluing of relational, anecdotal, and emotional data, reinforced by other characteristics such as one-right-way or either-or thinking, that can lead to reinforcing white supremacist narratives and power disparities inside organizations.

When I first learned of these traits, I, too, had a tough time reconciling my professional standards with the plainly written words that apparently characterized my work ethic as behaviors of white supremacy. *Sense of urgency is imperative in our business. How is that perpetuating white supremacy culture?* I've received similar questions from countless leaders who are baffled by the contradictions they find themselves in. In the example of sense of urgency, it was not until I reflected on my relationship to time and productivity, and their different historical contexts and culture norms, that I began to understand why a culture with a singular emphasis on urgency over the quality of time spent helps continue the legacy of white supremacy culture. Different cultures perceive time differently: for example, Western cultures tend to view time as linear and limited and punctuality as a way of showing respect for other people's time, while in Native cultures time is viewed as circular, and one shows respect not through punctuality but in the willingness to stay until the interaction is over or the task is complete.[25]

With professional spaces in the United States adopting the Western concept of time as being the superior way to work, we can see the interplay between white supremacy and capitalism in our society's obsession with urgency and efficiency, and its prioritization of profitability over human connection and well-being.

When I began my career in corporate America, I was told over and over again that "time is money." Quite literally, every minute of my time had a monetary value associated with it. As a junior analyst at a consulting firm, my time was worth a little below a hundred dollars per hour, which was billed to the client. I gasped when I saw our billable hourly rate sheet for the first time, which specified each staffed consultant's hourly rate by level, from the lowest-ranking employee (me) all the way to the firm's partner's hourly rate, which was many times higher than mine. My peers and I joked about the "break-even point" at which our employer would begin to profit off our labor, understanding exactly how much we were getting paid and how much the company was making from loaning us to its clients. Each person's worth was clearly calculated on the rate sheet, and each minute we wasted not billing our client was a minute the company delayed in breaking even on their investment in our salary and benefits. Looking at what I thought was an exorbitant amount of money per hour, I remembered how my dad, who lived in the United States as an undocumented immigrant for over a decade, used to pack his lunch—rice and some banchan, all mixed together in a Ziploc bag—for work. The store manager where he worked—a white man who was "generous enough" to hire undocumented immigrants under exploitative conditions in exchange for the promise to be an employer sponsor on their green card applications—did not allow his workers to take proper lunch breaks or even the luxury of sitting down, and my dad figured that eating out of a plastic bag while hiding behind the store counter was the most efficient way to sneak food into his growling stomach. In the eyes of white supremacy and capitalism, my dad's worth was determined by his productivity and usefulness to his employer's bottom line, not in his innate existence, rest, or dignity.

Capitalism in the United States was built on the backs of enslaved African people's unpaid labor and on land stolen from Indigenous peoples, and white supremacy was the necessary justification to legalize the dehumanizing practice of human ownership and labor exploitation. Black people's time was ruthlessly policed and exploited without compensation to produce wealth for white enslavers, which has fueled the entire economy of this country. Today, we see companies like Amazon being exposed for their inhumane labor practices, among them limiting the ability of their frontline workers, who are predominantly Black and Latine,[26] to take breaks,[27] all to increase their profit margins, which benefit their largely white leadership and shareholders. The relationships between time and money, white supremacy and capitalism, exploitation of the labor and time of people of color, and particularly Black and brown people, migrant workers, and underpaid laborers overseas, are all part of the intricate web of white supremacy culture that thrives off our false belief that speed and timeliness are a badge of honor that "good employees" get to wear. A blanket sense of urgency at the expense of the humane treatment of workers produces conditions that devalue people of color who continue to occupy the most exploited jobs in our society today.

Organizational culture steeped in white supremacy culture builds processes and policies that reinforce and reward people, behaviors, traits, and beliefs that conform to these standards of whiteness (e.g., perfectionism, quantity over quality, legitimacy based in perceived objectivity and quantifiable data, etc.), which are falsely dubbed as "strong work ethic," "culture fit," and "professionalism." Meanwhile, it punishes and discards people, behaviors, traits, and beliefs that challenge the status quo. One such example is biased hiring practices that privilege graduates from majority elite white institutions over others (e.g., historically Black colleges and universities, community colleges, trade schools, educational institutions overseas, online universities, etc.), immigrants with white European accents over immigrants of color with "ethnic" accents, abled people over disabled people, and people without dependents over those with caregiving responsibilities. It is now a well-known statistic that white names receive 50 percent more callbacks for interviews when compared to candidates with more "ethnic-sounding" names, such as Lakisha and Jamal (names used in the study).[28] A different research study found that companies are more than twice as likely to call Black and Asian applicants for interviews if they submit whitened résumés than candidates who reveal their race—and this discriminatory practice is just as prevalent in organizations that claim to value diversity as those that don't.[29] HR and legal practices that only give legitimacy to documented and quantitatively measured data produced by credentialed consultants, over the emotional wisdom and lived experiences of their marginalized employees, is another manifestation of white supremacy culture ("worship of the written word"), as is the rampant and insidious retaliation marginalized employees face when they blow the whistle on unjust working conditions ("fear of open conflict").

We have been taught to value the "executive presence" that teaches us to act with the level of confidence exemplified by tall white men in suits. Through the enforcement of these regulated culture norms (e.g., *white* executive presence, *white* confidence, or *white* culture fit), white supremacy culture becomes institutionalized and structurally normalized. And because of this, unless we work to recognize and dismantle this institutionally reinforced rubric of whiteness, even when an organization is filled with people of color, we can continue to perpetuate the culture of white supremacy as non-white people. Remember: white supremacy is the air we all breathe, and its toxicity flows through each of our veins no matter the color of our skin.

It is critically important to emphasize that though white supremacy was built by and for the benefit of white people, it resides within *everyone,* including people of color. This is why representation alone cannot solve white supremacy culture and systems, as we will discuss in Chapter 6, The Double-Edged Sword of Representation, and why we need to interrogate the ways we spread it through our own internalization. While we all perform whiteness to different degrees to survive, internalized white supremacist delusion tricks us into actually believing the false narrative that those who conform to the standards of whiteness are more deserving—of success, respect, dignity, validation, comfort, immunity, benefit of the doubt, money, care, attention, grace, compassion, understanding, opportunities, and forgiveness. So some of us live our entire lives trying to meet the standards defined by whiteness, intoxicated by the lure that one day, we, too, will become worthy of living dignified, abundant, and expansively expressed lives, only to find out we will never be seen as fully human in a society plagued by white supremacy.

It is equally crucial to understand that white supremacy doesn't just hurt people of color. Damon Young, writer and author of *What Doesn't Kill You Makes You Blacker,* said in reference to white supremacy's disproportionately deadly impact of COVID-19 on the Black community, "But it's not just affecting us. White people are dying too. White supremacy has always mattered more than white lives do."[30] Because white supremacy's primary goal is maintaining systemic white dominance, it does not hesitate to dispose of human lives in service of its goals and therefore hurts everyone, including white people. To keep its power, white supremacy bulldozes over anything that gets in its way, as exemplified by the frequent police violence against *all* protestors fighting for Black and brown lives or the continued exploitation of the poor and working class, including white people. White supremacy does not value individual lives—only white power. White supremacy will come for you, too, believe you me.

White protestors not prosecuted.

> White supremacy targets and violates BIPOC people and communities
> with the intent to destroy them directly; white supremacy targets and
> violates white people with a persistent invitation to collude that will
> inevitably destroy their humanity.
> —Tema Okun[31]

WHITE SUPREMACY IS INHERENT IN OTHER FORMS OF OPPRESSION

CONTENT NOTE: *descriptions of how white supremacy manifests, including but not limited to mentions of eugenics, ableism, pathologizing LGBTQ people, genocide, deportation, and detailed descriptions of anti-Asian violence and the police murder of George Floyd*

The further entrenched I become in the work of social justice, the more I realize that the forces and legacy of white supremacy are omnipresent and impossible to untangle from other forms of oppression, whether it is capitalism—as we unpacked in this chapter—or colonialism, imperialism, homophobia, transphobia, sexism, misogyny, ableism, xenophobia, fatphobia, ageism, and so on. By honing in on what white supremacy is and how it manifests, we can begin to understand how these different interlocking systems of oppression, a concept introduced by the Combahee River Collective in 1977,[32] also mirror the foundational ideals, principles, and practices of white supremacy: they all revolve around hoarding power and using that power *over* others through various false narratives around the superiority of one group over another. Once we understand how these systems of

oppression feed off one another to sustain themselves, while also understanding each oppression's unique application in different communities, we
can commit ourselves to the fact that to fight one, we must fight all forms
of oppression.

The disability justice* community has taught me a great deal about how
ableism is central to understanding racism, anti-Blackness, white supremacy, capitalism, and other forms of oppression. Throughout history, white
supremacy has used the language and tactics of ableism to dehumanize,
pathologize, and incriminate not only disabled people but also Native people, Black and brown people, Asian and Latine people, queer and trans people, poor people, and anyone who is deemed less than the perfect portrayal
of whiteness as an idea. For example, in the 1920s, eugenics lobbyists and
proponents of racist IQ tests argued that Black and Native people had nat-
urally inferior intellectual abilities, which helped justify racial segregation
and discriminatory treatments.[34] And it wasn't until 1987 that homosexual-
ity was removed completely from the Diagnostic and Statistical Manual of
Mental Disorders (DSM),[35] and it wasn't until 2019 that the World Health
Organization stopped classifying being transgender as a mental disorder,[36]
which had played a major role in stigmatizing and pathologizing trans people as being mentally ill or otherwise disabled, allowing extreme forms of
transphobic and homophobic violence and practices to exist, such as conversion therapy, which sought to "cure the disease" through tactics widely
condemned as being harmful and unethical.[37] (Unfortunately, conversion
therapy is still legal in many states,[38] and being intersex is still considered
a disorder, according to the fifth edition of the DSM.[39]) White supremacy,
aided by other forms of oppression like ableism, gave birth to structural and
societal barriers for people of color, disabled people, and other marginalized
people and created conditions that are inherently inaccessible and unsafe to
those deviating from the mythology of white perfection.

On our path to collective liberation, we must continuously strive to understand the web of interconnectedness of different systemic oppressions

---

*The term *disability justice* was coined in 2005 by a group of disabled queer women of color
activists including Patty Berne, Mia Mingus, and Stacy Milbern, as well as Leroy Moore, Eli
Clare, and Sebastian Margaret in order to "centralize the needs and experiences of folks experiencing intersectional oppression."[33]

while reminding ourselves that these interdependencies, while complex, are also what bind us together in solidarity. I first learned of intersectionality in 2007 when I was at UC Berkeley leading a queer student organization I cofounded. A term coined by the civil rights lawyer and critical race theory scholar Dr. Kimberlé Crenshaw in 1989,[40] *intersectionality* offers a framework for understanding how multiple marginalized identities intersect to create a set of unique and complex convergence of experiences of oppression. In a 2020 interview with *Time* magazine, Dr. Crenshaw defines intersectionality as "a lens, a prism, for seeing the way in which various forms of inequality often operate together and exacerbate each other," and notes how people who are subject to multiple forms of inequality—based on "race, gender, class, sexuality, or immigrant status"—have an experience that is beyond "just the sum of its parts."[41] Using myself as an example, as an Asian woman, I do not just experience sexism in men-dominated spaces and racism in white-dominated spaces; I also experience a form of oppression that combines both forces of patriarchy and white supremacy that is unique to my identity. This can show up in the way I experience a particular type of fetishization and exotification as an Asian woman. In a different example, a Black woman may experience *misogynoir*, a term coined in 2008 by Dr. Moya Bailey[42] that describes "the specific hatred, dislike, distrust, and prejudice directed toward Black women."[43] Intersectionality has been a critical tool for ensuring we understand the unique manifestations of the interlocking systems of oppression, and I've found it is impossible to engage in coalition-building work without a thorough understanding of the concept.

> *Within the lesbian community I am Black, and within the Black community I am a lesbian. Any attack against Black people is a lesbian and gay issue, because I and thousands of other Black women are part of the lesbian community. Any attack against lesbians and gays is a Black issue, because thousands of lesbians and gay men are Black. There is no hierarchy of oppression.*
> —Audre Lorde[44]

If we truly understand the functions and manifestations of white supremacy, and we chip away at it with criticality, then we can recognize just how far-reaching its effects are and how we cannot dismantle it without also understanding how other systemic oppressions operate with it in an inextricably interlocking manner. Similarly, we will be unable to fight any other systemic oppressions alone without also addressing the underlying foundation of white supremacy. By cutting at the root of our oppressions, we will see that while our struggles may look different, the source of our trauma is shared. The same force of white supremacy and capitalism that enslaved African people also massacred Indigenous people for their land, exploited Asian migrant labor, and bombed innocent lives abroad. The same force that brutalizes and murders innocent Black lives rips children away from their refugee parents' arms and puts them in cages. The same force that vilifies Muslim, Sikh, and Jewish people criminalizes queerness and being trans. All of our struggles are interconnected.

Efforts that do not begin with a foundational understanding of how these systems reinforce one another often end up replicating the harmful characteristics of white supremacy culture once again. For example, feminist movements that do not address the effects of white supremacy quickly end up with limited solutions to sexism through the narrow lens of white women, which does not account for the experiences of women of color. In the workplace, it is all too common to observe women's employee resource groups turn into what appear to be *white* women's groups without meaningful participation of or leadership by women of color, who often find a stronger sense of belonging in race-based affinity groups. Without the inclusion of diverse perspectives, such groups end up struggling to effect meaningful change. Limited analyses lead to limited solutions, and in the end, we arrive back where we began, only now with more mistrust, fractures, and repeated harm.

When COVID-19 began gaining national attention, there was such a surge in anti-Asian violence that the FBI put out an official warning.[45] Fueled by the forty-fifth administration's xenophobic and Sinophobic remarks that dubbed coronavirus as "kung flu," "Wuhan virus," and "China virus," Asians, particularly East Asians who are often lumped into one monolithic group despite the myriad ethnicities that exist, faced both verbal and physical assaults at an alarming frequency. Between March 2020 and March 2021, Stop AAPI Hate received over 6,603 reports of anti-Asian hate incidents nationwide.[46] In 2020 in Texas, a nineteen-year-old man stabbed three members of an Asian American family, including two children, because he believed they were "Chinese and infecting people with the coronavirus."[47] A sixteen-year-old boy in California ended up in an emergency room after being physically attacked by bullies who accused him of having the coronavirus.[48] My friend, a Filipino American born and raised in the Bay Area, was spat on in the street and told to go back to his country. My dad, who now works as a real estate appraiser, was asked to wear a hazmat suit when his client found out he was Korean.

As many Asians in America entered their own racial reckoning and the community conversation around fighting anti-Asian racism started to take off, a different global uprising was spreading in response to the unjust and racist murder of George Floyd by a Minneapolis police officer, Derek Chauvin. As Chauvin knelt on George Floyd's neck for nine minutes and twenty-nine seconds, Tou Thao, a Hmong American cop, stood idly by while Floyd called out for his mother with his dying breath. Multiple traumas converged that summer, and it felt as though the Black Lives Matter movement was the rallying cry that burst open our pained hearts, ready to demand change. The call to action from the Black activist community for non-Black people was loud and clear: organize your communities, acknowledge and condemn anti-Black racism, and follow the leadership of Black people. My team and I worked around the clock to create educational resources specific to combating anti-Black racism and white supremacy. I went into overdrive, writing, protesting, sharing, amplifying, and facilitating conversations about anti-Blackness and police brutality, while shedding light on the insidious forces of white supremacy that impact *all* marginalized people, including Asians in America. I published articles about the urgency of fighting anti-Black racism within Asian communities and held virtual spaces with other Asian racial justice advocates like Ellen Pao and Kim Tran, in which Asians gathered to discuss both our historical and present-day complicity in anti-Blackness and white supremacy culture, our oppression from it, and the ongoing activism work done by progressive Asian organizers.

Over the next few weeks, I started to see impassioned responses to my blog posts. Some expressed gratitude while others spewed nasty anti-Asian rhetoric. Some Black readers shared their personal experiences of anti-Blackness perpetrated by Asian store owners, neighbors, colleagues, and bosses and expressed their exasperation at being oppressed by not only white people but also by other people of color. Among the flurry of messages I received, the ones that pained me the most were the messages of disappointment and hurt from those in my own Asian community, people who felt worried that all of the attention was being diverted to Black Lives Matter while our people continued to suffer. They wrote to me about their pain, which they felt was unseen, trivialized, and dismissed, like much of our historical struggles: "I support BLM, but what about us? We're hurting too." Some Asians asked how I could be focused on supporting Black people when they were part of the force vilifying and victimizing us, making problematic anti-Black generalizations based on a handful of now-viral videos of attacks on Asian elders perpetrated by Black individuals.

Fast-forward to early 2021, when another surge of videos documenting anti-Asian hate incidents flooded social media, this time even more intense in frequency and violence, breaking open a renewed uproar of Asian voices once again demanding justice. While most mainstream media outlets initially remained silent, AAPI activists and public figures mobilized to capture the nation's attention, seeking to dismantle the pervasive model minority myth in order to shed light on the ongoing anti-Asian racism dating back to the 1800s. Some Asian people, undoubtedly from a place of desperation and hurt, began sharing posts to the tune of: "We showed up for Black Lives Matter. Now it's your turn to show up for us." While the desire for support was understandable, what these messages ended up revealing was a limited understanding around the interconnectedness of all our struggles under white supremacy, which resulted in the symptom of transactional allyship, where our solidarity was reduced to a mere exchange or a tit-for-tat scorekeeping.

Herein lies the issue with only discussing certain types of racism (anti-Black racism or anti-Asian racism) in silos without naming the source. In failing to shed light on the shared root of white supremacy, we mistakenly believe our rallying for one group means turning our backs on others, and that efforts and resources are being *taken away* from our issues rather than being shared in a way that strengthens our collective fight. This type of thinking, rooted in scarcity mindset and either-or binary thinking, is in and of itself the function of white supremacy, and it often leads us to resorting to problematic narratives that perpetuate different forms of oppression. What some of my readers failed to acknowledge was that when we show up for Black lives, we're showing up for *all of us,* not only because there are Black and brown Asians who are subjected to anti-Black violence but also because, while our struggles may take different forms, we share the common enemy of white supremacy. Our divesting from anti-Black racism gets us closer to dismantling white supremacy that harms us, too, and without Black people's freedom, there can be no liberation for us all. And perhaps more honestly, we must show up not only in the spirit of solidarity but also out of the recognition that many of us have been complicit in perpetuating anti-Blackness and violence against Black people. It is incumbent upon us to understand that though we are impacted by white supremacy, sometimes we also act as vessels for its proliferation. Understanding all the ways white supremacy manifests, not just as forces that hold us down but also as poison we've internalized and weaponized against others, is critical to building principled solidarity that is not artificial.

When I reflect on the famous quote, "Our liberation is bound together,"[49] I think about both the connected shackles of oppression across different marginalized communities, as well as the ways in which we play an active role in either advancing or thwarting one another's liberation, often using the same tools and remnants of white supremacy. Make no mistake, as Asians living in the United States, our pain deserves to be seen, and we have a rightful place in the social justice movement as costrugglers, not just allies,* *and* we also have a responsibility to recognize when we are acting as perpetrators of oppression against other marginalized groups. Our capacity to hold multiple realities, struggles, solutions, and truths in our intertwined lives is vast, and growing such capacity is core to social justice work. Acknowledging our shared oppression and our complicity does not diminish our pain; it strengthens our power and allows us to fight and heal together. So, let's practice *yes, and. Both and.*

---

*I credit Hyejin Shim, a second-generation queer Korean American organizer, writer, and friend, for this framing. Her 2017 Medium article "Questions on (the Limits & Effects of) (Asian American) Allyship" was imperative to my own perspective shift. Hyejin is also the cofounder of Survived and Punished, a national advocacy project dedicated to supporting criminalized and incarcerated survivors of violence.[50]

GRAPPLING TOWARD POSSIBILITIES

Trying one thing after another and trying to learn from everything that I try—that's the only way. The illusion that there's a quick answer leads to burnout.
  —Grace Lee Boggs[51]

Since the initial rise of anti-Asian violence, I've been asked by countless well-intentioned folks of all races, "What can we do to stop the violence?" My answer often involves a quote from Brea Baker, a writer, abolition activist, and friend: "We need to stop underestimating racism. There's nothing we can do today that's going to stop anti-Asian racism *by tomorrow*."[52] If stopping violence rooted in white supremacy and racism was as simple as following a one-two-three checklist, we would have done it by now.

White supremacy wants us to believe there are simple, efficient solutions to complex problems, thereby encouraging us to prematurely ditch the necessary grappling when we can't find a simple answer to a problem at hand. During an executive session, a white man CEO of a fast-growing tech company in San Francisco asked me, "How can our for-profit company possibly be antiracist?" This question came out of his recent reading of Dr. Ibram X. Kendi's *How to Be an Antiracist*, in which Dr. Kendi explains the inextricable and reinforcing relationship between capitalism and racism.[53] The well-intentioned CEO was genuinely baffled by the notion that, in order to be truly antiracist, one must also practice anticapitalism. A C-level executive at a Fortune 500 financial data services company had a similar reaction when an employee brought up this point during an all-company meeting, only this executive was much quicker to squash any mention of anticapitalism by stating, "We are definitely *not* going to be anticapitalist." She laughed it off and ensured no conversation around capitalism surfaced ever again.

Binary thinking and perfectionism force people to throw up their hands the moment they realize they cannot find or accomplish the "perfect" answer. "What's the point of us even trying if we're never going to be anticapitalist?" But what if the answers reside within the trying? What if the tension *is* the point that breaks open the pathways—not to a simple, singular, and reductive solution but to multilayered, collective, and complex *solutioning* toward possibilities?

What would it look like for company executives to actually grapple with the fact that to be antiracist is to be anticapitalist and to begin to align themselves closer to their proclaimed ideals of equity and justice? What would it look like for us to sit with the discomfort of not being either-or but both-and and work toward being less of the thing we don't want and more of the thing we do want, always in pursuit of staying in integrity with our values and our collective liberation? What would it look like for us to welcome the tension and contradictions we find ourselves in, to become a little or a lot less exploitative, oppressive, and white supremacist with each decision every day? What possibilities exist when we can break free from the binary thinking that white supremacy has taught us and embrace the messiness in the in-betweens and keep trying to do the next right thing?

As we continue on our social justice journey together, we must choose to actively and continuously unlearn white supremacy that lives within each of us and in every system we inhabit. Radical—which etymologically means to relate from a *root*—approaches to our collective healing and liberation begin with our unlearning what's been taught to us as a way to oppress and replacing our attachment to perfectionism, binary thinking, oversimplification, and conflict avoidance with something much more vulnerable, complex, loving, and courageous.

CHAPTER 5

THE ONLY CONSTANT
IS CONTEXT

Have you ever stared at your phone and said, "Should I really be sending this photo to my coworker?" as you look at a half-naked photo of yourself and imagine your receiver's reaction. No? OK.

Well, my new coworker didn't hesitate to send me such a photo on my first week at a tech company through our work chat. He also asked me to "return the favor" with a photo of me in a bikini. What a welcome.

We had been exchanging friendly chats for a few days. He was based in a different city and had been quick to offer support and background information on who's who, making me, a junior employee trying to prove myself, feel less alone at a brand-new company. At first, I was appreciative of his proactive outreach and kind gestures. He asked a lot of questions about me, and though my gut sensed he might be a bit *too* friendly, I didn't want him to feel written off by the new girl or cause him to run off and tell others I was a bitch. I also knew he had been at the company for a long time and was known by everyone and that he reported directly to one of the top executives, whose office my cubicle happened to be right outside of.

When he asked me for my bikini photo after sending his wild-night-in-Vegas snapshot, which showed him wearing a feathered boa around his neck, with his arms around two women in lingerie, I knew it had gone too far. I consulted with a coworker who was a college friend of mine, and with his reassurance, I printed out the chat history and presented it to my direct manager. Being a typical early-stage tech start-up, we did not have HR, only an executive team led one hundred percent by men.

Everything escalated quickly, and the next day, I overheard his boss yelling at him over the phone. Through the thick glass wall, I could hear faintly the sentence that made my gut sick: "I told you this can't happen again!"

He was fired. My boss's boss met with me to share the news. He told me how sorry he was that I had to experience that and said I had done the right thing by reporting it. I felt grateful. Then he said, "I wish you didn't lead him on, though. I read through the chat, and you should have stopped when he started making inappropriate jokes. You kept him going by laughing along. It was like you were flirting back." I was stunned, and embarrassed. *He's right. I should have stopped him way sooner. Why didn't I?* Whenever he made a sexually charged or inappropriate remark, I just laughed it off, typing "lol" and "gotta go!" into the message box, hoping he would lose interest and just go away. I never confronted him or told him off directly. I went back to my desk and sat there with my face hot. I felt relieved that my harasser was gone, but I couldn't shake the feeling of deep shame and a sense of having brought this upon myself. I didn't want anyone else to see the chat history or find out that I had failed to stop him from harassing me. I didn't want people to know *I* was the reason he got fired.

This is where we stop the film and hit the brakes and where my thirty-something self tells the younger me, *No, that's bullshit.*

If we were to look at the incident in isolation as something that happened between two individuals, then *maybe* the statement of my boss's boss has some merit. But we do not live in a vacuum. We live in a society filled with complex history, diverse identities attached to those histories, and different power dynamics that govern the way we experience the world. This is why understanding the broader context is so critical whenever we are analyzing any given situation. For instance, it matters that I was a brand-new employee and that he had been at the company for years. It matters that I was in a junior role while he had a direct line to an executive leader. It matters that I had just come from a corporate culture riddled with hierarchy and permissiveness that had trained me to second-guess myself and let go of anything not "egregiously bad." It matters that all I wanted was to prove myself and fit in without being defined as the "difficult one" for once in my life. It matters that I was twenty-three and he was in his forties. It matters that I am an Asian woman and he, a white man. It matters that I had experienced sexual violence before, not once, but many times to different degrees, and that

being fetishized, sexualized, and exoticized as an Asian woman is a recurring theme in my life. It matters that I was one of only six or seven women
out of forty or so employees, and that my boss, my boss's boss, and the entire
executive team were men. It matters that there was no HR and no evidence
that such a function was valued—and even if there had been one, that I
already had very little faith in its ability to protect me over the company's interest. And it matters that we live in a society that puts the burden of defense
on survivors rather than putting the mandate on would-be perpetrators to
not violate. All of it matters.

THE PITFALLS OF MISSING CONTEXT

Context—history, cultural and social conditions, identities, power dynamics—matters, always. And yet, in my work as an equity consultant and facilitator, I've witnessed just how lacking in context most organizations and
individuals are in their approach to understanding the issues of systemic
injustice.

One of the key skills we look to develop as facilitators is the ability to
identify the root of any conflict, which requires an understanding of context.
If someone is posing a problem or asking a question, rather than jumping
to provide a surface-level answer, we need to first identify the context from
which they are coming. For example, when, in response to efforts to build
designated resource groups for women, LGBTQ+, or BIPOC professionals
in the workplace, someone asks, "Why can't we have a white man's club?" it
is not difficult to gather that this person is likely coming from a place where
he does not fully understand the structural inequities that exist, where creating such a club would be redundant to the society we already live in—the
entire world is already a white man's club. This person is missing the broader
context as it relates to the history of white supremacy and the unequal dis-
tribution of systemic power that exists today, among other legacies, that ne-
cessitates deliberately creating safe spaces for marginalized people.

So many DEI initiatives fail because people get stuck in the never-ending
loop of false equivalencies rooted in vast misunderstanding and a lack of
contextual analysis: "Programs like diversity hiring and affirmative action
are reverse racism." "Yes, Black lives matter. But don't *all* lives matter?" "Men
no longer feel safe in the age of #MeToo; we can't even go to lunch with

women colleagues without fear of being accused of harassment." "Cancel culture is toxic, and it doesn't allow for diversity of thought." "Why can't we appreciate each other's culture without calling it appropriation?" "Introverts are at a disadvantage too. Why not create an inclusion category for them?" At a glance, these questions may appear to be natural reactions to the issues, but the truth is we've already gone off topic, and we're no longer having the same conversation precisely because these questions have failed to consider context. If we can't even agree on what the problem is, how could we possibly agree on the solutions?

Without contextual analysis that takes into consideration the long history of systemic oppression and its present-day manifestations, any type of equity and inclusion efforts can quickly turn into a shallow marketing campaign without a solid foundation, a check-box exercise susceptible to co-option, distorted to maintain the status quo. In tech, this lack of critical contextual and historical analysis has led to a number of public debates and scandals. In 2017, a now-former employee at Google published a memo criticizing Google's diversity programs, using strikingly ill-informed "logic" that lacked context and nuance: "To achieve a more equal gender and race representation, Google has created several discriminatory practices: Programs, mentoring, and classes only for people with a certain gender or race, a high priority queue and special treatment for 'diversity' candidates."[1] That same year, Apple's then head of diversity received harsh public criticism for stating that there could be diversity when there are "twelve white, blue-eyed, blond men in a room" because they're going to bring different life experiences and perspectives,[2] and despite her clarification and apology that followed, her initial statement fueled some tech leaders' eager adoption of the notion of "diversity of thought" over social identity-based representation, which, sadly, continues today. Even now, it has been disappointing to see so many self-proclaimed progressive intellectuals use "diversity of thought," or sometimes "diversity of personalities,"* as a convenient excuse to not challenge systemic oppression, while comforting themselves in being complicit in the continued exclusion of marginalized groups in the organizations they

---

*This would be a different, and useful, conversation if they were fighting for equity and access for neurodivergent people, autistic people, or disabled people. However, this is usually not what people mean when they use the phrases *diversity of thought or diversity of personalities*.

inhabit. For example, consider some white people's assertion that design-ing inclusion for introverts is just as important as supporting historically marginalized groups, using this as a way to claim a cut of the diversity pie for themselves without fully understanding how systemic oppression has impacted marginalized social groups throughout history. While there may be cultural biases against introverted personalities, there have never been government-sanctioned discrimination policies that rendered the entire group of introverts oppressed.

In 2020, a group of writers and artists cosigned and published what is now known as the Harper's Letter, which condemned an increasingly "in-tolerant climate" and "censoriousness" of the left that "weaken our norms of open debate and toleration of differences in favor of ideological conformity," likening the series of public calls for accountability to stifling atmospheres created by a "repressive government."[3] "Cancel culture" is a concept that has been widely debated in many spaces, from politics to social media to social justice organizing. When people denounce cancel culture, most people are condemning the tactic—the sensationalized and ruthless public takedowns through mass shaming with the ultimate goal of "canceling" individuals or entities, namely through losing their platform, job, company, or social sta-tus. What some people forget to take into consideration is, again, context: *Whom* are we canceling and *why*? *When* is a call to cancel someone or some-thing appropriate, and when is it not? *How* does such cancelation actually materialize?

When examined within context, cancel culture is a boycott tactic seeking to utilize mass mobilization, usually online, to hold people in positions of power accountable for abusing their power for an extended period of time despite multiple unsuccessful attempts to have them correct their behavior, or for an act so egregiously harmful it must be stopped immediately to re-duce future harm (think Harvey Weinstein, Louis C. K., Paula Deen, etc.). When utilized strategically and deliberately, it can be a highly effective way to deplatform individuals who have repeatedly caused harm using their power, or those whose lack of willingness to change could continue to jeopardize the safety of marginalized communities. Canceling, or what I'd rather call a public boycott, is not to be confused with the act of calling people out or calling people in, which are valid and necessary interpersonal intervention tools for shaping culture so that it's rooted in accountability, inclusion, and continuous learning.* But without paying attention to how and why public protest tactics are used, the phrase *cancel culture* has been co-opted by those most resistant to the idea of accountability to weaponize and fearmonger, changing the perception of this intervention tool from that of a strategic tactic to a blunt instrument for reactionary public takedowns for seemingly innocuous mistakes or an outright constitutional threat to free speech.

Cultural appropriation is another hot topic that gets conflated with cultural appreciation when missing the much-needed contextual analysis. Author Susan Scafidi in her book *Who Owns Culture?* defines cultural appropriation as "taking intellectual property, traditional knowledge, cultural expressions or artifacts from someone else's culture without permission."[4] Marginalized people can enact cultural appropriation and exploitation too, for example, when non-Black people of color use AAVE/BVE (African American Vernacular English/Black Vernacular English) temporarily to mock or for social clout, or when non-Indigenous people of color wear traditional Native headdress and clothing as costumes for their own entertainment, whether for Halloween or a music festival or as sports mascots. In January 2021, The Mahjong Line, a company founded by three white women, came under fire for culturally appropriating mahjong, a traditional Chinese game whose history goes back centuries and carries deep cultural significance. On their website, they shared their mission to bring a "refreshed" and "modernized" version of mahjong to the "stylish masses," and featured photos of white women playing their version of mahjong while seated at tables on a lawn, sipping white wine. They wrote that "there was so much potential in the words and expressions called out during a game," which implicitly positioned themselves, three white founders, as saviors who could "elevate" another culture that they deemed antiquated and primitive, while neglecting

---

*Calling *in* is typically thought of as a more compassionate approach to interrupting someone's problematic behavior, in which tactics like asking questions, pulling them aside in private, or encouraging a shift (versus directly naming and requesting change) are used. It's important to note, though, that when our defenses are activated, even being called *in* can feel like we're being called *out*, making it difficult to distinguish between the approaches. Both approaches of calling out and in are valid, and both help advance our practicing accountability. There are many nuanced debates around the dangers and/or usefulness of callout culture and disposability politics, all of which deserve contextual analyses and discernment (see Chapter 8, Permission to Be Called Out).

to mention any of the cultural significance of mahjong to the Chinese community or its lineage.[5] Though their intention to bring more awareness to mahjong may have been sincere, their complete disregard for the deep history of mahjong, blatant whitewashing of the game they deemed not stylish enough for the *white* masses, and ultimately their intention to profit off their savior complex and exploitation made this particular rendition of mahjong highly offensive and put it squarely in the category of cultural appropriation, not cultural exchange. Against the backdrop of escalating anti-Asian hate incidents, which was fueled by the same xenophobic, Sinophobic, and anti-Asian rhetoric mirrored by the three white women, this particular example served as a sobering reminder of our unjust reality, which made the pain sting even more.

> That power imbalance allows the culture being appropriated to be distorted and redefined by the dominant culture and siphons any material or financial benefit of that piece of culture away to the dominant culture, while marginalized cultures are still persecuted for living in that culture.
> —Ijeoma Oluo[6]

NO CONTEXT, NO CHANGE

CONTENT NOTE: *murder, anti-Blackness*

Before legitimizing uninformed commentaries and questions by engaging reactively, which then serves to give credence to these false narratives situated outside of context, we ought to practice first naming the contextual discrepancies and work to close the gap.

The false equivalencies and lack of contextual awareness apparent in all of the above examples are incredibly distracting to the work we're ultimately trying to do. In facilitating what most corporate leaders call "difficult conversations," we often remind people to distinguish between the idea of *safety* and *comfort*. When we fight for *safety* for the marginalized, what we're talking about is safety from being discriminated against, harassed, assaulted, fired, or killed by the system and supremacist culture, which has historically criminalized, subjugated, exploited, and violated them and continues to do so. This need for safety is not the same thing as cis, heterosexual white men wanting to avoid feeling *uncomfortable* while having difficult conversations around DEI, feeling "excluded" from initiatives centering marginalized identities, or feeling shame for making a mistake. And yet, the notions of safety and comfort are so often mistaken as the same thing, making it difficult for advocates to discern when to push or pull back the intensity of equity and inclusion programs and for whom these programs should exist. Without employing principled and informed contextual analysis, concepts like safety can be easily flattened, co-opted, and misunderstood.

When I moved to Oakland, my dad, whose only exposure to Oakland was the mainstream media's portrayal of it as a predominantly Black city ridden with poverty, homelessness, and crime, asked me with a concerned look on his face, "Is that a safe neighborhood?" In contrast, when talking to a local real estate agent about neighborhoods I should consider buying a home in, they pointed to a number of neighborhoods experiencing gentrification (or, in their words, "up-and-coming neighborhoods") by mostly white, Chinese, and Indian tech workers and emphasized how "safe" these neighborhoods were compared to other parts of Oakland. But what is safety without context? Trayvon Martin, a seventeen-year-old Black teen, was shot and killed inside a gated community in Sanford, Florida, while wearing a hoodie and holding a bag of Skittles. My partner, a dark-skinned brown man with a beard, hurries me along when I marvel at someone else's garden on our walks because he doesn't want anyone to call the cops on him for being "suspicious." "Don't put your hood on!" I shout at him as he leaves the house at night for a walk in his black hoodie. Who he fears is not another brown or Black person in a hoodie—it's our white neighbors who might conflate their discomfort with their safety being threatened and who, despite the known deadly risk, might call the police on Black and brown people to manage that discomfort. So again, what is safety, really, and for whom? What does safety look like for different people? How does safety manifest in different contexts? And how can we prioritize the safety of the most marginalized without being distracted by the discomfort of the privileged?

We cannot succeed in bringing about diversity, equity, inclusion, or justice unless we cling to context. For example, while there may be individual and interpersonal levels of prejudice enacted by people of color against white people, there can be no such thing as "reverse racism" because the current power disparity makes it so that people of color do not have systemic power over white people to materially change the lives of white people en masse whether through policy changes, hiring, wealth redistribution, and so forth. Here, we must remember that racism is not merely an interpersonal act of prejudice but also a complex set of systems, policies, and beliefs that reinforce the marginalization of people of color while privileging white people in society. Given this context, diversity goals or affirmative action are efforts that seek to *correct* the historical and present-day injustices faced by marginalized groups. The negative reactions to this "special treatment" incorrectly assume that the world is already a level playing field for all, and therefore these efforts are not only unnecessary but also unfair. Of course, corrective actions seem *unfair* when devoid of historical context. We saw similar illogical reactions during the COVID-19 pandemic, where ample data confirmed the disproportionate and deadly impact of the pandemic on Black people due to the continuing effects of systemic racism, including inequitable access to health care and overrepresentation in crowded housing conditions and essential jobs.[7] To remedy this, in July 2020, the state of Oregon approved the proposal of civic leaders and designated $62 million of its $1.4 billion in federal relief money to specifically address the needs of its Black residents, business owners, and community organizations. Despite the need for this deliberate attempt to address the disparity, millions of dollars of emergency aid were put on hold after two lawsuits surfaced, one class-action case led by a white business owner and another by a Mexican American business owner alleging racial discrimination, which followed the decades-old pattern of ahistorical reactions to antiracist policies, thwarting any attempts to restore equity and justice for the historically marginalized.[8] Instead of providing urgently needed resources to those most impacted by the convergence of the pandemic and systemic racism, advocates were forced to exhaust their energies fighting the misguided lawsuits, hoping to untangle the misunderstanding and get back to actually addressing the problem.

> The only remedy to racist discrimination is antiracist discrimination.
> —Dr. Ibram X. Kendi[9]

We need to have dedicated initiatives focused on increasing diversity, equity, and inclusion for specific groups of people because there is, and has

of them in the reality we live in. We cannot solve for in- if we don't first agree there is *exclusion* and *inequity* for people. We cannot achieve justice unless we acknowledge first. Creating change begins with a shared understand- ...ge is, in fact, necessary.

REMEMBER THE ABC: ALWAYS BE CONTEXTUAL

A lack of contextual analysis accompanying our journey ultimately serves to uphold existing systemic injustices by (1) erasing the long history of systemic oppression, (2) disregarding the continuing legacy of those oppressions, traumas, violence, and injustices, and (3) creating distractions that force us to expend energy trying to get back on the same page, rather than solving the actual problem. This chaotic cycle is incredibly exhausting and yet so common, and its ability to distort the work's integrity while creating mass confusion is second to none. Contextual analysis is key to ensuring we do not fall into the trap of false equivalence or reductive solutions that target the wrong problems. Here are some questions that can help guide us:

- **Who has or has had power?** Power, or the ability to influence and make decisions that impact others,[10] can come from organizational hierarchy or belonging to a dominant social identity group.* Notice any imbalance in power and determine who has power at interpersonal, organizational, and systemic levels.
- **How is the power being used?** Examine how power is being used and whether it's power *over (coercive)* or power *with (coactive).*† Is someone

---

*Social identity is different from personal identity. Social identities are derived from our perceived or actual membership in social groups (e.g., race, gender, sexual orientation, socioeconomic class, religion, etc.). Social identities influence the way our society is designed and experienced at both systemic levels (e.g., laws, policies, etc.) and personal levels (daily life). In contrast, personal identities are related to our sense of self and do not necessarily have a bearing on the way our society is structured (e.g., there are no specific bathrooms assigned for introverts or historical examples of discrimination against people who value compassion).[11]

†The earliest mention of the distinction between power *over* versus power *with* that I could find was from Mary Parker Follett, an American social worker and management theorist who, in the 1920s, wrote "power usually means power-over, the power of some person or

or an entity using or abusing power to diminish, harm, or exploit those with less power? Or is this a situation where a marginalized person or community is trying to *reclaim* power as a way to resist abuse? How might the response strategy and approach differ based on who is using the power and how it is being used?

- **Who benefits?** Who benefits from this action, situation, or use of power? In the case of borrowing from someone else's culture, who is the ultimate beneficiary in terms of social and material capital?
- **Who is harmed?** Who is harmed in the process? What was the harm (try to be as specific as possible)? How far does the harm extend? At whose or what expense is the situation happening?
- **What historical, social, cultural, or political context might I be missing?** What do I know for certain, and what am I unsure of? What beliefs and narratives have I been taught, and how might I validate or invalidate them through additional exploration? How might this additional context and understanding shift the way I view this particular situation?

Without full context, our justice work becomes a mere politically correct way of being polite on the surface rather than creating systemic shifts to restore dignity, respect, and power to historically oppressed people. When we fight for inclusion and equity, we're not just campaigning to "be nice to everyone"; we are doing so in the context of centuries of systemic oppression and exclusion that have marginalized people from specific social identity groups, prevented them from entering the workforce, barred them access to building generational wealth, and forced them to play catchup just to get to the same starting place as those who did not face those barriers. And when we fight for representation, it's not an intellectual thought exercise of gathering diverse perspectives for the sake of variety or innovation; it's a fight that seeks to address the historical legacies of slavery, genocide, disenfranchisement, misogyny, xenophobia, transphobia, homophobia, ableism and the

---

group over some other person or group, it is possible to develop the conception of power-with, a jointly developed power, a coactive, not a coercive power."[12] There are many different analyses and frameworks for understanding power. Some may find two additional concepts helpful: power *to* and power *within*. I've found the Power Matrix developed by Just Associates particularly helpful, which explores different dimensions of power and their interactions.[13]

likes that made any representation of marginalized groups an *impossibility*, especially in positions of power.

Fighting for inclusion, equity, representation, and justice is a continuation of the struggle that began with the founding of this country, and we cannot let sloppy ahistorical analyses and out-of-context false equivalencies get in the way of remembering the root of our fight.

CHAPTER 6

THE DOUBLE-EDGED SWORD
OF REPRESENTATION

In 2020, I was invited to take part in a daytime talk show on national TV for a segment on building trust and solidarity across women of different races. I was excited by the potential to be a cast member and for the opportunity to engage in an important conversation. Of course, I was also a tiny bit excited (translation: ecstatic) about my TV debut! Before they confirmed my role, a couple of different people interviewed me, asking screening questions to make sure I was the right fit. During my first call with an associate producer, a young white woman, I was asked to speak about my experience of being an Asian woman in America.

And so I shared my background as an immigrant, as well as the nuance of being a queer woman, and how my work in social justice activism shaped my worldview and how I experienced the for-profit workplace. I talked about my struggle with defying stereotypes of the "quiet, submissive Asian woman" as a loud, assertive, and vocal advocate for equity in the organizational setting. I talked about the casual biphobia and fetishization I experienced as a queer Asian woman navigating the misogynistic and racist corporate culture, as well as the daily microaggressions I endured while clenching my jaw trying to "make it" so I could achieve the financial stability that my parents so desperately wanted, and needed, for me. After each story, I was met with the same question: "Right . . . uh-huh, yup. What else?" I racked my brain to pull out any memories that would accentuate my narrative as an Asian woman, and I felt as though I was circling around the right answer that the producer had in mind. I wanted to impress her so that she would pick me, but it seemed as though the only way to do this was to tell the most obvious and blatant stories of anti-Asian discrimination and trauma. I found myself simultaneously resisting the one-dimensional immigrant narrative, trying to insert nuance and highly undervalued subtlety into my stories, while inching closer to the stories that I knew the producer and the audience were expecting and wanted to hear. "Well, with COVID, I've been told to go back to my country," I said. The assistant producer's voice brightened as the light bulb finally went off. "Yes! Tell me more about that."

> *The lie that Asians have it good is so insidious that even now as I write, I'm shadowed by doubt that I didn't have it bad compared to others. But racial trauma is not a competitive sport. The problem is not that my childhood was exceptionally traumatic but that it was in fact rather typical. Most white Americans can only understand racial trauma as a spectacle.*
> —Cathy Park Hong[1]

COMPLICATE THE NARRATIVE

The experience left me wondering, *Where's the line between representation and single-narrative exploitation?* Surface-level representation, or diversity as a mere symbol for justice without substantive systemic shifts, is one of the most common ways our society showcases and prematurely celebrates progress. Representation, when artificially curated using the same tools and approaches of oppression, obscures the enduring need for real change while offering a false sense of relief. Representation without a deeper analysis can quickly turn into another Band-Aid solution that perpetuates harm, for example through tokenization, generalization, appropriation, and erasure. Having more of the same story that feeds into people's thirst for our flattened, one-dimensional narratives is not *better* representation.

Media representation is one major way that shapes our awareness, so let's spend a moment examining Hollywood. While the representation of people of color in top film roles has been steadily improving at a rate of 30.9 percent according to the annual Hollywood Diversity Report by UCLA (still disproportionately underrepresented for Latine, Asian, and Native people at 4.9 percent, 4.8 percent, and 0.3 percent respectively), in 2019, only 1.5 out of 10 film directors were people of color, while the rest were white, and only 1.4 out of 10 film writers were people of color.[2] Representation on the surface of the screen is not enough—who is behind the scenes selecting, writing, and illustrating our stories matters too. Without adequate representation at all levels, especially in roles with real decision-making power to influence *how* we are represented, we are at risk of being limited to one-dimensional narratives written by and for our spectators, not us. These are the kinds of mainstream-gaze-driven narratives that seek to tug at the heartstrings of the audience—the rags-to-riches immigrant story, the heart-wrenching coming-out story, the resilience and earnest rehabilitation of the previously incarcerated person story, the "overcoming" disability story, and more—where the audience indulges in the trauma of the oppressed as inspiration, feeling a momentary satisfaction that comes from validating their tender hearts' ability to feel empathy for others. Of course, many of these narratives have merit and are important to be told, but the mainstream depiction of the marginalized tends to be narrow in its range and its purpose, rendering it shallow, predictable, and voyeuristic.

So many of our stories are told through the *interpretation* of our lived experiences by the dominant culture and for the betterment of its audience, whether it is for their education, awareness, inspiration, or action, rather than to center the honest and nuanced truth telling by and for the story owners. Sometimes we're even robbed of the opportunity to play the roles that are supposed to be about us. Scarlett Johansson, a white woman, playing an Asian character in *Ghost in the Shell*, or heterosexual and cisgender actors being applauded for their "realistic" acting while playing queer or trans characters, or the fact that 95 percent of characters with disabilities are played by nondisabled people[3] point to the disheartening resistance to granting true ownership and power to marginalized people with real lived experiences to tell their stories. Having our stories written, directed, and played without us is not representation; it's exploitation, or patronizing interpretation at best. And this long-standing historical pattern is found outside of Hollywood too, from corporate America to politics, where we see white antiracism "experts" be given more opportunities (and more money) than people of color to teach others about our traumas, and where feminist men are given more recognition than women for fighting against sexism on a daily basis. What type of representation and change can we expect from putting people who have no clue about our lived experiences in charge of changing our lives?

When we can take full control of our own stories—from the why to the how to the what to the who—what would those stories say? What do our stories sound, look, and feel like when our traumas aren't told for the sole purpose of convincing, entertaining, or educating our anthropologist audience? What stories of our joy, triumph, levity, dreaming, and tenderness are being robbed from our collective consciousness when the dominant culture feeds off our trauma, reducing our pain to yet another sensationalized news cycle that cements our expansive humanity into tragic moments? In addition to seeing the triumphant immigrant story of chasing the American Dream, I want to see a wildly mediocre immigrant character grappling with the ordinary issues of being a teenager. I want to see ridiculous, cringeworthy romantic comedies starring nonbinary and disabled people that are not patronizing, and I want to see a badass Asian action heroine whose superpower is not math or being an exotic femme fatale.

Korean American poet and writer Cathy Park Hong, in her book *Minor Feelings*, warns about the danger of defining ourselves through the white gaze: "Racial self-hatred is seeing yourself the way the whites see you, which turns you into your own worst enemy."[4] White supremacy culture and other forms of oppression disregard our desire to stretch our potential beyond their imagination. It edits, butchers, and retells our stories. It lowers the volume on truths it doesn't want the world to hear and turns up the volume when the message quenches its thirst for validation. And we become disposable the minute we veer off script. To achieve fuller, expansive, and complete representation, we ought to search for, appreciate, celebrate, and honor the *diverse experiences within diversity* and create room for stories that do not exist for the sole purpose of whetting the appetite of a culture that has been trained to expect a single narrative.

MAKING SPACE FOR *ALL* OF OUR STORIES:
AN ASIAN AMERICAN* EXPERIENCE

CONTENT NOTE: *colonization, mentions of torture and sexual violence*

Growing up in South Korea, I never thought about representation as a matter of struggle. I grew up seeing people who looked like me in different positions

---

*I use the term *Asian American* to refer to those who identify as Asians in the United States regardless of their documentation or citizenship status. I am not using the umbrella terms

of influence in society: teachers, politicians, inventors, athletes, musicians, actors, CEOs, comedians, writers, singers, artists, chefs; virtually everyone in the media and the figures featured in my history books were Korean. I never knew the experience of longing for familiar faces in the mainstream media until I moved to the United States.

Once in America, I felt weird claiming the Asian American identity at first, knowing how different my culture is from the other ethnicities lumped into the category. In fact, it offended me when I observed how no one in the United States seemed to care, or know, about Japan's colonization of Korea between 1910 and 1945 and would so casually collapse Korean people's struggles in this country with the struggles of Japanese Americans as if they were synonymous, despite the national trauma that still haunts my people's souls. I grew up being taught about my people's fight for survival and independence under Japanese rule, overcoming years of inhumane treatment, cultural erasure, torture, exploitation, and systematic rape of our women and girls by the Japanese Imperial army. Given the historical tension and precarity of the relationship between the two nations even to this day, being sorted alongside each other under one category felt odd and dismissive of our historical context.

My reservations began to diminish, however, once I realized the way American society views my people and those who once oppressed my people, how little white supremacy cares to distinguish or understand the complex humanity of those outside whiteness, and how uniformly oppressive xenophobia and racism are in this country dominated by white power. I realized how connected our struggles are, and how the term *Asian American*, coined by Emma Gee and Yuji Ichioka, was born out of a strategic political necessity to build pan-Asian solidarity and power in the late sixties, inspired by other social justice movements at the time like the Black Power movement and the antiwar movement.[5] It wasn't until later that I also learned about the history of Japanese incarceration on US soil beginning in

---

AAPI (Asian American and Pacific Islander) or AAPINH (Asian American, Pacific Islander, and Native Hawaiian) because I do not believe the following text sufficiently addresses the issues challenging the Native Hawaiian and Pacific Islander communities. And while I use Asian American, it is important to acknowledge that this coalitionary term born out of political activism is comprised of more than thirty-five different ethnic and national identities and that I certainly will not, nor am I attempting to, be able to capture the multitudes and complexities of all of our important stories.

1942, which forcibly relocated Japanese Americans to concentration camps, and that both my ancestors in Korea and Japanese Americans in the United States had been fighting for their lives and dignity at the same time, albeit in different contexts. With this glimpse into Asian American marginalization, I needed to find solace in *any* representation of Asian people, even if that meant looking into the faces of my ancestors' colonizers and being grateful for their mirrored features that resembled mine on the TV screen.

Part of rejecting the one-dimensional narrative is building our collective tolerance for different stories while resisting the urge to generalize and to-kenize, even when the stories do not meet our criteria of excellence or serve the movement, while still preserving our right to critique them. "This is not the type of representation we asked for" is a common response I've observed, and one I have used myself, when we lament a story, public figure, or work that does not accurately or respectfully depict the realities of our community. Within the Asian American community, this happened when the block-buster movie *Crazy Rich Asians* came out, portraying stories of, well, crazy rich Asians in all their glory and wealth, and similarly when Netflix launched *Bling Empire*, starring obscenely and unapologetically wealthy Asians in Los Angeles flaunting their power and political ignorance. Similar reactions oc-curred when Andrew Yang, who ran in the 2020 Democratic presidential primaries, fed into the problematic narrative of Asians as the model minority when his response to the increasing anti-Asian bigotry during the pandemic was for Asians to "show our American-ness" and prove that we, too, are wor-thy of respect and dignity through more service and hard work: "We need to step up; help our neighbors; donate gear; vote; wear red, white, and blue; volunteer; fund aid organizations; and do everything in our power to accel-erate the end of this crisis."[6] When I staunchly criticized his call to action on social media, I received messages from some Asian people (or, presumably, the "Yang Gang") who called me anti-Asian for "betraying my own kind" while decreasing our chances of being able to hold political power. I expe-rienced a similar reaction when I criticized the highly anticipated movie re-make of *Mulan* for having a predominantly white behind-the-scenes crew and for filming in Xinjiang,[7] a region in China where at least one million Ui-ghur Muslims are believed to be held in concentration camps.[8] In response, passionate Asian fans complained that I was destroying our opportunity for future productions starring a majority Asian cast.

Herein lies the problem in its complexities: the challenge with being limited representation in the first place is that we mistake valid critique as a call for no representation ("So, you'd rather us *not* have this person/story/ movie?"), or we fear that harsh critique will lead to even fewer opportunities for us to be represented; meanwhile, our hypervigilance around policing the kinds of stories that get told, particularly ones we perceive to be unfavorable to our justice movement, can also be unhelpful because we know no single story can encapsulate our multiple truths and diverse experiences. When our reaction, understandably, is to say, "That's not the kind of representation I want," what some of us are reacting to is the frustrating reality of being afforded limited opportunities to shape our narratives without the *privilege of individuality*, a form of white privilege coined by writer Michael Harriot. "Sins of one become the sins of all," says Harriot, citing examples of how Black and brown people and Muslims and Sikhs are so often collectively reduced to the violent acts of a few, while white people continue to exist as individuals with layers of complexity.[9]

The complex issue of representation within the Asian diaspora and more broadly the Pacific Islander, Native Hawaiian, and other historically under-represented and excluded communities, too, must be understood within its specific context, where there is perpetual anxiety and fear around erasure, tokenization, generalization, appropriation, and misrepresentation given the historical and present-day patterns of oppression we face in the United States. Asians in America are often gaslighted by a society that is committed to seeing us either as the model minority, where we're anything but oppressed, or as perpetual foreigners who will never fully belong.

What we might be reacting to is the anticipated erasure of our community's continued struggles and untold stories, that of undocumented Asian immigrants, migrant workers, and criminalized and incarcerated people, as well as radical AAPI activists in prison abolition, sex work decriminalization, labor organizing, disability justice, queer and trans liberation, and more who continue to be left out of public discourse. Like how the death-ridden labor of twelve thousand Chinese workers on the first transcontinental railroad was deliberately left out of historic photographs, and how the names of those who fought for equality alongside Black activists—Yuri Kochiyama, Grace Lee Boggs, Larry Itliong, and the likes—are so often unknown and their fights forgotten.

What we might be reacting to is the minimization or whitewashing of our struggles. The successes of the "crazy rich" few have outshone the many who live in poverty: the Asian community has the greatest and fastest-growing wealth gap in the country; according to Pew Research Center, between 1970 and 2016, the top 10 percent of Asian income earners made 10.7 times as much as those in the bottom 10 percent.[10] Despite the model minority stereotype, a 2021 Pew report showed that 12 out of 19 different Asian origin groups had poverty rates that were as high as or higher than the US average in 2019.[11] In the workplace, the bamboo ceiling continues to exist: Asian Americans are the least likely group to be promoted to leadership positions despite some ethnicities' overrepresentation in certain industries.[12] What many are rightfully reacting to is the very real repercussions of these reductive one-dimensional stories materializing in increased anti-Asian violence as well as structural discrimination that often target the most marginalized and vulnerable among us. Despite this dire situation, less than 1 percent of all philanthropic investments made by grant-making foundations goes to funding AAPI organizations.[13] So the reaction makes sense given that monolithic erasure is a particular flavor of oppression Asians have been experiencing in the United States for centuries, flattening our vastly diverse realities by painting over it with a singular brushstroke and ultimately contributing to increased levels of inequities and violence.

Thus, white supremacy culture and its scarcity and either-or mindset (either single-narrative representation or none at all) force us to be satisfied with limited representation without real power: a token Asian movie once every four decades; limited on- and off-screen opportunities for Asians; Asian stories told by and for the white gaze, often leading us to uphold the model minority myth even when we are seeking to escape it. White supremacy has trained us to be grateful for the pettiest amount of tasteless crumbs, while so much of our diversity and expansiveness continue to be invisibilized without a trace in the American psyche. Instead of accepting this frustrating reality, we must continue to demand *more space* for counterstereotypical and expansive stories while also allowing for constructive critiques of stories that cause harm. When I lived in Korea, I was not only exposed to Korean doctors, lawyers, or celebrities on TV, I was also exposed to Koreans who were struggling entrepreneurs, corrupt politicians, and perpetrators and victims of violence. I believe both breadth and depth of representation are necessary to telling the most complete and honest stories about our humanness. Welcoming multiple, and at times contradictory, stories to exist while granting ourselves the freedom to express our dissent and criticism enables us to achieve truly diverse and multidimensional representation beyond a one-dimensional narrative.

The real sign of progress would be when we can allow all of these stories and images, in their full authenticity, to coexist without fearing that we had *one shot* and we blew it, because somehow the world has gotten enough of our stories after one blockbuster hit, one problematic TV series, and one tokenized politician. When we, too, are able to exist on a spectrum, from *The Avengers* to *Jersey Shore*, from *David Letterman* to *Game of Thrones*, while also giving ourselves permission to unabashedly criticize stories we do not resonate with. When the audience is able to resist the urge to generalize and cement a single narrative that ends up causing irreparable harm and lasting repercussions on our ability to demand equity, justice, and freedom. When we are allowed to be unexceptional but *real*. And when we no longer live in a perpetual state of anxiety about mattering. . . . Then perhaps we'll know we've gotten somewhere. I want to take up space without the burden of representing my entire community, not only because that is an unfair and arduous task but also because I simply cannot.

THE LIMITS OF REPRESENTATION

Diverse representation is important in its own right: it allows society's consciousness to shift, normalizing perceived differences within our communities and helping to reshape the narratives that have largely been "male, pale, and stale." More importantly, seeing ourselves represented affects how we see our own potential. It acknowledges realities beyond our imagination of what we thought previously possible, for example, that a Black, South Asian woman can become the vice president of the United States of America. We need more representation of marginalized people and historically underrepresented people in all areas of society, always. However, let us not fool ourselves into believing that representation alone will get us collective liberation. A community can be represented, or even overrepresented, and still be marginalized and lacking real power all at the same time; this is why the terms *marginalized* and *underrepresented*, though often related, are not interchangeable.

Representation has its limits. We've seen time and again how representation can be perceived and treated as the ultimate goal, when in reality, it is just one of many milestones toward change mistakenly dressed as completion. It is not enough to insert diversity into oppressive systems and expect immediate transformation, as the changed faces can still enact the same patterns of violence to uphold systemic oppression. Even when a select few break through ceilings, the unfortunate reality is that they often still lack real power to enact change inside toxic systems overwhelmingly controlled by white men. Additionally, there are two other key reasons why we can't rely on representation alone for systemic transformation: (1) internalized oppression in marginalized people is real, and (2) we cannot keep putting blanket, disproportionate expectations on already marginalized people to shoulder the additional burdens that come with representation.

Over the years, I've had the opportunity to meet with hundreds of heads of diversity at prominent organizations all across America, as well as CEOs, some of whom hold marginalized identities. One of the most disappointing parts about working to create change from within harmful systems has been the dissonance my team and I feel when we witness marginalized people working to serve and protect the interests of those in positions of power rather than fighting for the marginalized, including their own communities. There have been times when I've found myself walking away from opportunities not because white men executives were not receptive to our message but because we were never granted access by those who sought to preemptively protect their fragility from being unleashed:

"We're just not there yet."

"Can you just focus on gender [translation: cis, heterosexual, white women] and not race for now?"

"Can you maybe not use *those* words? You know how defensive they can get."

At one global tech company, my team and I spent over six months delivering workshops designed to combat white supremacy culture and anti-Black racism. We received overwhelmingly positive feedback from its employees, especially its Black employees, who repeatedly asked that their executive team be exposed to the same level of honest conversation and explicit education. Despite this, the Asian woman director of diversity assured us that the executive team was "not ready" for the conversation and instead proposed an hour-long presentation on cognitive bias and high-level diversity trends they should be aware of. "You know how they are," she said, with a shrug and a laugh, as if I should agree. A different company, a multibillion-dollar financial conglomerate, received troubling accounts of biased hiring and promotion practices and toxic workplace culture for marginalized employees via its employee engagement survey results. The head of HR, a white woman who favored our critical yet compassionate approach, hired my company to address these issues but then quit a few months later while we were in the midst of our engagement. During this time, the company brought on a new senior vice president of diversity, a Black man whose legal background was seen as a huge asset to the firm. During my first conversation with him, I found myself in a delicate standstill, with me trying to tactfully decline his request to put together a custom workshop targeting the company's employee resource group (ERG) leaders. Having previously come from an even more hierarchical and toxic employer, the new diversity leader was impressed by the surface-level commitment of the all-white executive team and was gravely alarmed by the "angry" and "militant" demands of the ERG leaders. He believed the young and passionate ERG leaders needed more professionalism, patience, and appreciation and "to learn how to influence without getting angry and realize how good they have it here." Less rage, more diplomacy. Fewer demands, more gratitude. He, like many other gatekeepers I've met in this work, was quick to offer credit and praise to the well-intentioned white men leaders who displayed the bare minimum level of awareness and care, before paying any respect or curiosity to understanding the agonizing battle scars endured by marginalized employees. And make no mistake, gatekeeping, respectability politics, and power-coddling behaviors by those in relatrive positions of power are seen widely across all industries beyond the for-profit sector, in academic institutions, nonprofits, and government agencies.

> *The oppressed internalize the values of the oppressor. Therefore, any group that achieves power, no matter how oppressed, is not going to act differently from their oppressors as long as they have not confronted the values that they have internalized and consciously adopted different values.*
> —Grace Lee Boggs[14]

Respectability politics and exceptionalism are survival skills mastered by many marginalized people (including myself, as you will see in Chapter 12, Hold Trauma with Care), and they can become deeply internalized as we taste the rewards of momentary acceptance, belonging, and proximity to power. Internalized oppression misleads us to believing that the way we gain respect and are given power is through compliance and conformity to the rules of oppressive systems. Internalized white supremacy, coupled with the ever-present need to survive within violent systems through covering* (downplaying or toning down stigmatized identity to assimilate or to survive), code-switching† ("adjusting one's style of speech, appearance, behavior, and expression in ways that will optimize the comfort of others in exchange for fair treatment, quality service, and employment opportunities"),[17] and appeasing, interferes with one's ability to advocate for real change by disrupting the status quo. It is difficult to find marginalized people in positions of *real* power, and it is even more difficult to find people in such positions who are able and willing to *exercise* that power in favor of the broader justice movement, perhaps because not doing so is rewarded with upward mobility and protection and doing so is punished and penalized. We sometimes trade in radical change for incremental wins, not because we don't believe in the need for radical shifts but because we believe that it is the *only* way to achieve *any* change at all and to mitigate further harm within highly policed systems upon which our survival depends. And while I am all about changes of all shapes, sizes, and increments, when we preemptively downsize our actions to appease the powerful, we risk having even that incremental shift be directed toward maintaining the status quo. When marginalized people in relative positions of power uphold systems of oppression, their representation is merely symbolic for what could truly be possible: transformation from the inside out, toxicity excavated from within each system and each of us.

---

*Covering was first coined by sociologist Erving Goffman in 1963, and the concept was further studied and expanded by legal scholar Kenji Yoshino.[15]

†Code-switching was first coined by sociolinguist Einar Haugen in 1954 to describe the shifting between two or more languages in a conversation. The particular definition I use in this chapter is one provided by Courtney L. McCluney, Kathrina Robotham, Serenity Lee, Richard Smith, and Myles Durkee in a Harvard Business Review article entitled "The Costs of Code-Switching,"[16] which I believe most accurately encapsulates the modern-day usage and understanding of the term.

There is a fine line between conforming to the pressures of oppressive systems to survive and enthusiastically upholding oppressive structures to gain access to the same power. The line can sometimes be frustratingly difficult to discern, but there is a difference, and being able to hold the complexity of both circumstances is instrumental to our ability to course-correct as we go. Recognizing the challenging circumstances doesn't mean we absolve marginalized people who aid in the oppression of their own or other marginalized communities, but it does mean we ought to examine the conditions they are navigating and who ultimately holds power to create change. We should use our discernment to distinguish between who is using strategic foresight versus relying on respectability politics; who is influencing to advocate for real change versus coddling those in positions of power; who is actually serving the most marginalized versus protecting and shielding the powerful; who is stretching with limited power and resources versus using what limited power and resources they have to uphold the status quo; who is aligned with the politics of the movement versus projecting their internalized oppression. As mentioned before, discerning between motivations to obtain safety and desires to avoid discomfort becomes a critical practice here.

And it is worth repeating: when people of color replicate white supremacy culture, intentionally or unintentionally, it is not the same thing as white people perpetuating white supremacy culture. As noted in Chapter 5, The Only Constant Is Context, analyzing who holds power, who is impacted by the power, and who is ultimately responsible for systemic violence and oppression is important to ensuring we do not shift the blame of white supremacy entirely onto those who are seeking to survive within an oppressive structure. I'm not calling for absolution of complicity based on one's marginalization; rather, I'm asking us to pause and consider what equitable consequences might look like, in a way that is rooted in principled discernment of context.

THE INEQUITABLE BURDEN OF REPRESENTATION

The second reason representation alone is not enough to effect change is because we cannot continue to place a blanket expectation on marginalized people in relative positions of power to take on the disproportionately heavy burden of representing and fighting for their identity groups' needs. A CEO of a well-funded tech company once told me she didn't want to be described as a woman of color CEO; she wanted to be known only for her ability to lead her company and nothing else. She explained that she did not feel she had ever been treated differently because of her race or gender and that emphasizing her social identities felt like she would be playing the "victim" rather than being seen as an equal to white men CEOs known simply for their merit.

I was disappointed by the missed opportunity for her to create a more empowering narrative that could shed a light on the inequities women of color face at work. Though I understood, to a degree, her desire to be known just for her accomplishments and to avoid the inevitability of tokenization and other pressures, there was nothing more I would have liked than to see every marginalized person in visibly influential roles claiming, loudly and proudly, their experiences of oppression and resilience as a way to own their identities, demand justice, and smash the myth of meritocracy as a shining example for others. I used to feel intense frustration and even resentment toward such public figures who didn't seem interested in taking up space with all of their opportunities; I called them sellouts, not yet self-actualized under the spell of internalized oppression, intoxicated by their proximity to power while their communities suffered. I was a harsh critic. And then I realized how I, too, was inadvertently enforcing another form of tokenization, forcing my own reductive, single-narrative expectations on them instead of allowing them to exist in their own story. I realized just how much more I was expecting from marginalized and underrepresented people who had managed to succeed in unwelcoming spaces, in contrast to the low expectations I had set for white men leaders who have far less to lose besides their comfort and slivers of hoarded power. I realized how often I demanded to be seen *through* those who shared my bodily reflections and assumed that they, too, shared my pain, context, and desire to be stewards of our movement. I started noticing how frequently and nonchalantly we as a society rob marginalized people of their freedom to just *be* and to exist without having to shoulder the burden of solving injustices they did not create while also suffering from them in their daily lives.* I also learned that the quicker I ac-

---

*I do believe it is important to expect different levels of responsibility and accountability from those who hold positions that are *explicitly* about dismantling systemic oppression (e.g., DEI leaders, government officials, etc.). Part of the job of leading DEI efforts inside organizations

cept the fact that I cannot expect marginalized people in positions of power to want to share the responsibilities of the movement, the less heartache I experience and the faster I'm able to employ more effective tactics to work within this context.

We say, "With great power comes great responsibility" (thank you, Spider-Man!). But do we demand the same type of responsibility from those with the *most power*, those who are direct beneficiaries of the oppressive systems, and hold them to the same standards of accountability as we do for marginalized communities with fractions of such power? Of course, everyone who holds power should be held to a standard that seeks to reduce harm and cultivate equity and justice, and those who perpetuate violence, regardless of their identities, must practice accountability. The answer isn't to stop expecting anything from anyone, but I believe we ought to shift our demands to those who benefit the most from perpetuating systemic oppressions, or at the very least extend to them the same level of fervor and scrutiny we give to marginalized people in positions of power. In this process, we intentionally give marginalized people agency to exist without the *disproportionate* expectation to be martyrs and lift the automatic pressure of assuming that they will represent their community's needs in all ways.

The same need is especially true for marginalized people *without* organizational power who exist within toxic systems. I've worked with countless "Onlys"[18] inside workplaces—the only person of color, the only trans person, the only disabled person, the only woman—who, even when they are not expected to lead diversity initiatives, feel the pressure of being a model employee to defy negative stereotypes and to ensure paths can be cleared for more of their folks to come through the doors they're holding open. In our workshops, I often see these Onlys in the room—probably more nervous than the rest of the room about how this DEI conversation is going to go and how much additional emotional and educational labor they'll need to take on either during or after the workshop. The pressure for them to represent their community in a positive light while honoring their own needs and boundaries can feel like an overfilled balloon ready to explode.

---

is taking risks to challenge the status quo. The expectation of that risk taking should be even greater for people working as independent consultants, because they are likely to face fewer penalties and diversified risks compared to those who are employed within one organization.

I've been there, too, often as the only queer woman of color employee in rooms filled with people who expect me to be their social justice encyclopedia. This experience of being seen as a token of a community can feel exhausting, isolating, and threatening, especially when no one around us notices the unequal and unfair pressure to represent our identity group(s) or expects us to speak up against bias and educate others who "just want to learn" at the expense of our emotional labor. This is heightened in professional settings when we are trying our best to show up as a positive, hardworking team player, but a part of us remains in a constant state of censorship because we don't want to sound like we're complaining or being too aggressive when bringing up concerns around being tokenized. The permission to represent ourselves, and ourselves only, isn't the type of privilege that is granted to marginalized and underrepresented people by default. We are constantly performing, rather than just being.

While it may feel like it is our duty to represent our community in a favorable light so we don't perpetuate stereotypes or jeopardize others' chances to succeed, we must remember it is also purposeful to allow ourselves to exist without centering the gaze of the privileged and to fully embrace our own complex, diverse, and layered narratives. The burden lies on the gazers to resist the temptation to generalize or flatten the narratives of marginalized communities based on the actions of a few. And *all of us* must be vigilant to avoid becoming the imposers of reductive narratives when we find ourselves bearing witness to others' stories.

Remember that the conscious act of establishing boundaries and allowing ourselves agency is a liberatory practice necessary to resist exploitation and reclaim our own stories. Liberation does not come at the expense of marginalized people; justice without our agency is no justice at all.

PART 3

SHOWING UP

CHAPTER 7

CENTER THE
MOST MARGINALIZED

I did not have health insurance all throughout high school because my family couldn't afford it. Whenever I got seriously ill, instead of visiting a nearby doctor's office like other kids, my dad woke me up at five in the morning to drive us to an unnamed clinic run by a Vietnamese doctor in a predominantly Mexican neighborhood, about an hour away from where we lived. There would always be a line, as most of the visitors were anxious to be seen before having to go to work. I still remember the stench from the rundown butcher shop next door, which always reeked of spoiled meat and blood, as soon as we pulled into the parking lot. The minute my dad parked the car, I would jump out to write my name down on a piece of paper hanging on the not-yet-open clinic's door to secure my spot, which would come in two to three hours' time. That was about all the "paperwork" we ever needed to do. They never asked for any documents—no proof of insurance, driver's license, or state ID—and the visit always cost twenty dollars flat, then another twenty if you received a shot or an unmarked bottle of mystery antibiotics. *Cash only*. I envied my friends who talked about their "primary care physician"—it sounded like such luxury to have someone who understands your holistic health needs, is fully equipped with your medical history and is willing and able to take the time to explain different treatment options. Unless the pain was absolutely unbearable, I avoided going to the clinic at all cost.

Not being able to see a doctor whenever I was sick wasn't the only downside to the precarious circumstance of living without health insurance. It also meant not being able to present a doctor's note, which some teachers required to avoid an absence penalty, having to explain why it was difficult for me to obtain an immunization record, and sometimes being precluded from participating in certain activities or programs. Not having access to one thing, it turns out, means losing out on many things, because our systems and policies are often designed with an assumption that everyone already has equal and blanket access to everything. I often wonder how our education system—and our society at large—might look like if designed by and from the perspective of those who do not have equal access to various needs that are required to navigate today's world without friction.

WHAT DOES "CENTERING THE MOST MARGINALIZED" MEAN?

To me, centering the most marginalized is an approach rooted in the foundational belief that by centering and valuing those most impacted by systemic oppressions we are able to create the most comprehensive and effective solutions that can ultimately benefit *all* of us. The approach acknowledges that the most marginalized are also ones with the most clarity around the unmet needs and realities of systemic inequities and therefore should be given *real power* to lead, beyond mere inclusion or consideration. It means prioritizing their voices and demands while deliberately shifting resources and decision-making powers to enable their top-level leadership. It means destroying the assumption that people who have more privileges know more or better and designing systems, processes, policies, cultures, and products that value the full and complex humanity of marginalized people, including their lived experiences, wisdom, agency, and dignity.

> *Living as we did—on the edge—we developed a particular way of seeing reality. We looked both from the outside in and from the inside out. We focused our attention on the center as well as on the margin. We understood both. This mode of seeing reminded us of the existence of a whole universe, a main body made up of both margin and center. Our survival depended on an ongoing public awareness of the separation between margin and center and an ongoing private acknowledgment that we were a necessary, vital part of that whole.*
> —bell hooks[1]

So, *who* exactly are the "most marginalized"?

It's important to note that focusing on the most marginalized is not about engaging in the "Oppression Olympics,"* where we stack rank and compete to determine who is more or less oppressed than others while trivializing the experiences of those who are thought to be "less" marginalized. Rather, the approach demands that we recognize the impacts of systemic oppression that have marginalized specific social identities for centuries (e.g., Black, Indigenous, and people of color; disabled people; queer and trans people; women; etc.), while privileging others (e.g., white people, heterosexual and cisgender people, abled people, men, etc.). And it guides us to take an intersectional approach (thank you, Dr. Kimberlé Crenshaw!) to understand the compounding effects of multiple systems of oppression that create unique experiences even among already marginalized groups. For instance, we cannot solve issues of sexism just by listening to white cisgender women; instead, we need to seek out the needs of women of color and beyond that center the experiences of Black, Indigenous, disabled, trans, undocumented, fat, queer, poor women in order to design much more comprehensive solutions that ultimately benefit *all women*. Within the AAPI community, too, there is colorism and classism that leave darker-skinned people in lower social or socioeconomic statuses more vulnerable to the impacts of multiple systems of oppression than those who are light-skinned and belonging to a higher social or socioeconomic status. This doesn't mean light-skinned AAPI people don't experience marginalization or do not deserve to be listened to, but it does mean that efforts seeking to dismantle oppressions faced by AAPI people will be incomplete unless they solve for the experiences of those at multiple different intersections of oppression.

The acronym BIPOC (Black, Indigenous, and people of color) has been gaining popularity in recent years over the acronym POC (people of color), which dates back to 1796, in an effort to acknowledge and center the experiences of Black and Indigenous communities[4] that have been prone to erasure and flattening when we speak of people of color communities in general. Without diving into the debate around the efficacy of these acronyms, which

---

*According to Wikipedia, the first potential recorded use of the term was by Chicana feminist Elizabeth "Betita" Martínez in a conversation with Dr. Angela Davis at UC San Diego in 1993.[2] Professor and author Ange-Marie Hancock defines Oppression Olympics as "an evocative term to describe intergroup competition and victimhood" in her book, *Solidarity Politics for Millennials*.[3]

I discuss in Chapter 9, Change Through Language, let's pause to reflect on why some may be advocating for this distinction. In understanding racism in America, I've found it impossible to arrive at meaningful antiracist solutions that center the most marginalized without a rigorous understanding of anti-Black racism, anti-Indigeneity, and, though often skipped over, imperialism. This is because these forces, undergirded by white supremacy and racial capitalism, have fundamentally shaped the experiences of all people of color in the United States (and abroad) through the specific US histories of chattel slavery, the genocide of Indigenous peoples, and imperialist wars waged globally, setting the foundation upon which every system was built and how and why certain racial groups took root in the United States. These complex and evolving historical legacies continue to proliferate today, manifesting themselves through mass incarceration, the racial wealth gap, immigration and refugee policies, and more. It is imperative that we remain grounded in this country's history and stay alert to recognize its continuing impacts as we hone our approach to centering the most marginalized in the context of fighting racism and other forms of oppression.

Centering the most marginalized is an approach that helps us proactively recognize any deficiencies in vital perspectives outside our bubble of privilege that can only come from the lived experiences of those most impacted by the issues we're trying to solve. It is not an absolute rubric but rather an approach adaptable to any context and scope of the work. Take, for example, the urgent issue of climate change. We cannot adequately solve climate change unless we take into full account the disproportionate impact it has on communities of color, particularly Black and brown people, Indigenous people, poor people, disabled people,[5] and, more broadly, poor and low-income countries, who are left to shoulder its most devastating impacts.[6] Numerous studies have shown that Black and low-income communities are disproportionately exposed to toxic air pollution in the United States and face the least amount of reinvestment after natural disasters compared to their white and wealthier counterparts,[7] both as a result of centuries-old systemic racism and legacies of racist policies like redlining.[8] Indigenous peoples "who are impacted first and worst by climate change," as explained by Tara Houska of Couchiching First Nation,[9] have been sounding the alarm on climate change for a long time based on their vast knowledge and reliance on the environment, despite Western science's early dismissal and delayed acknowledgment.[10] Indigenous peoples have been at the forefront of the environmental justice movement, fighting corporate extractions and oil pipeline constructions, while sharing their invaluable wisdom to protect and preserve the land, water, air, and human lives. Talia Buford of ProPublica reminds us, "Knowledge comes from people who have been here all along, and from whom we could learn a lot, if we are willing to listen."[11]

By "center the most marginalized," I'm imploring that we take an intentional approach to ensure we do not exclude or disregard sets of experiences that are essential to a fuller analysis of the issues in front of us by asking: Who are the people most impacted? Who is *not* in the room but should be? How can we ensure that the most marginalized are moved from the margins to the center, not as temporary guests but as leaders with the power to transform the room itself?

> The biggest issue we face is shifting human consciousness, not saving the planet. The planet does not need saving, we do.
> —Xiuhtezcatl Martinez[12]

HOW DO WE DO IT?

CONTENT NOTE: *transphobia*

1. Decenter the Needs of the Privileged

A few years ago, I came across a YouTube video starring a group of people in what appeared to be a diversity workshop. The group consisted of various individuals of different races. After reviewing the importance of cross-cultural dialogue, the white man facilitator turned to a Black participant and said, "Go ahead, tell them about your pain," gesturing to a couple of white people sitting near them. I promptly closed the browser.

One of the most common ways we fail to center the most marginalized is by shifting the burden of emotional and educational labor onto them as a way to center the needs of the privileged. Marginalized people are asked to retell and relive their traumatic moments so others can learn from them; they are expected to tone down their anger and hurt for others' comfort; they are forced to speed up their healing process—or skip it entirely—so that they can be a resource to others. Just like the white woman host who encouraged white women to befriend other women of color in Chapter 2, Know Your Why, no matter how genuine our intentions are, this pattern of centering and prioritizing the needs of the privileged reproduces unjust dynamics that continue to harm the most marginalized.

Nonbinary actor and activist Indya Moore, in one of their Instagram Live sessions during Trans Awareness Week, shared a recent encounter they had while getting waxed. They recalled how the person who was waxing them, a cis woman, asked Moore where they got their "vagina done" because she "didn't like the way hers looked." Moore continued, "Do you understand what that feels like? . . . Why am I suddenly in a space where I'm needing to hold and be present and be a resource for you?"[13]

Despite Moore's thorough and heartfelt explanation, a dizzying number of people commented on Moore's video still defending the cis woman and her "genuine curiosity," while calling Indya "overly sensitive," "angry," and "mean." "Why are you offended by this?" "Why can't you just teach her?" "She was just trying to connect." Yes, it is human for us to want to develop connections and identify on common grounds (note, however, that the cis woman's disliking her labia's appearance is *not* comparable to trans people's decision to medically transition*). But what so many failed to recognize was the incredibly predictable pattern of how we, as a society, expect marginalized people to serve as a "vessel," as Moore called out, or a resource for others to become more educated, feel at ease, and be validated. Adding insult to injury, the cis woman's question followed the dehumanizing impulse of many cisgender people who too often reduce trans and nonbinary people's expansive humanity to their body parts.

The experience of being asked to explain ourselves, provide analysis of our traumas, hold space for others' learning and processing, and affirm their "genuine efforts," all despite the crushing weight placed on us, is all too common among people with any marginalized identity. As an immigrant, I'm often asked about my experience of moving to the States and learning English, and as a queer woman I'm asked about my coming-out story and when I first realized I was queer. It is not that I don't want people to ever ask me

---

*The process of transitioning looks different for different people. Not everyone who identifies as trans goes through medical transitions. Everyone's gender identity is valid and deserves full respect, regardless of what their transition process looks like.

these questions as a way to learn or connect, but it is important for people to understand just how often I am faced with these questions—almost always without first being asked about my boundaries or capacity to share and very rarely with any purpose other than to satiate others' curiosity. Despite the genuine attempts, sometimes people, eager to learn and connect, end up causing harm by forgetting the importance of honoring the needs, boundaries, and desires of the marginalized. Sometimes, we need the space to just *be* without having to explain our *being*.

> *Being visible and trans is not an invitation to be studied.*
> —Indya Moore[14]

The burden society puts on the marginalized to perform in a way that caters to the privileged can be seen similarly when we engage in tone-policing—when we are hyperfocused on the tone in which a message is delivered rather than on the message itself. When a marginalized person calls us out and we ask for "civility" and "respect," we are yet again prioritizing our own emotional needs over the pain, anger, sadness, disappointment, and hurt felt by those experiencing the actual pain. (Imagine our loved one telling us to "calm down" when we're really upset, except it's not over dirty dishes but centuries of systemic oppression; and instead of being able to fire back, marginalized people are often forced to comply due to negative repercussions.) When we engage in tone-policing, we spend our energy demanding the message be presented to us on a silver platter of politeness and compassion, instead of focusing on creating space for honest and righteous reactions to injustice. It is a different way of saying, *My emotional well-being matters more than yours*, yet again perpetuating the unjust patterns of supremacy culture that devalue the humanity of the marginalized while centering the entitlement of the privileged.

To help recognize these patterns, here are additional examples that show how we unwittingly center ourselves over the needs of the marginalized, and how we can correct this dynamic:

- Prioritizing our education over the labor of marginalized people: "Can you educate me?" "Tell me why you're so upset." "What resources would you recommend?" Instead, engage in proactive and continuous self-education and use existing resources. Always ask for permission before asking someone to educate us. Whenever appropriate, offer to compensate people for their educational labor.

- Prioritizing our comfort by diluting, whitewashing, or tone-policing uncomfortable truths that activate our defensiveness. Instead, practice discerning between discomfort and safety and lowering our defenses when we feel challenged. Validate marginalized people's lived experiences fully and create a culture where honest and precise language is welcomed over euphemisms.

- Adopting a sense of superiority (savior complex) when we attempt to meet a need: for example, hesitating to give money to an unhoused person because we worry about how they will spend it ("Will they use it to buy drugs?"), which centers ourselves even in moments of supposed selflessness because *we* want to dictate how *our* money is spent. Instead, respect marginalized people's (including those leading organizations and movements) agency and trust that they have the ability, power, and knowledge to act in ways that best serve them.

- Disrespecting boundaries set by marginalized people: ignoring marginalized people's request to not engage in certain conversations, especially ones pertaining to their identities or lived experiences, or failing to ask for consent before jumping into venting or unloading our thoughts on issues that require emotional labor. Instead, always ask for consent to gauge the other person's capacity and willingness to engage.

- "Creating change" at the expense of the marginalized: in the social media age, many argue that sharing videos of racial violence—whether it's police brutality against Black people or anti-Asian violence—can play an important role in building groundswell public outrage and demand for accountability, especially where traditional media has failed; on the flip side, many in the Black community have criticized the sensationalization of Black trauma, perpetuation of the single narrative, and retraumatizing of the community by replaying these images over and over for the education and mobilization of the masses. A similar conversation is taking place within the Asian community in response to the rapid rise in videos depicting anti-Asian violence. As someone who has both criticized and shared such videos, I practice pausing and reflecting before indiscriminately hitting the "share" button: What is the request from the impacted community with regards to amplifying this incident? Do we need this video to spread awareness or to believe the existence of this violence? And more broadly, we must continue to ask: Whose needs are we centering when we require visual proof beyond the words of survivors before being moved to act? Is retraumatizing those most impacted by the trauma a necessary by-product of fighting for justice? I don't believe there is one right answer to these questions in our current reality, but I implore all of us to grapple with these tensions nonetheless.

- Looking for credit or public acknowledgment for every self-proclaimed allyship action to virtue signal or to avoid practicing accountability when we've caused harm (e.g., "But I was at the Women's March!" "I donated to Black Lives Matter; I can't be racist."). Instead, revisit the foundation of allyship and the deeper why for being on this journey. Our allyship actions are time bound and should not be used to elevate ourselves or to absolve us from practicing accountability. Remember, allyship is about consistency and achieving equity and justice, while holding ourselves accountable to the needs of the most marginalized.
- Rushing to be forgiven when we've caused harm (and worse, lashing out when we're not forgiven immediately) and wanting to be reassured that we're still a "good person." Instead, focus on fully understanding and repairing the harm we caused and practice accountability without the expectation of being forgiven (more on this in Chapter 8, Permission to Be Called Out).

Sometimes, it might feel like we're getting contradicting pieces of advice: "How are we supposed to not put the burden on marginalized people but also listen to them at the same time?" "Aren't we supposed to be following their lead? Now you're telling us to figure it out and do the work ourselves?" Let's tease this out, since the answer is usually somewhere in the both-and. Both practices—listening to the most marginalized and not shifting the labor burden on marginalized people—when coupled with contextual analysis and the continual practice of decentering ourselves will get us closer to centering the most marginalized.

Take for example a well-intentioned white man CEO who is just waking up to the reality of white supremacy culture and hastily engages one of his only Black employees, whose job isn't to lead racial equity trainings, to hold space for his processing without their enthusiastic consent. In this instance, the CEO is prioritizing his own need for education at the expense of the Black employee's agency and (likely free) labor while wielding his organizational power. What could he have done instead? For starters, he could begin by regulating his own desires and reflecting on his sense of urgency and other emotions that may be coming up, asking questions like, "Why is it that I'm only now waking up to this reality?" or "Why is it that I don't know what to say or do in this moment?" Then, rather than assuming his employee has the capacity, knowledge, or desire to educate him, he could ask for permission to ask questions after having done his own homework and offer additional compensation for the employee's time and expertise (which the employee may or may not have beyond speaking about their lived experiences), or better yet actually hire willing and prepared Black racial justice educators to support his delayed learning.

Decentering our needs and centering the most marginalized involve shifting the burden of emotional and educational labor onto ourselves, be it de-escalating our defenses, checking our sense of entitlement, or educating ourselves, so that the same group of people do not have to continuously expend their energy beyond what they consented to.

2. Design Solutions Beginning with the Most Marginalized

My first major opportunity to practice the approach of "centering the most marginalized" happened in college when I launched Queer Youth Leadership Camp (QYLC) with a number of other queer and trans youth activists on campus. QYLC was a weekend summer camp experience geared toward empowering low-income LGBTQ+ youth of color who were not yet out, who often experienced isolation and bullying, and who were left out of receiving critical resources only accessible through public channels. One major issue they faced in accessing services, participating in programs, and receiving resources was the legal requirement of obtaining parental consent, which made it difficult for youth nonprofits and community-based organizations to provide support. We wanted to address this unmet need by creating a covert opportunity for not-yet-out queer and trans youth to gather and build community while learning various activism and self-empowerment skills.

Our planning began by gaining a detailed understanding of the young people's circumstances and designing our programs to meet them where they were. Ensuring their safety, access, and dignified empowerment remained our top priority throughout. Many of us had been in similar circumstances only a year or two prior to entering college, so we let our lived experiences guide our planning. Instead of mass-promoting the event on popular LGBTQ+ resource websites (this was when we were using flip phones and Blackberries and when many young people without laptops had to go to the school library to "surf the web" using public computers), we engaged in one-on-one outreach to local high schools and encouraged school counselors and Gay Straight Alliance (GSA) advisers to pass on the information discretely so as not to inadvertently out them to their family or friends. Our fundraising covered 100 percent of the Camp's expenses, and we received in-kind donations from local restaurants and shops to ensure money was not a barrier to the students' participation. We drafted two different versions of the event overview—one for the young people and one for their parents and guardians who may not have been amenable to sending them to a "queer camp" by rebranding QYLC to Quarterly Youth Leadership Camp (there weren't very many words that began with the letter q!), overemphasizing the portions focusing on the college application process, scholarships and grants, and leadership development to increase the chances of them granting permission. We trained all of our volunteer student staff to treat each student with dignity and respect, ensuring we did not replicate the harmful cycle of violent disciplinary actions that Black and brown queer and trans young people were all too familiar with; instead, we practiced de-escalation, mediation, and self-management skills. Miraculously, young people who had been hiding themselves started to find us, and reading their applications validated the need for the space we had sought to create: "Please don't tell my parents." "I don't know anyone else who is gay." "I want to meet other kids who are like me."

When we finally gathered, in just three short days, we bonded over sharing and witnessing one another's pain and experienced precious moments of levity, joy, and connection free from judgment and threat of violence. My favorite part of the Camp was the grand finale talent show, where fired-up teens performed drag, sang their own songs, read poetry, danced, acted, told jokes, and expressed parts of themselves they had previously hidden in all their glory on a made-up stage in the rec room of the dorm building. There were tears and belly laughs, lots of claps and finger snaps. As I looked around, basking in the rare sense of belonging as we held space for one another, I was reminded of the power of community and the simple and crucial act of bearing witness to each other's full, unobstructed humanity. Days after the event, I got a message via Facebook from one of the students who had attended the Camp: "The Camp saved my life."

To this day, creating the Camp remains one of the most fulfilling and proudest moments of my life. Some might say we were reckless and dishonest in our tactics—and as a thirty-something-year-old looking back, I can't fully disagree that we had taken some questionable risks. But we had also done what we thought was the most necessary thing for the marginalized young people within our community. As people who recognized what limited yet relative privileges we had as students at an elite university, with access to resources and, most of all, a level of protection and forgiveness based on our status as young people ourselves, we wanted to empower and create a sense of community for other young people whose daily lives consisted of hiding from their family and friends and surviving bullies, suicidal thoughts, depression, and loneliness. We knew, from experience, how this newfound sense of community could transform young people's lives. By truly centering the needs of those we sought to support, we were able to design an experience that was accessible and inclusive, and one that made everyone feel seen, honored, and celebrated.

Unfortunately, our world is filled with counterexamples of the Camp, where the needs of the marginalized remain as an afterthought or, worse, where marginalized people end up with *additional* burdens in order to access resources. So many programs that seek to create equitable opportunities for all—from financial aid to scholarship conference tickets to supplier diversity certifications—end up putting extra burdens on the very people they seek to support by asking them to earn the benefits through additional time and labor, while offering distinctly subpar experiences through limited or degraded options: financial aid that restrict how you can spend the money, complimentary or discounted conference tickets that limit your access to certain programs, or a supplier diversity certification process that is cumbersome for small businesses that are already resource strapped.

By not prioritizing dignified and equitable experiences, we end up treating and marking marginalized people as *needy*—as if this need originates from their personal lack—instead of recognizing that it is the *systems* that have rendered them marginalized and in need in the first place. The problematic mentality of "helping the needy," even when the on-paper outcome is ultimately good, shifts the burden onto the marginalized, who must earn what they rightfully deserve, and maintains the status quo pattern of power imbalance, while still keeping marginalized people firmly in the margins.

The pattern of leaving behind the most marginalized continues even in spaces that claim to be solving for the very people they've alienated. Time after time, I've seen nonprofit boards that do not include the actual beneficiary of the organization's core services: youth nonprofits without a youth board member, nonprofits serving houseless people without having a single member who has experienced house- or homelessness, and NGOs serving low-income and poorer countries through the sole leadership of US-based, majority white leaders. Then there's the process of reporting sexual violence, which is notoriously awful for survivors—from having to explain the trauma over and over to an accusatory and gaslighting line of questioning, to being criminalized as a result of their other marginalized identities—reminding us that the legal system was not designed to truly center the needs of those harmed by violence. Educational institutions utilize virtual education platforms without regard to the fact that students from low-income households may not have adequate access to high-speed internet or private laptops. Countless companies limit the provision of valuable internship opportunities only to those who are willing and able to work without compensation. Some vendors and shops only accept credit card payments when an estimated 39 percent of Americans do not own a credit card for various reasons,[15] including low credit scores, undocumented status, or mistrust in the financial system. "Progressive" events are held at inaccessible locations and without sharing accessibility information in advance or at sites that only offer gendered restrooms. Critical information about community health or financial resources is delivered only in English and not in other languages spoken by its local residents. Annual Pride parades contract with the local police to provide security, making the event increasingly hostile for Black, brown, undocumented, disabled, trans, and queer people of color, the very communities that gave birth to Pride by rioting against police brutality.* The list of how we continue to leave the most marginalized behind goes on, and I'm reminded just how easily history repeats itself, remembering how the women's suffrage movement left behind women of color because race was deemed too controversial, while the gay rights movement of the sixties (and to an extent, today's mainstream LGBTQ+ movement too) left behind trans and nonbinary people because challenging the gender binary was considered too controversial a fight.

> Access is a last-minute add-on. When we're thought of at the very
> end, that's a real blow to our confidence, our identities, and it has a
> ripple effect through all aspects of life.
> —Christine Sun Kim[16]

Solving for the most marginalized does not mean building solutions that will only serve a small, limited minority. As a matter of fact, policies, products, and cultures designed to meet the needs of the most marginalized often end up benefiting a much wider net of people. Inclusive Design, a design methodology explained by Kat Holmes, author of *Mismatch: How Inclusion Shapes Design*, and her colleagues at Microsoft, prioritizes the inclusion of the "fullest range of human diversity" in their designs, which is made possible by focusing on the needs of those who are most often excluded and marginalized. They share that while this approach "can seem like a significant constraint . . . the resulting designs can actually benefit a much larger number of people."[17] For example, they illustrate how an important innovation like closed captioning not only makes visual content accessible to the D/deaf† and hard-of-hearing communities, it also supports English-language

---

*There is a long history of resistance against police brutality by the LGBTQ+ community, much of it led by trans women of color, as exemplified by the 1959 Cooper's Do-nuts Riot in Los Angeles, 1966 Compton's Cafeteria Riot in San Francisco, and 1969 Stonewall Riots in New York City that led to what we now know as Pride. Learn about the fierce activism of Marsha P. Johnson, Sylvia Rivera, Miss Major, and many more!

†According to Start ASL, "in Deaf culture, 'D,' 'd,' and 'd/Deaf' are extremely significant."[18] Ai-Media explains the distinction by explaining that the use of uppercase *D*, Deaf, is used by people who identify as culturally Deaf, or part of the Deaf community, while lowercase d, deaf, refers to the physical condition of having hearing loss. To honor both communities, many advocate for the use of "D/deaf" or "d/Deaf."[19]

learners like my family or people navigating crowded places like airports or train terminals. Providing subtitles has an added bonus of being a smarter digital strategy, where videos with subtitles reach 40 percent more views than ones without them.[20]

By intentionally centering the needs of the most marginalized in our design processes, we are bucking the old recipe of baking inequities into our systems and instead allowing completely reimagined solutions to emerge that can ultimately benefit all of us.

> *Designing with constraints in mind is simply designing well.*
> —Inclusive Design Toolkit[21]

3. Make Space, Shift Resources, Redistribute Power

To truly center the most marginalized in our equity and justice work, we must shift resources and reallocate power to those belonging to marginalized communities to lead the solutioning, rather than making assumptions about their needs from a position of privilege.

In the second quarter of 2020, organizations braced themselves for the financial impacts of COVID-19. By April 2020, my company's sales leads had plummeted by 60 percent since January and our profit by a whopping 90 percent, and we barely avoided a loss that month. By early June, our sales had dropped so far below our projections that our entire business model had to be turned upside down. But before we went belly up, the entire world flipped instead, catalyzed by the brutal murder of George Floyd and people's outrage breaking open onto the streets in search of justice for Black lives. All of a sudden, we received a disorienting number of requests from companies. Many of these companies had just slashed their diversity budgets to zero and laid off their most marginalized employees, but now they were clamoring to figure out how to respond to the undeniable political and social turning point, completely unequipped and underresourced. We saw a 1,538 percent month-over-month increase in leads, and that summer, nearly nine hundred different organizations reached out to my small business through referrals, word of mouth, and internet search.

The sense of relief that others expected me to feel never came—instead, I felt anger and exhaustion from witnessing and processing so much cumulative trauma, and the sudden surge of corporate motivation tasted more bitter than sweet. I had two choices: I could aggressively expand my team to take on as many clients as we possibly could and make up for the prior months' losses. Or I could redistribute the leads to other DEI firms, specifically ones led by Black people, not as an act of charity but because I believed they were the *most qualified* leaders to steward the movement. My initial calls for Black-owned DEI firms willing and available to take on new clients quickly snowballed into a massive thread of comments on my social media platforms, so I created a spreadsheet where consultants could put down their contact information and specialty for potential clients to see. Within days, the spreadsheet became a robust directory of hundreds of Black-owned DEI consultancies, and I received messages affirming the redirect was working. The most impacted—and therefore the most qualified—got hired and paid, on their own terms. The database continues to exist today,[22] with over eight hundred entries, and serves as an important counter to corporations' lazy excuse of "not being able to find" willing and available Black DEI consultants to support their efforts to overcome anti-Blackness and white supremacy culture.

We don't need freshly awakened white allies to start another nonprofit to solve racial inequities or another AI-powered bot teaching people how to be inclusive. We just need them to funnel their money and connections to existing organizations already doing great work with limited resources. We don't need cisgender and straight allies to be on speaking panels talking about trans and queer people's struggles; we need them to give up their seats and fill them with actual trans and queer people. We don't need another white cisgender man politician advocating on behalf of all of us; we need them to fundraise on behalf of candidates who are BIPOC, women, trans and nonbinary, disabled, Muslim and Sikh, immigrants, and poor. Don't just put yourself in their shoes; give up your shoes and trust them to do what they need to do to create better paths beyond your imagination.

> *[Marginality] nourishes one's capacity to resist. It offers the possibility of radical perspectives from which to see and create, to imagine alternatives, new worlds.*
> —bell hooks[23]

CHAPTER 8

PERMISSION TO BE
CALLED OUT

I was scrolling through my Twitter feed while boiling a pot of pasta when I spotted a tweet from a Black woman activist I admire announcing her admission to a prestigious graduate school program. Thrilled for her, I quickly drafted a congratulatory message and replied to the tweet: "Amazing news! They're so lucky to have you. In fact, they should pay YOU to attend given how much others will learn from you." A few minutes and a couple of likes on my tweet later, I received an unexpected response from her asking me to reconsider my tweet.

My head spun. *Wait, what I said was offensive? How? But other people liked my tweet.* Practicing what I train others to do, I responded immediately and apologized, saying I would think about what I had said. With her feedback, it was not difficult for me to see that though I meant to highlight her brilliance, my flippant comment devalued her accomplishment, and tacitly diminished her deliberate choice to attend a program that she deemed valuable. I stared at my initial tweet now with disgust and shame. *Am I supposed to delete this thing or leave it for everyone else to learn from?* I didn't want more people to see my thoughtless tweet, so without much thought (again), I deleted it. I wish there had been a rule book for how to handle this sort of thing—"How to manage tweets you regret tweeting," "Recovering from Twitter foolishness 101"—and in retrospect, if I could go back in time, I wouldn't have deleted it.

The final gut punch that made my now-soggy pasta completely unsalvageable was her next tweet, which reminded people to think before tweeting. At this point I was completely flustered. I wanted to simultaneously disappear forever while proving that I was still a good person, deserving of her and other people's respect. So, I went on a retweeting frenzy, using other people's witty insights to cover up my Twitter page. *See? I'm a good person! Don't look at that other stuff I messed up on, look over here instead!*

Fighting for social justice is often described as courageous, fearless, and inspiring. Yet, feelings of fear, anxiety, shame, and inadequacy accompany nearly everyone I know who is trekking through the journey. Many of us desire to have good impacts, but sometimes, even our best intentions can bring unintended consequences of harm. And this unpredictable potential, coupled with our terrifying fear of being called out, sometimes holds us back from taking any action at all, which in turn makes our dreaded fear of causing harm a reality through inaction.

Maybe you've been called out before in a way that has scarred you forever. Maybe you're seeing other people get called out publicly in ways that make you squirm. Maybe you've never been called out and don't ever want to experience it. Or maybe you're like me, prone to anxiety and overthinking your every action, which my therapist has been witness to for years as she listens to me babble about my impending doom every week. But somehow, she always manages to help me return to my center, reminding me, despite all of my irritating flaws and reprehensible mistakes, that I am still whole and worthy, and that while the fear of being called out is valid and human, it should not dictate my future actions or define me. Whatever the reason may be, in order to become effective change agents in this journey, we need to get intimately familiar with our fears and what they represent for us, and practice countering our fears with a greater desire for change and accountability so that we can act while being fearful anyway.

BEFORE WE BEGIN: PUTTING THINGS INTO PERSPECTIVE

While the rest of this chapter focuses on how we hold ourselves accountable while simultaneously making room for our own humanity, remember that our accountability practice should always be first rooted in centering the person or people who were harmed by our actions.

I've observed over and over how people who are called out or called in react by focusing on the way the feedback was delivered, their innocent intentions behind the action, the possible misunderstanding, or quite literally anything and everything *but* the actual harm they've caused, causing the person who experienced the harm to do additional emotional labor of explaining, adjusting, or holding space for them. I've also made the mistake of asking the person I've harmed to extend me the benefit of the doubt before being curious about *their* context or honoring *their* truths. Sometimes, even when we're getting called *in* in the most gentle, compassionate, and thoughtful way possible, it can still feel like we're being called *out*, because of our ego, our internalized biases about the person giving us the feedback, our past experiences, or our current state of mind, which may cause us to activate our flight, fight, or freeze response.

Accountability is hard. Getting called out is hard. But is it as hard as, or should it be compared to, experiencing harm on a daily basis as a marginalized person or facing retaliation for fighting for equity and justice? No, of course not. This is why we continue to advocate for survivor-centered approaches to harm, ensuring that we do not continue the pattern of coddling those who caused harm at the expense of those who have been harmed. Rather than holding on to the intent of the former, we focus on the actual impact experienced by the latter.

It is also important to note that most of the examples of harm I use in this chapter are commonplace interpersonal harms that happen all around us, not prolonged abuse or severe forms of violence. I do not believe there is one right way to address all types of harm, violence, or abuse, and it's crucial we use our discernment to identify the most appropriate tools for accountability depending on context. The distinction between harm and abuse is an important one too, as Da'Shaun L. Harrison, a Black trans writer, abolitionist, community organizer, and the managing editor of *Wear Your Voice* magazine, notes: "Whereas harm is a one-time act of violence or infliction of pain, that can be either intentional or unintentional, abuse is about a continued and repeated force of violence that mistreats, mishandles, or exploits someone's body, being, and/or feelings. It is about a commitment—interrogated or uninterrogated—to enforcing violence onto someone else with no interest in stopping."[1] The lessons in this chapter are most appropriate for handling interpersonal conflicts, one-time harms, and everyday mistakes in our lives.

WHAT TO DO WHEN YOU GET CALLED OUT

So, let's say you've just been called out for using outdated and insensitive language, or maybe you shared something on social media that perpetuated problematic stereotypes about a marginalized identity group. Maybe you're an executive leader facing criticism from your employees for not following through on your promises to foster diversity, equity, and inclusion, or maybe you've been called out by a friend for making an insensitive joke at a social event. Whatever the reason may be, when you've caused harm, remember that this is an opportunity to practice accountability and take a step toward rebuilding eroded trust. Early on in Awaken's curriculum design journey, I pored over every apology framework and research I could find, trying to identify consistent advice across multiple sources and disciplines. Luckily, many apology frameworks shared a similar set of principles, whether they are rooted in social justice, social psychology, behavioral economics, or one of my favorite YouTube videos by Franchesca Ramsey entitled "Getting Called Out: How to Apologize."[2] And luckily for you, here is a compilation of the best advice collected from numerous experts across disciplines to help you respond when you've been called out:

1. Listen and Calm Your Defenses

Most apology frameworks skip this part, but as a certified mediator and a student of nonviolent communication, I believe active listening and self-management are core, foundational skills in any conflict situation. Before doing or saying anything, focus on listening and practicing self-management. Notice what is going on in your body as you listen to the other person share how you've caused harm. Listen to understand, not to respond, and focus on the message not the tone in which the message is delivered. Breathe, unclench your jaw, wiggle your toes (no, really). Notice and manage your immediate defensive reactions that want to jump to explaining yourself or defending your character. The frantic energy is a signal that you need to take a breath, buy yourself time to reflect, and recenter before reacting hastily. The most important thing in these initial moments of accountability is that we minimize the risk of causing more harm, because when we are activated we are prone to reacting in self-defense rather than listening for understanding. Accept their concerns as their truth, no matter your intentions. "But what if they're wrong?"

Remember: while our perceptions of what happened may differ, each person's emotions are *always* valid. Honor and validate their emotional reactions and do not prescribe how others should or should not feel about what happened.

2. Apologize and Acknowledge the Harm (or Ask for Time to Reflect First)

"I'm sorry."

First and foremost, apologize. Apologize clearly, and with sincerity. Mirror back what was shared with you to reassure the person harmed that you understand the impact (e.g., "I can see why when I did _____ [harmful action], that made you feel _____ [the impact].") You can ask if they'd be willing to clarify or elaborate on the harm they experienced, depending on your relationship and situation. Avoid diluting your apology by saying "if" or "but," which are all too commonplace in boilerplate performative corporate nonapology apology statements. For example, "I'm sorry *if* you were offended" implies that it was the person's choice to take offense, rather than your action being offensive, which ultimately shifts the blame onto the person who was harmed. The best apologies I've received always included detailed naming of the harm I experienced, which showed the person's full understanding of my hurt. Given how rare it is to experience apologies that sincerely acknowledge the harm without defensiveness, it's no surprise why, for me, even just the accurate naming of the harm can often feel like a complete amend all on its own.

Mia Mingus, whose written series "The Four Parts of Accountability: How to Give a Genuine Apology" should be required reading for everyone, writes "If you are not genuine in your apology, you can cause more hurt/harm. I cannot emphasize this enough: if you don't want to apologize, don't apologize."[3] Don't say you're sorry just so you can get past this moment of discomfort. If you need time to reflect on your actions, then ask for that and circle back when your apology can be genuinely rooted in your understanding of the harm caused (e.g., "Thank you so much for bringing this up. Would it be OK with you if I took some time to reflect so I can be thoughtful in my response?").

3. Express Gratitude for the Feedback

"Thank you for caring enough to bring this to my attention."

When marginalized people take time to educate others, that additional emotional and educational labor often goes unappreciated or, worse, penalized. Appreciate the fact that someone is calling you out because they believe in your ability to do better, or that they care enough about being in relationship with you, or simply that they've given you an opportunity to learn and do better. In many instances, it takes a tremendous amount of courage to call someone out or in—honor their courage by expressing your gratitude and ensuring they feel safe to do so again if they observe harm in the future. In an organizational setting, power dynamics and a culture of psychological safety play an important role in creating an environment where honest feedback can occur. Continuously modeling gratitude for constructive feedback and welcoming honesty without penalty can help nurture this culture of psychological safety in which marginalized people and those with limited power can feel safe enough to share valuable feedback.

4. Make Amends Without Expecting Forgiveness

"I'd like to _____ to make this right. Is there anything I can do to help regain your trust?"

Many apology experts deem this as the most challenging step, because what is needed to repair the broken trust can look different for different people, and making amends cannot be done alone. In his book *On Apology*, Aaron Lazare, a professor of psychiatry whose research focuses on the psychology of shame, humiliation, and apology, describes the process of apologizing as being relational and not unilateral, in which "an apology often involves more than a unilateral offering of one party to another but can be a dialogue and even a negotiation between two parties."[4] Other fascinating research by Yohsuke Ohtsubo, a psychologist at Kobe University who has studied apologies for over a decade, discovered that "costly apologies tend to be perceived as more sincere than noncostly apologies (e.g., merely saying 'sorry')." In other words, Ohtsubo clarifies, "It's the *cost to the offender* that matters," not necessarily the value to the harmed, when it comes to signaling genuine remorse and sincere intention.[5] Whether it is a corporation committing millions of dollars to regain the trust of its customers or a politician resigning from their position to accept responsibility, there are various forms of interpersonal and institutional amends we can consider, depending on the context. The best way to determine how to make amends is by understanding the actual desires and needs of the person harmed. Note, however, that depending on the situation, sometimes it may not be possible to collaborate on the reparative steps or even be able to achieve full repair or be granted forgiveness. It's important to remember that seeking to repair the harm *without* expecting immediate forgiveness is key to ensuring we do not center ourselves in moments of taking accountability—a sincere apology should seek to restore the dignity of the harmed person and to meet their needs. When we make amends to prioritize our immediate relief rather than the healing of the person harmed, it is no longer a genuine apology but a tool for manipulation. Lazare, in a 2005 *Washington Post* article, writes that when used as a manipulative tool, apologizing can turn "what should be a powerful act of reconciliation into a meaningless travesty." He continues, "Instead of healing breaches, these sorry exercises widen the gulfs between people."[6] As you seek to repair and make amends, come back to your why often to help you stay in alignment with your values.

5. Commit to Doing Better, Then Actually Do Better

"I commit to _____ to ensure it doesn't happen again."

Building, and rebuilding, trust requires consistency and time. Depending on the circumstance, you may be able to communicate a plan of action beyond the present moment that will help the harmed party understand how you will ensure you won't repeat the same harm in the future. For example, in my current intimate relationship, that commitment looks like each of us going to therapy once a week to take care of our own mental health and learning to communicate our needs honestly and directly. In organizational settings, it can look like committing to a multipronged strategic plan and specific metrics to achieve more equitable hiring, promotion, and compensation practices. But before you make any commitments, make sure there is a genuine desire and plans to follow through because promises without actions can cause more harm and mistrust than healing.

6. Get Support for Yourself

It is not comfortable to be called out, nor is it easy to make amends. When I am called out, I have a terrible habit of dehumanizing myself through punishing self-criticism and forced isolation. Practicing self-compassion in these moments is a nice idea, but remembering to make room for it is much more challenging than it seems. My support network of trusted advisers and friends has been critical to sustaining myself in this work, and I believe this

is an integral part of everyone who is committed to the social justice journey for the long haul. My support system is comprised of people who hold
me accountable with unfiltered honesty and also with immense compassion.
They help me process my mistakes so that the emotional labor doesn't fall
on the person I harmed, while also holding space for my messy emotions
and insecurities triggered by the situation. When I am unable to get out
of my shame spiral, they gently remind me that I am a human capable of
making mistakes, while ensuring I stay in integrity throughout my accountability process. Sometimes the only way we move through these difficult
moments is to let time play its role (after we've apologized) and acknowledge
that tough feelings *are* part of the process of taking accountability. Sulking indefinitely in self-hatred and shame won't make the harm we've caused
disappear or lead anyone to grant us forgiveness. Even in these painful moments when we feel like we don't deserve support or understanding, we
need to remember that our deep introspection, self-compassion, behavioral
change, consistency, and eventual healing are all critical parts of being able
to bounce back to continue the work. In restoring our own humanity, we
also model our belief that everyone is capable—and worthy—of growth and
transformation. And we don't have to do this alone.

EMBRACING THE DISCOMFORT OF BEING CALLED OUT

Most of us do not yet live in a culture where accountability is an organic,
normalized part of our lives. Instead of a culture of psychological safety in
which we are encouraged to try new things and make mistakes, we have a
culture of retribution and shame that motivates us to hide our failures. Instead of slowing down to allow for nuance, complexity, and multiplicity to
emerge, we rush to categorize and criminalize people using rigid standards
of perfection defined by white supremacy and capitalism. We have been
taught that vulnerability is weakness, while people who harm others must
be inherently "bad" who need to be exiled and punished. These limiting,
binary beliefs make it challenging for us to differentiate our intentions from
our impacts, and our actions from our humanity.

When we are made aware of our fallibility, we are quick to defend our
intentions rather than being curious about the impact of our actions and
possibility for amends. At the first sign of being called in, our self-protective

mechanisms kick in, and we rush to preserve our innocence and expend all our energy trying to prove we have not caused harm. We desperately want to fast-forward to the place where the accuser realizes they are mistaken and *we* get to be the real victim. From a place of fear, we prioritize rejecting being categorically mislabeled as a "bad person" rather than acknowledging our own complex, multilayered humanity, which makes making mistakes inevitable. With this instinctive defensiveness as a primitive coping mechanism, we rob ourselves of the opportunity to repair damaged trust and relationships, along with the permission to change and grow. But if there is anything that I've learned from years of experience being called out and calling others out, it is that tuning into our own feelings and allowing them to be fully validated, interrogated, and integrated is the only way we can ensure our reactions and future actions remain in alignment with our values.

But what does it mean to really *sit with your feelings*? Like, do you actually just sit there, mulling over your emotions? Here are some tips I've learned along my journey:

- **Pay attention to your body.** When I try to feel my feelings, I end up thinking and analyzing instead, trying to *solve* my feelings intellectually. What I've learned over the years from people much more enlightened than me, like my therapist, is that our feelings live physically in our bodies, not just in our heads. We feel them through our stomach churning, our heart palpitating, our legs anxiously shaking. We feel them through our hot faces, our clenched throats, and our sweaty palms. When we are called in or called out, especially by people we love and respect, we first feel it in our bodies. So pay attention to what's happening in your body and practice de-escalation techniques (e.g., breathing, tapping, stretching, shaking off, etc.) to slow your body and restore your calm.
- **Acknowledge and name your emotions.** Research has shown that the mere act of naming our feelings, or *affect labeling*, can decrease the intensity of negative emotions we experience by "hitting the brakes on your emotional responses" that trigger our fight or flight survival reaction, according to psychologist Matthew D. Lieberman.[7] Explicitly naming and acknowledging our feelings through journaling, therapy, venting, and so on and getting granular about the emotions we

experience (the Feeling Wheel developed by Dr. Gloria Willcox[8] or the Emotional Word Wheel by Geoffrey Roberts[9] are great tools for this) can be helpful in regulating our emotions and making space for further reflection and accountability practices.

- **Take your time.** Despite our best efforts, it may take some time to come out of the cycle of shame and blame and be ready to jump back into the work. I've never been able to recover quickly from my own mistakes and being called out. I usually spend days feeling intense emotions that mirror the stages of grief, from anger to denial to sadness to acceptance, with a whole lot of self-pity, criticism, and feelings of unworthiness. In these moments, it's important to fight the temptation to rush our reflections or to evade difficult emotions. Rather, practice self-compassion and gentleness to move through them intentionally.

Through intentional reflection and processing our feelings, we can work to fully metabolize and turn them into something other than trapped energy that eventually leaks out to cause additional harm. Our hyperintellectual culture teaches us to value logic and data over our emotions and instinctive bodily wisdom and to dissociate, intellectualize, or diminish negative emotions. But the introspective practice of sitting with our feelings is an integral part of practicing accountability. In remembering and valuing our ability to stay in touch with our emotions while allowing ourselves the spaciousness to explore the stories they're trying to tell, we align our minds, bodies, and souls to be able to continue the work of fighting for justice and healing.

CALLING OUT IN CONTEXT

As mentioned in Chapter 5, The Only Constant Is Context, the tools we use to practice accountability should differ based on context—the approach we take to holding abusers in positions of power accountable should differ from the way we hold the people in our lives with different positionality accountable for making one-off mistakes. Our own positionality matters too. A white person calling out other white people is different than a person of color calling out white people. Historical context, power dynamics, and our identities are always at play.

When I first began my social justice journey, I was an indiscriminately vocal and punishing critic of *everyone* around me. As soon as I learned a new concept or terminology, I used it to call people out left and right, no matter the context: *That's not how you should be doing this or that. You're racist/sexist/oppressive!* Coupled with my flaming rage fueled by a newfound awareness of the injustices in the world, as a teenage activist I was determined to hold *everyone* accountable. Criticizing and shaming people newer to the journey, regardless of context, was my way of quieting my own insecurities and developing my voice, while also being righteously angry about the harm I and so many other marginalized people were experiencing. I thought being as critical and harsh as possible, no matter the nuance or my positionality, was the best and only way to fight for all of us. Along the way, I disposed of people whose curiosity wasn't strong enough to withstand the harshness of my criticism and lost the attention of those who hadn't figured out a resilient-enough why to stay in the movement while feeling unappreciated. I made people feel inadequate, ashamed, and unworthy of calling themselves activists or allies. Ultimately, I wasn't an effective change agent or ally myself; I had become a successful gatekeeper to the change work.

We all play different roles in different contexts. We do not get to hold up the bar and decide whether someone is "good enough" of an ally to communities we do not belong to. For example, as a non-Indigenous person, I don't get to go around shaming others for not being "good enough allies" to Indigenous communities, performing anger louder than those most impacted but without doing any of the necessary education work, when all that achieves is shifting the labor onto others while dismissing potential allies, all for my own need to feel morally superior. That is my ego wanting validation, my self-indulgence centering myself through the facade of solidarity, and not a strategic way to achieve change nor a critical way to act based on my own positionality.

Whenever there is a power imbalance, the burden of compassionate call-ins, added emotional labor, and repetitive education tends to fall disproportionately on the shoulders of the most marginalized in the service of those more privileged. This uniquely exhausting burden must instead be taken up equitably by those who experience less harm due to their positions in society, understanding that such positionality grants the privilege of emotional spaciousness and energy to engage. When I am hurting from forces of oppression that harm my community, I want to be able to process and express my anger without penalty. Meanwhile, I need those who are hurting less to take on the emotional burden of guiding others who require more explanation and education. Marginalized people reserve the right to be direct in challenging those in positions of power and privilege because part of the act of calling out is allowing for freedom to express frustration and hurt without filtering them for the comfort of those who caused harm or who continue to benefit from the systems that cause harm. These callouts are vessels through which marginalized communities seek to restore the dignity and justice that have been taken, and those in positions of privilege must refrain from co-opting or weaponizing the concept of respect against marginalized people in the form of tone policing ("Why can't you be more civil?" "Why are you so angry all the time?"), gaslighting ("It's not always about race," "You're overreacting"), spiritual bypassing ("You create your own reality," "Raise your vibration!"), or penalizing (e.g., withholding promotion, firing, ostracizing, etc.).

Being discerning and disciplined with our anger is an ongoing practice that will help us stay principled throughout our journey. I want us to be committed to taking down all systems of oppression with utmost criticality and unforgiving sharpness, while using contextual discernment in calling out or calling in those who fumble while fighting alongside us. Anchored to my own fumbled beginnings, I remember the people much wiser and much more hurt than me who consented to educating and bringing me along when my consciousness was just beginning to expand. Yes, I did my own homework too, but those compassionate call-ins were the fuel that fed me to stay in the work, building up my capacity to handle harsher criticisms later on with a thicker skin. While there should never be an expectation placed on marginalized people to extend compassion or grace when calling out harm, I frequently remind myself of the generosity and grace I was, and still am, afforded by my fierce and compassionate friends, mentors, and teachers, and I, too, commit to practicing humility as a lifelong learner, guiding newcomers to stay and fight better with us.

WE HAVE THE CAPACITY TO TRANSFORM

For me, forgiveness and compassion are always linked: how do
we hold people accountable for wrongdoing and yet at the same

time remain in touch with their humanity enough to believe in their
capacity to be transformed?
—bell hooks[10]

A daily recurring thought since I began writing this book has been, *Wow, I hope I don't get canceled.* As a Virgo and an intensely anxious person, thinking through the worst-case scenarios is part of my unshakeable habit and a coping mechanism that I learned from surviving a rather unstable childhood. On my bad anxiety days, I paint a gruesomely detailed picture of my worst nightmares coming true, beginning with my favorite writers rolling their eyes at the sound of my name and Asian activists disowning me on behalf of the Asian community. I shudder at the thought of bringing shame onto every human being who has breathed within six feet of me: all of my clients disavowing our previous work together, and my friends denying ever having known me, or worse, offering up my ugliest stories of that one time I pissed them off. I imagine my mom crying every day, and my dad shaking his head, telling me I should've never left that corporate job I got right out of college. At this stage of my imagination, I've surpassed my stress-eating phase, and I'm contemplating fleeing the country, except I can't find a country where Twitter doesn't exist. At the end of my melodramatic saga, I ask myself, *Why the hell am I writing a book again that's probably going to disappoint everyone?* After I've sufficiently degraded my own work and buried my initial why, I contemplate preemptively writing an apology letter to the world for my editor to review.

> *[Accountability] will never be easy or comfortable, but what if it wasn't scary? What if our own accountability wasn't something we ran from, but something we ran towards and desired, appreciated, cherished, held as sacred? . . . What if it wasn't rooted in punishment, revenge, or superficiality, but rooted in our values, growth, transformation, healing, freedom, and liberation?*
> —Mia Mingus[11]

I reflect on this question by Mia Mingus often: "What if accountability wasn't scary?" When I turn inward to reflect on all the moments that I have felt worried about being canceled or publicly called out, I discover my deeper fears that underpin my anxiety: fear of being seen in the depth of my vulnerability, fear of letting others' judgment dictate the truest reflection of who I am, fear of being misunderstood, fear of being abandoned by people I love, and fear of the world validating my inner critic that tells me I am not enough and will never be enough. *But what if accountability wasn't scary?* What if instead of fearing being wrong, I trust my ability to receive feedback with gratitude and a commitment to doing better? What if instead of fearing being misunderstood, I take the opportunity to better understand whatever conflict I find myself in, while affirming who I am to myself by staying tethered to my values? What if instead of fearing being abandoned, I trust in the resilience of my relationships, which have been built on a foundation of mutual accountability and years of showing up for one another?

As a lifelong student of this work, one thing I know for certain is that, despite my most genuine efforts, I will continue to make mistakes that cause harm and I will never *not* feel bad about them. But I also know that while I am capable of making mistakes and causing harm, I am also just as capable of reflecting, taking accountability, repairing, learning, growing, and forgiving myself.

When fighting within systems of oppression, no one comes out stain-free. We can do what we can to avoid touching wet paint while dismantling the walls, but anyone who manages to stand clean perhaps wasn't doing much of the dismantling at all. Even with our best efforts to avoid causing harm along this journey, there is no doubt we will make mistakes. Of course, we should continue to do our best to minimize harm by educating ourselves, considering context, and centering the most marginalized, and sometimes we will need to act using our best judgment, knowing that even if we don't get it exactly right, we will be able to learn in real time as we go. It is important that we don't become so consumed with trying to avoid harm that it leads to a cycle of inertia fueled by overanalyzing, where we remain complicit in moments that require intervention. Perfection is a mandate of white supremacy culture, and we cannot let this impossible, racist standard drive our (in)actions. While we fidget in discomfort trying to find the "perfect" way to show up, systems of oppression are killing us and the people we love. When we remain stuck in our desire to be conflict-free, we not only miss the opportunity to intervene to create positive change, but we also end up actively centering our needs, at all cost, *over* the needs of the most marginalized. We also miss invaluable opportunities to learn about our deep-seated fears and wounds and chances to build even more resilient relationships.

Instead, let's build capacity to receive critical feedback without defensiveness, practice accountability, and course-correct. This is one of the most important skills we need to continue doing the work. And when you've caused harm amid the hard work, always remember that you, too, are worthy of forgiveness. We owe it to the movement to believe in everyone's capacity to transform, including yours.

Do the best you can until you know better. Then when you know better, do better.
   —Maya Angelou[12]

CHAPTER 9

CHANGE THROUGH LANGUAGE

"I don't want to say the wrong thing" or "Tell me what to say" remain some of the most popular sentiments and requests I receive as an equity educator and consultant. Those of us who wish to do the right thing are tormented first by our desire to *say* the right thing. The topic of inclusive language is enduringly popular, and the desire to focus on adopting correct terminology is understandable, since language is perhaps the most obvious gauge we use to judge someone's level of awareness and knowledge—or their ignorance and potential to cause harm. For example, it's easier to make judgment calls about someone who addresses a mixed-gender audience with "hey guys" than trying to discern their actual beliefs and actions around sexism and patriarchy. Feeling like you've got a handle on the most up-to-date language can also bring about a false sense of safety from being found out, even if you haven't spent much time thinking or learning about different communities. Sometimes there is even a mild sense of accomplishment when we remember to say BIPOC (Black, Indigenous, and people of color) instead of "just" people of color, or when we say queer without hesitating instead of gay. We feel a little bit more in the know and maybe a tad edgy. Given this low-hanging fruit and seemingly practical impacts, it's no wonder people ask for the latest list of "what to say and what not to say" all the time.

Part of the problem with providing people with a rigid list of the right things to say, however, is that once a situation changes, many fail to adapt, use discernment, and consider context, which can quickly turn those "right things" into "wrong things." As much as I'd love for us to be able to arrive at justice as a result of memorizing all the right words, we can't "inclusion-dictionary" our way through the social justice movement. Just like a checklist of one-time tasks, memorizing a static list of terms may provide temporary relief but is unsustainable in the long run. Inclusive language is an approach and an ongoing practice rather than a fixed glossary of cultural faux pas to avoid. Language is always evolving as the needs of marginalized communities shift and time changes, and new language is being created constantly to capture the myriad nuances and beauties of our existence. Rather than focusing on the what, I once again implore all of us to focus on learning the why and the how to create a more enduring and sustainable foundation. Noam Chomsky, a philosopher, political activist, and "the father of modern linguistics," puts it succinctly: "Do you train for passing tests or do you train for creative inquiry?"[1] Let's train ourselves for the latter.

Let's first talk about the different types of language. Now, I'm no linguist, and the following categorization and nonexhaustive list of examples were born out of the need to start a conversation on the basics of inclusive language, so if you're a linguist I hope you'll forgive me for any linguistic sins I may have committed!

Examples of Harmful Language

- **Exclusionary language:** insulting, insensitive, or otherwise violent language that harms, excludes, or degrades marginalized identities, ultimately contributing to their systemic oppression (e.g., "that's gay," "man up," *illegal immigrant, faggot, ghetto,* etc.).
- **Microaggressive language:** Derald Wing Sue defines *microaggression** as "brief and commonplace daily indignities . . . whether intentional or unintentional, that communicate hostile, derogatory, or negative attitudes toward stigmatized or culturally marginalized groups"[3] (e.g., "All lives matter"; "Where are you *really* from?"; "We believe in diversity,

---

*The term *microaggression* was coined by Harvard University psychiatrist Chester M. Pierce in 1970 to describe insults and dismissals regularly committed by non-Black Americans against Black people,[2] and it has since been expanded to apply to various marginalized communities. While microaggressions can be behaviors (e.g., touching a Black person's hair) or environmental (e.g., being the only student of color in a school filled with white people), for the purpose of this chapter, we'll focus on microaggressions expressed through language.

but we don't want to lower the bar"; complimenting a Black person for being "articulate").

- **Culturally appropriative*** **language:** language that has been selectively taken, co-opted, or repurposed from others' cultures for the benefit of self, often without permission, proper education, or acknowledgment (e.g., *powwow, spirit animal,* non-Black people engaging in digital blackface to communicate online,[†] etc.).

Examples of Inclusive Language

- **Empowering language:** universally inclusive (e.g., "hey team" versus "hey guys") and respectful language that honors, empowers, and acknowledges marginalized people as they wish to be addressed or identified (e.g., *Asian American* versus *Oriental, undocumented* versus *illegal immigrant, transgender* versus *transsexual*).

- **Reclaimed or reappropriated language:** marginalized people taking back pejoratives or other historically disparaging language in an act of self-empowerment and protest (e.g., *queer,* the N-word, *disabled, fat,* etc.). Ample context is required prior to using, which we'll discuss below.

Though I caution people against rushing to prioritize learning the latest terminology over doing the deeper work of understanding the why first, the undebatable truth is that language *does* play an important role in creating change. Language can literally shape our thoughts and the world around us. Cognitive scientist Lera Boroditsky spent years researching the causal relationship between language and the way we think and found that "the structures

---

*Similar to microaggressions, cultural appropriation can appear in various forms, including attire, customs, behaviors, and language. Context plays a key role in determining whether something is appropriative or appropriate/appreciative (see Chapter 5, The Only Constant Is Context).

†Lauren Michele Jackson defines digital blackface as "the act of inhabiting a black persona. Employing digital technology to co-opt a perceived cache or black cool . . . [which] involves playacting blackness in a minstrel-like tradition."[4] Digital blackface happens when non-Black people utilize internet memes and graphics of Black people and AAVE to express a message and tone, usually with hyperbolic, excessive, or theatrical intentions, which is why I've included it in this list on language.

that exist in our languages profoundly shape how we construct reality," where the languages we speak "not only reflect or express our thoughts, but also shape the very thoughts we wish to express." She shares a number of fascinating examples to illustrate this point in her 2010 article in the *Wall Street Journal*. For example, Russian speakers have more words to describe light and dark blues, which results in their ability to distinguish different shades of blue much more quickly than English speakers. The Pormpuraaw Aboriginal community, in their Indigenous languages, only use absolute cardinal directions (north, south, east, west) rather than relative terms like left and right, and this constant linguistic training makes them "remarkably good at staying oriented and keeping track of where they are, even in unfamiliar landscapes," Boroditsky writes.[5] In their book *Words Can Change Your Brain*, neuroscientists Andrew B. Newberg and Mark Robert Waldman validate the impact of language on our brains by sharing that "a single word has the power to influence the expression of genes that regulate physical and emotional stress."[6]

Given that language plays such a critical role in the way we think and organize our society, it is imperative that we equip ourselves with the skills to adapt and be intentional with our practice of it.

THE FIVE PRINCIPLES OF INCLUSIVE LANGUAGE

Rather than providing a static list of the latest terms (the what), which may become quickly outdated or be used out of context, here are five foundational principles (the why and the how) to help navigate language in a thoughtful, adaptive way.

1. Use the Most Universally Inclusive Language

We begin the practice by first identifying language that inadvertently, or sometimes purposely, alienates others, and consciously decide to broaden our scope of language to include historically excluded and marginalized people. Common examples in this practice are using nongendered language when addressing groups of people, like "hi *team*," "greetings *everyone*," and "welcome *folks*" instead of "ladies and gentlemen" or "hey guys." There has also been a movement to use gender-neutral terms when describing occupations (e.g., *congressperson* versus *congressman/woman*, *firefighter* versus *fireman*, etc.), products that can be used by multiple genders (e.g., *menstrual product* versus *feminine product*), and not equating body parts to gender identities (e.g., *people who menstruate* versus *women*—because folks with different gender identities, like trans men, nonbinary people, and gender-queer people, can menstruate too), while normalizing the use of the singular *they* pronoun rather than defaulting to pronouns that reinforce the gender binary (*he* or *she*). Inside companies, there have been calls to shift ableist language, such as *company all-hands* being replaced with *company-wide meeting*, or *daily stand-up* with *daily check-in*. Exclusionary language sends overt and subtle signals that certain people do not belong in certain spaces, that their existence is not valuable enough to be acknowledged even in something as flexible as the language we use. Using and maintaining harmful language is the gateway to perpetuating more harmful patterns, while replacing exclusionary language with universally inclusive language helps disrupt that by neutralizing the underlying bias.

Being able to use the most universally inclusive language requires us to train ourselves to recognize when certain terms and language we use are exclusionary in the first place. Terms and phrases that are rooted in oppressive history or cultural appropriation are difficult to spot without additional knowledge and awareness, so continuing to educate ourselves and proactively seeking out resources is important. For example, it wasn't that long ago that I learned the problematic history behind *grandfathered in*, a phrase I had become accustomed to using while working in the tech industry, widely used to describe contract terms or customers that were considered exempt from any new changes made. Little did I know that the phrase's origin dates all the way back to the late nineteenth century. With the ratification of the Fifteenth Amendment in 1870, Black men were granted the right to vote—in theory. In reality, state requirements, such as literacy tests and poll taxes, were deliberately set as obstacles to disenfranchise the Black voter. To keep these same requirements from disenfranchising illiterate white men, a "grandfather clause" was created in the 1890s in a number of southern states like North Carolina and Georgia that allowed men to vote on the basis of their lineal ancestor's (i.e., grandfather's) ability to vote prior to 1867, effectively excluding Black voters.[7] Understanding our history and habitually interrogating where certain ideas, terms, and language originate will give us practical tools to broaden our scope of knowledge while challenging us to rewrite our stories using the most accurate and empowering language devoid of an oppressive legacy.

2. Respect People's Agency to Self-Identify

As we do our best to keep up with the evolution of language, it is important to keep in mind that no community is a monolith. When it comes to
language that is about one's identity or identities, it is far more important
to respect each person's agency to self-identify than it is to flex our knowledge about the most "technically correct" way to identify. I have met gay
people, especially elders who have survived brutal violence as a result of
homophobia, shudder at the reclaimed word *queer*. I continue to learn from
a diverse group of disability justice activists and advocates, some who prefer people-first language (*people with disabilities, a person with autism*, etc.)
while others prefer to use identity-first language that asserts their disability
as an inextricable part of their identity (*disabled, autistic, blind, D/deaf*, etc.).
Here's a rule not to be messed with: don't correct someone else's identity
based on your intellectual analysis or personal opinion.

Self-identification has always been an integral practice within the
LGBTQ+ community. The language I use to describe my sexuality has
evolved over the years, along with my ongoing self-discovery. It took trying on different labels at different times to get to the most precise label that
made me feel most seen, validated, and honored, even if it was just for me
to feel closer to myself. When I was in high school, I had my first crush on a
girl. She was an amazing hip-hop dancer and a little older than me. I would
swoon as I watched her dance, royally confused about my feelings. I didn't
feel like I was a lesbian because I liked boys too. *Bisexual* felt like too rigid
a word, and I didn't like the implied gender binary. I wasn't ready to lean so
quickly into identifying with a community I had only read about before. I
was scared—scared of my feelings, of what it meant about who I was and
how my life might change. The kids who everyone knew were gay, or who
were *suspected* to be gay (I know, high school is *awful*), were goths or mega
nerds who had lunch in our openly gay biology teacher's classroom, and I
felt like I had nothing in common with them. When I finally mustered up
the courage to share my very secretive "feelings" with the only lesbian person I knew at the time—the *other* openly gay biology teacher (what's up with
queer people making biology cool?)—she helped me find an underground
support group for LGBTQ+ students on campus.

The group consisted of four to six students depending on the week, facilitated by Mrs. Morton from the programs office. Every week during a different

period, we gathered in a circle and talked about our latest crushes, our feelings, our family, our fears, and our dreams. Each person got their turn, and everyone else listened, while nodding, laughing, and crying. I talked about my confusion and discomfort, my feeling of not being ready for any of it. Another student, B, who had an obsession with all things Hello Kitty and rocked his hair purple and blue, gave me the identity that felt perfect for me then: *questioning*. "You're *questioning*." YES. *That's who I am.* Despite the uncertainty inherent in the word, I had never felt more certain about who I was. I was *questioning*! I felt empowered and understood, not just by these kind people holding space for me—goths and nerds who were much more comfortable in their skin than I was—but also by myself.

Over the years, I learned to no longer fear my desires, and I began to claim my identity more boldly. I identified as bisexual, then briefly as pansexual, and eventually landed at queer, which has been the home of my identity for over a decade. During my self-exploration, a lot of people had very strong opinions about my identity, and they weren't afraid to share them, unsolicited: "You're basically straight." "How many girls have you been with?" "Just wait until you meet the right guy."* "You're just confused." This type of identity gaslighting happens all the time to so many marginalized individuals. Trans people's gender identities are questioned and doubted not only by individuals but also by institutions (e.g., medical, legal, educational, etc.), and their ability to self-identify is policed through institutionalized policies and legal ramifications that delegitimize or criminalize their identity. Terms like *illegal* and *alien* are thrust upon immigrants, and people are cast away from society on a daily basis with labels like *criminal* and *prisoner*, which strip away their innate personhood while replacing it with a set of numbers. When we destroy someone's ability to declare their own identity by replacing it with unilaterally imposed demarcations intended to degrade, we actively participate in erasing their history, agency, and humanity, mirroring centuries of oppressive tactics that have dehumanized and subjugated marginalized people.

---

*There's something alarming about the way our society so desperately wants to see stereotypically feminine women express and understand their sexuality as it relates to their relationship with men rather than their own expressed desires and innate sense of self. Note that one's sexual orientation is not about the gender of the person or people with whom one is partnered currently but rather based on one's own definition and sense of self.

Respect people's agency to self-identify, and give yourself and others space to explore language that best captures each person's needs. When you are not sure about how someone identifies, and if such knowledge is imperative to the context (for example, you are writing someone's introduction in an email or for a speech), it is better to ask for clarification than to use incorrectly assumed identities. You can do this at an organizational level too: more and more organizations are providing options for people to self-identify on surveys and form fields that request demographic information. I encourage organizations to replace the category "other"—which quite literally *others* identities that sit outside the default groups perceived as the norm—with "prefer to self-describe/self-identify" to give back agency and allow for expansive diversity to emerge.

3. Who Says It Matters

"How come Black people can say the N-word but I can't?" I hope none of you are asking this question, though it's one I've heard one too many times in my life in school, at work, inside workshops—non-Black people who love rap and hip-hop and desire to sing the *whole* thing without pause; non-Black coworkers who want to be able to retell jokes made by famous Black comedians without altering the "flavor"; or non-Black queer and trans people using AAVE/BVE to keep up with the "trends." When called out on it, people often argue that they are engaging in cultural *appreciation* and not appropriation, leading with their innocent desire to share culture and often ending with the assertion of their First Amendment rights. The thing is, when it comes to inclusive language, or anything related to social justice for that matter, context, including *identities*—yours and others'—*matter.* In other words, who says what matters.

Each of our identities carries with it our own lived experiences and our communities' historical legacies. At one point or another, some of us will desire to be seen just as a *person* without any of the identifiers that define us; maybe we want to be known for our soul and our personality, our unique talents or our accomplishments. I've observed white people demanding to be seen as just people too (and truthfully, they often are from the perspective of the media and storytelling, as mentioned in Chapter 6, The Double-Edged Sword of Representation), and I've desired the same, especially when I've been the target of racism, sexism, or tokenism. But the truth is we can never separate ourselves from our identities or the dynamics that our identities create each time we interact with others. What our identities represent and have represented throughout history matters a whole lot when it comes to language and how it is used. Context, once again, is key.

When a pejorative word is being reclaimed, it is done as an act of protest and empowerment by the community historically harmed by the term. Only the community that has been the direct target of the oppressive term can reclaim the use of it as empowerment; the oppressing group does not get to dictate when and how terms that were weaponized to subjugate others are brought back to life. The important point here, or perhaps the entire point, is the shift of power from the oppressor to the oppressed. Over time, the term may become popularized and mainstream enough to be used by people outside the community (e.g., *queer*), but this requires a degree of permissioning and consent from the marginalized community at large, as well as an accompanying societal shift in attitude, beliefs, and behaviors. With varying forms of oppression—racism, sexism, transphobia, homophobia, ableism, and more—still so prevalent and viscerally felt by marginalized people, when the words they're trying to reclaim as a way to take back power are used casually by people who continue to benefit from the system that oppresses them, it reinflicts the very violence the language had been created to perpetuate while simultaneously eroding trust. Without heightened care and contextual understanding, casually using reclaimed or reappropriated language as a nonimpacted community member can cause harm by violating the community's agency and ownership over their righteous protest.

As a general rule, with regard to the use of reclaimed language, consider your own identity and its historical relationship to the community that is doing the reclaiming, as well as the present-day context of oppression. Reflect on your own motivations behind wanting to use certain terms or phrases, and ask yourself, "Why do I want or need to use this language?" "Who benefits from my use of it?" "Who is harmed?" "What historical and present-day legacies have I considered?"

4. Be Precise, Especially When Describing Harm

Going to the doctor's office was often one of the most frustrating things I experienced while learning English. My inability to accurately describe the discomfort beyond "I'm in pain," "It hurts," or "dull or sharp pain" made me miss living in Korea where I could use a variety of colorful adjectives to describe uniquely different sensations. There are no direct translations that can fully capture these meanings, but let me try to give you a taste:*

- 칼칼해: feels like a whiff of chili pepper flakes got stuck in the throat, causing it to feel scratchy and raw; "my throat feels 칼칼해" (instead of "my throat hurts")
- 찌릿찌릿: feels like electricity coursing through my body in quick, staccato spurts; "my legs feel 찌릿찌릿" (instead of "my legs fell asleep")
- 시리다: feels like someone dumped a bucket of ice inside my spine, causing me to shiver; "my tooth is 시리다" (instead of "my tooth feels sensitive to cold")

During these doctor visits, I'd try to elicit the help of my electronic translator, which more often than not failed to capture the nuance of what I was trying to communicate. I used exaggerated facial expressions and animated body language, but I often left feeling frustrated and unsure if the doctor actually understood my suffering in detail enough to prescribe the right solution to my problems. If I can't even accurately convey my pain, how will the doctor help me feel better?

Precision in our language, especially when discussing harm, is critical to pinpointing the correct source of the harm and therefore the right solutions to treat it. Precise language allows us to hold the right parties accountable, while ensuring we tell the most truthful story we can. The good news is we don't need intricate Korean adjectives to accurately describe the problems we face in society. The bad news is that even with the existence of precise words, we often fail in using them to adequately capture the most honest realities of our situations.

Consider the difference in the following hypothetical headlines:

1a: "People of color are more likely to die from COVID-19."

1b: "Enduring systemic racism and inequitable access to quality care lead to higher death rates among people of color than white people."

---

*This is strictly me having a bit of fun imagining how I would describe each adjective and not how every Korean person would translate these words!

2a: "Women continue to experience workplace discrimination due to their gender."

2b: "Sexist culture and male dominance in the workplace lead to continued discrimination against women while advancing men."

Do you notice the subtle but important difference between sentences 1a and 1b, and 2a and 2b? In sentences 1a and 2a, the root causes of the harm (systemic racism and sexism) are hidden, making it difficult to pinpoint the driving forces behind the disproportionate death rates and workplace discrimination that marginalized groups face. The sentences trick our brains to associate the harm with the harmed parties, where a missing link erroneously ties them together to create a problematic causal relationship. The omission renders the forces of systemic oppression invisible, while successfully priming our brain to associate marginalized identities with the inequities they face. The sentences also fail to mention the unharmed parties, or rather the *beneficiaries*, of the disparate impacts caused by systemic bias and institutionalized oppressions. While these details may feel subtle and superfluous in the context of news headlines (after all, how many extra characters can possibly be squeezed into a single headline?), our overexposure to oversimplified and incomplete information has a lasting and broad-reaching impact on how we understand the world around us and how we make decisions based on our subconscious priming.

In her TED Talk "How Language Shapes the Way We Think," Lera Boroditsky states, "Language can fuss with tiny little perceptional decisions we make."[8] Her 2010 Stanford research paper, "Subtle Linguistic Cues Influence Perceived Blame and Financial Liability," coauthored with Caitlin M. Fausey, proved just that. They found that a simple change in language can influence the way we approach blame and punishment. The paper included a study in which participants were presented with a video clip of the widely watched 2004 Super Bowl half-time performance by Janet Jackson and Justin Timberlake, when the performance ended with the shocking exposure of Janet Jackson's breast on national television due to a "wardrobe malfunction." Participants were provided either an agentive report (e.g., "Timberlake ripped the costume") or a nonagentive report (e.g., "The costume ripped"), and were asked to assign blame and financial liability to the appropriate parties.[9]

The result showed a strong correlation between the type of linguistic framing used in the report and the participants' final judgment of blame and financial liability. Participants who were primed with agentive language ended up assigning an extra 53 percent financial penalty to Timberlake when compared to the group that received a nonagentive report. Fausey and Boroditsky concluded, "These results suggest that the form of this framing guides punishment."[10]

Subtle yet impressionable linguistic framing is *everywhere*—when we turn on the TV, read the news, share social media posts, or even when we engage in casual conversations. And coupled with the ubiquity of harmful stereotypes and biases, the repercussions of such framing extend into our schools, workplaces, courts, hospitals, and neighborhoods. It influences who we punish and blame more frequently (for example, schools are twice as likely to suspend or expel Black students, low-income students, and disabled students than their counterparts despite being engaged in the same or similar rule violations[11]), how severely we punish them, and how quickly we extend reparation or rehabilitation opportunities.

When discussing social justice and DEI issues, be vigilant about using the most accurate language to describe them. Ask yourself: What exactly was the harm? Who was harmed? Who or what caused the harm? When describing harm, avoid using diluted language or euphemisms. For example, when a white police officer murdered George Floyd, some opted to describe the incident as "racially charged," and many corporate statements did not even mention the terms *murder, racist,* or *police brutality** out of concerns that such terms could be too polarizing. But the reason why so many fear polarization caused by the mere use of the most accurate words is precisely because for so long we've prioritized artificial harmony over honest tension, and comfortable euphemism over uncomfortable truth telling, constantly adding more layers to obscure these truths. Don't be afraid to use words that may cause discomfort because of their directness. Directness and honesty are the point. In this instance, it would have been most accurate to describe the murder using words like *anti-Black racism* and *white supremacy* rather than just *racism* or *unconscious bias.* The latter type of framing led some organizations to rush to conduct diversity trainings on the topic of unconscious bias, missing the opportunity to have more direct and effective

---

*Out of thirty-five corporate statements analyzed by the *Wall Street Journal*, only eight used the term *murder*, four used the term *racist*, and one used the words *police brutality*.[12]

conversations about white supremacy culture and the history of anti-Black racism in policing and in the workplace.

Be direct, be clear, be accurate in describing the harm so we can prescribe the right solution for the pain. Similarly, when describing who was harmed, be as specific as possible. Coalitionary terms like *people of color* and *AAPI* tend to be overused when specificity is required, and while these terms serve a specific (and important) purpose of coalescing power and resources and building solidarity across different communities, when it comes to race-specific or ethnicity-specific issues, it is more helpful to name these differences. If we're discussing issues disproportionately impacting the Black community, don't use the term *people of color* or even *BIPOC* to describe the issues—say it is impacting the Black community. If we're discussing issues disproportionately impacting Native Hawaiians, don't use the umbrella term *AAPI*—say it is impacting the Native Hawaiian community. Be specific so the appropriate communities are centered in the movement.

Finally, use clear language to make apparent the causes of harm, and be sure to use phrasing that does not shift the blame onto the victim or the survivor of the harm. On April 29, 2020, the *New York Times* published a piece with the headline "Prisoner with Coronavirus Dies After Giving Birth While on Ventilator," and with a subtitle, "Andrea Circle Bear, the first female federal prisoner to die after getting the coronavirus, had just started serving a two-year drug sentence for selling methamphetamine."[13] The headline not only failed to capture the real and urgent problem of the unsafe and inhumane conditions inside prisons, it also dehumanized the victim by using a one-dimensional label, *prisoner*, and including the person's incarceration information, which was not pertinent to the issue at hand. This type of victim blaming is common throughout history and in our present day, where different biases are applied to associate certain populations with criminality and others with a presumption of innocence. Words like *terrorist* and *violent* are overused when describing Black, brown, or Muslim suspects, while biases that tend to soften criminality are used in favor of white suspects (e.g., *mentally ill* or *troubled* instead of *domestic terrorist*; *Stanford swimmer* instead of *rapist*).

Do not let harm exist passively without specific agents, whether that is a person, group of people, institutions, or systemic oppression, and ensure the accountability is pointed squarely at the actual source of the harm, not communities historically seen as an easy target to blame. We must be vigilant to not shift the responsibility of restoration onto individuals or communities harmed by oppressive systems. Using precise language is key not only to identify the right solutions to the right problems but also to help us hone the practice of being intentional with our language, where we understand that the words we use can shape how we remember historical events and how we choose to tell our stories. Language presents us with a powerful opportunity to remain in integrity and to change the way we build the world.

> When we say millions around the world are impacted by the global epidemic of famine, what we are saying is that millions of humans are experiencing physical deterioration of muscles and other tissues due to the lack of nutrients in their bodies. Injustice is an opaque word until we are willing to discuss its material reality.
> —Sonya Renee Taylor[14]

5. Don't Get Stuck in Arbitrary Rules

To allow ourselves to stay agile while prioritizing the needs of marginalized communities, watch out for our tendency to uphold existing norms that perpetuate white supremacy beliefs.

When someone says to me, "Oh wow, you speak such good English!" what do they mean by that? More often than not, they are expressing surprise and revealing their cognitive dissonance as they hear me speak in ways that are contrary to their assumption about how an Asian person would sound—an "unrefined" accent, improper grammar, elementary vocabulary. "You speak good English" is another way of saying, "You don't sound *Asian*." Though intended as a compliment, the underlying assumption lands only as a condescending insult. And then I'm left wondering, *What if I spoke with an "Asian" accent? Why wouldn't that not be considered "good English"?*

Linguist Noam Chomsky critiques this notion of "good English" in an interview at the University of Washington in which he explains, "These terms have no linguistic meaning, they have only sociopolitical meaning." He points to the importance of studying the authority structures in which good English is *legislated* to be deemed good English, rather than being inherently and linguistically superior to how people engage in casual "street speak." This is why it has to be *taught* in school, Chomsky explains, because the arbitrary rubric of "good" doesn't at all mirror the natural ways in which humans actually converse with each other.[15]

We are taught what is and isn't considered "proper" or "good" English (or ways to behave, things to believe, etc.) over and over in our lives, in our schools, workplaces, and interactions with authority figures and those around us. I used to obsess over grammar: I'd correct people's silly mistakes when distinguishing between *there, they're,* and *their* and be petulant about correcting "photo of he and I" to "photo of him and me." This irritating behavior was a subtle way for me to assert my sense of belonging in this country, showcasing that I knew how to speak good English despite people's assumptions based on my race and immigration status. Through my own work in understanding and unlearning white supremacy culture, I have, however, come to learn that policing one's way of communicating, whether in accent (particularly non-European accents), grammar, or even in tone, can perpetuate the arbitrary rules of properness defined by the establishment that seeks to separate wealthy white people from everyone else. This arbitrary policing of language justifies the marginalization and penalization of the latter group based on predefined rules that have been set to accommodate the dominant group, while deliberately excluding the full realities, complexities, and contexts of those outside them. People with accents originating from countries with majority non-white populations (e.g., China, Nigeria, Mexico, etc.) are seen as less intelligent and worse communicators than those with "no accent" (but *everyone* has an accent; we just have normalized some and not others) or those with white European accents (e.g., British, Australian, etc.), and this results in subtle and overt indignities and material consequences like reduced job opportunities, less frequent promotions to leadership positions, and limited access to certain spaces in society. The adherence to the rules of "proper" English is sometimes seen as a priority on its own, so much so that sometimes people push back on changes even when the proposed changes can bring about more inclusion: for example, many people have opposed, and some continue to oppose, the adoption of the singular *they* as a way to refer to a nonbinary individual or to avoid making assumptions when someone's pronouns are unknown, citing its "grammatical incorrectness." Sometimes, having a set of clearly defined rules gives us a shared understanding and a sense of comfort, but other times, we fall into the trap of protecting something that does not inherently hold value for the sake of keeping tradition, and our refusal to change can come at the expense of people we seek to support and care for.

Lastly, the tendency to abide by the guidelines of proper English (and by now, I hope I've made myself clear that "proper" more often than not means white) can also show up through the use of coded and covert language to cover up bias and different forms of oppression that harm others. Notice the next time someone says, "That's not a good neighborhood" (often coded language for describing a predominantly Black or brown and low-income neighborhood), or "She just doesn't seem like a culture fit" (coded language for dismissing candidates on the basis of perceived difference, often rooted in identity-based bias unrelated to job responsibilities), or "He lacks executive presence" (coded language for devaluing people who do not conform to the traditional characteristics of an executive, who are often tall, cis, heterosexual, abled white men). These are just a few common examples of how conscious or unconscious biases get expressed in a seemingly "polite" and "proper" way that is socially acceptable—because saying, "We don't want to live there because it's a Latino neighborhood" is much too crude. Over time, their cumulative and detrimental impacts contribute to sustaining systemic disparities.

In pursuing inclusive language, we must always be aware of our own conditioning—what we have been taught to respect and regard as superior—and consciously decide to let go of arbitrary rules to make room for the ever-changing and multidimensional ways of communicating that empower, expand, and embrace. We have to be careful not to be stuck in the properness of English or to mistake the adherence to the rules as the end goal—rather, we need to remember that language is one of the oldest tools we have that allows for deeper human connections, expressions, and understanding.

HOW FAR IS TOO FAR?

When I was first called in for casually blurting out the word *crazy* in a sentence, I did not have a positive reaction. With a skeptical look on my face I said, "Really? That's just taking it a little too far, even for me." My teammate Liz, who is always diligent about calling me in and helping me practice accountability, explained how the casual use of the word further stigmatizes people suffering from mental illness, and she shared her personal experience with the word being negatively tied to her past. Despite her compassionate explanation, I wasn't convinced right away. I clung to my feeling that the word was largely harmless and had become so mainstream that it was unlikely it would really offend anyone. Additionally, I felt annoyed that we were now focusing on this seemingly innocuous and trivial issue when people were still fighting to get rid of "much more" harmful language, such as the appropriated use of terms like *guru* and *spirit animal*. I was worried we were taking this so far that we'd lose the interest of well-intentioned people who would surely shake their heads and check out of the work of using inclusive language altogether, dismissing the ask as ridiculous. In other words, I was behaving exactly like the people I huff and puff about, choosing to be sensitive toward appealing to the majority over the needs of those most impacted by the language, resisting with fervor the simplest change requests made by marginalized people. Short of citing freedom of speech and reverse discrimination, in that moment, I had become *that guy.*

When we resist change despite having received clear feedback and explanation about the necessity of the change, what's really underlying the resistance isn't the validity of the request itself or our lack of understanding of the issue; it often unearths something deeper and hidden within us. What I was holding on to in that moment was my desire to not be a causer of harm: I wanted to continue using the word while denying any culpability. I wanted to have my cake and eat it too. Though the First Amendment prevents the government from "abridging the freedom of speech,"[16] our freedom of expression doesn't always guarantee freedom from causing harm. In his article "We're Still Living and Dying in the Slaveholders' Republic" in the *Atlantic*, Dr. Ibram X. Kendi writes about the importance of distinguishing between freedom *to* and freedom *from*.[17] This was a profound distinction for me, as I was able to articulate the difference between my desire to maintain my freedom *to cause harm* (without being told I was causing harm) and marginalized people's righteous fight to exist with freedom *from harm*. These needs are in stark contrast, which is why it is imperative that we use discernment and always choose to fight for our freedom *from* harm and not our freedom *to* harm without conflating them as equal.

Allergic reactions to "political correctness" have intensified these days, and the boundary between inclusive language and superfluous sensitivity is increasingly debated. In 2015, Donald Trump further fueled the hatred toward being politically correct by equating it to having his speech policed and censored, saying in an interview, "And this political correctness is just absolutely killing us as a country. You can't say anything. Anything you say today, they'll find a reason why it's not good."[18] Without considering historical and current context, using inclusive language has been mistakenly labeled as a merely politically correct way of being polite with one another that can quickly become a nuisance, rather than a systematic approach to restoring equity, dignity, and justice to marginalized people.

One of the earliest uses of the term *politically correct* can be found in a 1934 *New York Times* article entitled "Personal Liberty Vanishes in Reich," which describes the Nazi German government's propaganda and crackdown on all means of communications and journalism. "All journalists must have a permit to function and such permits are granted only to pure 'Aryans' whose opinions are politically correct."[19] During this time, anyone who defied this correctness as defined by the government was punished, and some were sent to concentration camps. Resisting political correctness in the context of Nazi Germany would have made sense, as it would have meant resisting systemic repression and government propaganda that sought to oppress. On the flip side, resisting political correctness as it is defined today, which is often about adopting more inclusive language, is quite literally doing the opposite of fighting for the marginalized, while repelling change that would support marginalized people. The modern-day weaponized use of the term *political correctness* to shut down inclusive language considerations is a surface-level reaction to the proposed language change (the what) instead of a deeper understanding and care for the underlying intention of the change (the why). My goal is not to champion political correctness per se, or any other form of perceived indoctrination for that matter, but rather to champion the why beyond the impulse of being politically correct on the surface.

When it comes to inclusive language, it's important to remember that the choice is always yours. Nobody can force you to say or not say certain things if you don't want to. But what inclusive language is all about is our *willingness to reconsider* our choices in relationship to our proclaimed values of inclusion, equity, and justice and our commitment to living in alignment with those said values. It's about challenging ourselves to consider the *potential impact and harm,* no matter how small we perceive them to be, and *deciding* it is worth our efforts and inconvenience to mitigate even the smallest potentiality.

I've since changed my mind about the words *crazy* and *insane,* and though I am not always spot-on in finding the most precise adjective to describe my reactions, I will say my vocabulary has gotten way better as my brain gets a workout every time I search for the replacement. "That's f-ing epic!" works decently well most of the time, and I enjoy the added bonus of knowing no one was harmed in my presence.

INCLUSIVE LANGUAGE AS AN ONGOING PRACTICE

Unless we are plugged into every single community that is at the forefront of spotting linguistic trends, we won't always have the latest and best language that is the most inclusive for, and desired by, various communities. It is never the expectation to know everything. But it *is* an expectation for a person committed to social justice to remain open to change and to stay accountable to the needs of marginalized people. And there is a plethora of readily accessible resources to help us stay informed and continuously learn. I've found it incredibly useful to immerse myself in the language of different communities by reading articles written by people of all identities, listening to podcasts and speeches given by grassroots organizers, diversifying my social media feed, and reading journalist style guides created by different communities. Learning about the untold history of historically oppressed people and being curious about the etymology of different words and phrases have also supported my ongoing learning journey.

And let's not stop at just *knowing* the right words—let's live the values of inclusive language by disrupting harmful language when we observe it and advocating for change. Let's support each other's learning by sharing resources and calling people in in real time. In a number of tech companies I've worked with, a group of engineers led the change to shift problematic engineering language like *blacklist, whitelist,* and *master/slave branches,* words widely used for decades in computing as a reference to the code hierarchy, to *blocklist, allowlist,* and *source/replica branches.* I've seen people on social media point to biased news headlines, pushing for more criticality and conscientiousness from journalists. Opportunities to practice inclusive language and disrupt the harmful cycle of biased linguistic framing are *everywhere*. We just need to start noticing and disrupt this passively active cycle of harm.

Language matters and words have consequences. We assign meaning through language, and even the slightest shift can fundamentally affect the way we view ourselves, one another, and the world. Language is a powerful tool at our disposal, and we must use it to create positive change. Studies have shown that simply using the correct chosen name and gender pronouns can decrease the suicide rate among transgender youth.[20] Shifting from *Oriental* to *Asian American*, a term born out of Asian political activism in the sixties, empowered Asian people living in the United States to form a collective, coalitionary, and political identity rooted in their shared oppression and lived experiences.[21] New words and identities are always being created to capture the beauty and expansiveness of our sexuality, and we continue to present each other with the gift of being seen, validated, and belonging in new and different ways. Having language for something that has not yet been named is incredibly important in shaping our society and allowing us to recognize and legitimize different lived experiences, identities, and concepts. And there is always room for more of us to be acknowledged and celebrated, to access freedom through the expression of our truest selves.

It's not the memorized words that make us effective change makers; it is our deep understanding of the power and weight of language, our measured and loving approach arising out of genuine care for other human beings, and our ongoing commitment to staying agile despite the inconvenience we may feel that get us closer to the change we all yearn for.

CHAPTER 10

DISRUPT THE PATTERN

What we practice at the small scale sets the patterns for the whole system.
—adrienne maree brown[1]

Imagine you're at a friend's baby shower, and she asks everyone to guess the gender of the baby by choosing either a blue sticker for a boy or a pink sticker for a girl. Others play along, remarking excitedly, "Oh, it's *definitely* a boy. I can just tell by your cravings!" You know activities like this further perpetuate the gender binary while contributing to tacit forms of transphobia. You feel uneasy. What would you do?

Imagine you're at a happy hour when your boss's boss asks an Asian employee where they're *really* from. Or imagine you're in line at a grocery store and the person in front of you says rudely to the cashier, "I can't understand what you're saying because of your accent." Imagine your neighbor telling you in passing how they had to call the police on a homeless person sleeping near their home over the weekend. Imagine your white coworker complimenting a Black candidate during an interview by saying they're "so articulate." Imagine you're at a networking event and the organizer asks everyone to share their *"spirit animal"* in an introduction activity. Imagine you're at a children's soccer practice and you overhear the coach yell out, "Come on, boy! Don't be a wuss!"

I invite you to picture yourself in these situations. Would you intervene? Really?

What would you do or say in each scenario? Which scenarios make you the most nervous or anxious? Angry, hesitant, or ready to act? What questions come up?

Intervening when we observe everyday harm, such as microaggressions, can feel incredibly uncomfortable and awkward. Over the years, I've noticed that many people find interrupting interpersonal-level harm more challenging than addressing apparently "bigger" forms of violence through mass action, like showing up to the Women's March or a Black Lives Matter protest. There is an undeniable dissonance permeating the air, caused by the gap between many people's proclaimed desires to be agents of change and their everyday actions that don't always align with their said values. Closing this gap *is* the work, and intervening when we observe harm is one major way for us to remain in integrity. These moments, particularly ones involving the everyday, seemingly negligible instances of harm, are crucial to developing our intervention muscles and shaping our immediate culture made up of people we can directly influence. And yet, despite our ample knowledge and robust intellectual analysis, many of us (myself included) have moments we can easily, and regretfully, recall when we've failed to interrupt harm in our own lives.

Despite the ubiquity of bystander trainings, many still lack the practice of day-to-day harm intervention. Common reasons why some people do not practice harm intervention include:

- **Not noticing harm in the moment.** Some people report not intervening simply because they did not realize that what was happening was harmful, or because by the time they realized the harm, it felt as though it was already too late to intervene (but it may not be!). People experience and interpret situations differently based on who they are and their context, so it is understandable that without shared lived experiences or awareness, something that is significant to some may appear as "not a big deal" to others (which, yet again, underscores the importance of diverse representation in positions of power, as well as continued building of social consciousness).
- **"It's not my place."** Some people feel as though it isn't their place to intervene, due to a variety of factors including their role, social identities, relationship to the person experiencing or perpetrating the harm, or the nature of the harm.
- **Lack of knowledge or skills.** Some fail to intervene because they do not know *how* to intervene—what words to use, whether they should

or should not intervene publicly, or even fearing that their flawed intervention may cause more harm than good.

- **Fear.** Some do not feel safe—physically or otherwise—intervening; some fear negative repercussions to their social standing, relationships, or reputation, while some fear losing their jobs, friendships, or access to certain spaces and privileges.

- **Low sense of accountability.** Some feel it is not *their* responsibility to intervene, either because no one else is doing it or because they believe other people will intervene (*bystander effect* and *diffusion of responsibility*); some may feel disconnected from the issue at hand because they, or their community, are not directly impacted by the observed harm.

- **Not a priority.** Some people, despite their awareness of the harm, decide not to engage due to their capacity or priorities they deem more urgent or important ("I don't have time for this").

- **Apathy.** Well, sometimes some people just don't give a damn.

The reasons why people do not interrupt harmful behaviors, patterns, cultures, and systems are limitless, and they shift based on their context and the nature of the harm. This is why proactively engaging in introspection to determine what may hold us back from acting in alignment with our values and building up our intervention strategies in advance can be incredibly helpful. Part of this practice is always coming back to our *why*: Why is intervening when you observe harm important for *you*? How does intervening harm in the moment help you be the person you want to be?

SMALL THINGS LEAD TO BIG THINGS

Sometimes I hear people say, "We should be focused on more important things," or "Is that really what's important right now? People are dying," when someone attempts to draw attention to something that could feel, well, less grave than people dying—like correcting someone's mispronunciation of another's name or misgendering, or proposing non-ableist terminology like "all-company meeting" instead of "all hands." I've been guilty of this, too, as I shared in Chapter 9, Change Through Language, when I resisted the request to stop using the word *crazy* in a derogatory way. These dismissive reactions are disappointing on many levels because they unveil the lack of understanding in how these seemingly trivial harms are, in fact, connected to the "more serious things." Addressing small infractions matters because if left alone, they lead to causing much greater levels of harm by contributing to a culture of permissiveness. These responses also replicate the binary thinking and scarcity mindset of white supremacy culture, where somehow tackling microlevel harms means we aren't able to focus on more serious forms of violence, which simply isn't true. In fact, by addressing both the small and big issues at the same time, we are able to connect the dots on how these issues are interconnected and how they uphold one another to perpetuate the dangerous cycles of violence over and over.

Weeks before the forty-sixth presidential inauguration, the *Wall Street Journal* published a column written by a white man that began: "Madame First Lady—Mrs. Biden—Jill—kiddo: a bit of advice on what may seem like a small but I think is a not unimportant matter. Any chance you might drop the 'Dr.' before your name?"[2] When I posted a brief commentary on this on social media, a cisgender white man friend commented on my post: "This is frustrating but is this really what's important right now?" But it *was* important because it showed yet another example of the insidious misogyny in the patriarchal system we live in. Additionally, people thinking this is not a big deal and choosing not to fully understand the implications of this harm lead to the creation of an increasingly permissive culture where it's OK for us to casually omit the successes of women, people of color, and women of color and to unwittingly engage in *untitling, uncredentialing,* or *unconscious demotion.*[3] Add to these infractions the backdrop of pay disparity between women and men (nonbinary people's pay gap data is still largely unavailable), especially between women of color and white men;[4] or the underrepresentation of women and women of color in positions of power across various institutions and systems;[5] or the fact that 48 percent of Black women and 47 percent of Latinas working in science report having been mistaken for administrative or custodial staff;[6] or the now widely known phenomenon of women being more likely to be interrupted (or mansplained!) more frequently than men[7] . . . you get the picture.

Being able to notice and call attention to these microlevel harms is critical to us growing the capacity to tackle bigger issues. The effects of these slights are not at all micro. They have lasting impacts on the way we perceive one another, make decisions, and create systems that privilege one group while marginalizing others. As Mia Mingus asks, "If we cannot handle the small things between us, how will we handle the big things?"

> *Learning how to address these smaller hurts or breaks in trust can help us learn the basic skills we need to address larger harms. It can also help to reduce and prevent larger forms of harm and violence (e.g., hurt becoming conflict, conflict becoming harm, harm becoming violence).*
> —Mia Mingus[8]

At the height of the #MeToo movement in 2017, the *Atlantic* published "The 3 Things That Make Organizations More Prone to Sexual Harassment." The article shared important research findings that showed how organizations that are "male dominated, super hierarchical, and forgiving when it comes to bad behavior" are more prone to sexual harassment and abuse.[9] Of the three factors—underrepresentation of women (especially at the leadership level), power imbalance, and permissive culture—researchers concluded, "The single biggest predictor of sexual harassment on the job is how permissive an organization is of this conduct."[10] This culture of permissiveness, in which there is a lack of accountability and people in positions of power do not take their employees' complaints seriously, isn't limited to the workplace. Many people listen to comedians make sexist and racist jokes and nervously laugh along, adults let children bully other kids and chuckle, "Boys will be boys," and we continue to witness powerful people get away with egregious misconduct despite multiple allegations over the years. Antidiscrimination and antiharassment laws and policies exist, yet our entire society is operating in a culture of permissiveness. Policy change can easily become cosmetic change unless there is real understanding and acceptance of the spirit of the shift, allowing for collective accountability whereby each one of us commits to doing our part to challenge the status quo and call attention to all levels of harm. We have a tremendous amount of power to change the direction of our immediate cultures—whether among our family members, friends, neighbors, schools, or workplaces. Our inaction is an active choice, and it is one of complicity.

I get it. Interrupting our social bonds is deeply uncomfortable. Risking our likeability and social standing, especially when the outcome of our intervention is unclear, can be really scary. But in these moments, we need to distinguish our *desire for comfort* from the *need for safety* for the targeted community and be willing to risk our comfort for their safety. As mentioned in Chapter 5, The Only Constant Is Context, people often conflate the need for *safety* for marginalized people with preserving the *comfort* of the privileged. When people with power get called out for causing harm and claim they feel "unsafe," what they really mean is they feel *challenged* and *uncomfortable*. When marginalized people experience harm and we demand safety, we mean safety in the most literal sense: safety from mental, emotional, and physical harm. What some fail to understand is how seemingly innocuous jokes; microaggressions that include microinsults, microassaults, and microinvalidations;[11] and verbal harassment serve as the bedrock of more egregious and obvious forms of violence. Left unaddressed, these insidious forms of violence become permissible and normalized, desensitizing us from noticing the slight escalations toward the top of the oppression pyramid. Today's "that's so gay" paves the way for tomorrow's "he's a fag," and the next day's verbal and physical harassment on school campuses, discriminatory policies against queer and trans people, mass shooting at a queer nightclub, and the epidemic of violence against trans people, especially Black trans women.

> *Revolution is not a one-time event. It is becoming always vigilant for the smallest opportunity to make a genuine change in established, outgrown responses.*
> —Audre Lorde[12]

TIPS ON HOW TO INTERVENE

What we needed to raise in others was this instinct. The ability to recognize, in an instant, right from wrong. The clarity of mind to face it rather than ignore it.
—Chanel Miller[13]

When you observe or experience a microaggression, it is helpful to remember to breathe and to engage in what is called *microresistance*, or "small-scale individual and/or collaborative efforts that empower targeted people and allies to cope with, respond to, and/or challenge microaggressions to ultimately dismantle systems of oppression."[14] This can take various forms, and here are some practical tips and strategies to keep in your toolbox for the next time someone says or does something problematic. Note that the following strategies are intended for commonplace microaggressions and insensitive jokes, rather than for more egregious levels of harm, harassment, abuse, or violence, and will work best in situations where you are engaging with people you have a vested interest in maintaining relationships with (as opposed to a stranger on Twitter!):

- **Wake up your gut.** Practice noticing harm in the moment, and trust your instinct. When something feels a little off, or you feel a bit of discomfort in your body, learn to hang on to that feeling and name it in real time, rather than dismissing or trivializing it.
- **Create a moment of pause.** Pick a go-to reaction or what my team and I call a *pause-word* (e.g., "Huh?" "Wait," etc.) so you can pause the situation and buy yourself time to think about your next move. Practice it until it becomes habitual and instinctive.
- **Ask clarifying questions.** Ask the person to elaborate (e.g., "I'm just curious, what made you say that?" "What did you mean by that?"). This can buy you more time to think through your approach and attain more information about where they are coming from. It may also help them to become aware of what they said or did.
- **Describe the impact.** "I felt _____ (feelings) when you said or did _____ (harmful comment or behavior), and it _____ (describe the impact)." Focus on communicating the impact of the other person's action on you, rather than blaming or labeling them (e.g., describe your feelings instead of retorting, "You're so racist for saying that"). This way, you are able to communicate the impact in a clear yet less-accusatory way without triggering their defensiveness and stonewalling.
- **Model your own learning.** Sharing your own learning journey is a great way to disarm the other person. I learned this popular education technique early on in my facilitation journey and have used it many times to diffuse tension and invite reflection: "I used to think _____, then I learned _____, so now I think _____" (e.g., "I used to think Thanksgiving is a holiday meant for expressing

gratitude, then I learned about its terrible history of white supremacy and genocide of Indigenous peoples, so now I think we need to educate our family about the real history of Thanksgiving to raise awareness").

- **Request behavior change.** If you are able to, provide an alternative behavior to replace the problematic one. "Instead of _____ (behavior to be changed), can you do _____ (desired behavior)?" "I'd love for you to say _____ (desired language) instead." It's OK to simply request the behavior to stop, too. "I need you to stop saying _____ (language to be changed)."
- **Suggest additional education or resources.** If you have the capacity to support their learning, offer time to check in again (e.g., "I'd be happy to chat with you more about it later. Would that be helpful?"). You also have the option to share resources that may further support their awareness building (e.g., books, articles, etc.).
- **Check in with others who may have been harmed, if appropriate.** If there were other people present who may have been harmed, check in with them and offer support (e.g., "I'm so sorry you had to go through that, is there anything I can do to support you?" "Do you want to talk about how you feel?" "I'm here to hold space for you if that might be helpful").

Depending on the situation, you may use a mix of these strategies. Some situations will feel trickier and require extra care and discernment in your approach to minimize further harm. For example, in the past when I've been mistakenly called by the wrong name (of another Asian woman or by my last name, Kim), I've appreciated someone else intervening to correct the mistake but without launching into a lecture about how it is a common microaggression to "not be able to tell Asians apart," which perpetuates many racist tropes against Asian people, or a full-blown history lesson on xenophobia in the United States since the 1800s, yada yada. Sure, the person who caused harm *should* learn about the impact and reflect on what happened but not necessarily in my presence where I am suddenly under an unwanted spotlight as the subject of their education. In situations like this, it is usually best to quickly correct the mistake and move on, and then continue the conversation with the person who made the mistake at a later time to unpack the impact fully. Sometimes indirect interventions, such as changing the subject or creating a distraction to change the course of the conversation (a personal favorite tactic for when non-Asian men start talking about their Asian wives as they try to relate to me), may prove more effective and, in some cases, safer for the person who is being targeted. Remember, the aim in these interpersonal conflict scenarios shouldn't be to escalate the situation or to shame the person who caused harm for the sake of punishment. Rather, it is to meet the needs of the most impacted person or community* with utmost respect and dignity by clearly naming the harm and helping practice collective accountability toward positive change.

Part of practicing harm intervention is learning about your own style, strengths, and areas of improvement in intervening and refining your approach over time with practice. And if you've missed your opportunity to intervene, you can always circle back and revisit the situation (if you know the person who caused harm). Work up your courage for a redo: "Hey, can we check in about something that happened last week?" "I'm sorry I didn't address this earlier, but I've given it some thought and want to share this." "I've not been able to get this off my mind, can we have a quick chat?" You won't always get the gift of a second chance, but when you do, I hope you take it. And if you are in a position of power, or have relative privileges in a given situation, you *must* use your positionality to intervene and interrupt harm. The burden and responsibility of harm intervention must *always* fall on the shoulders of the most privileged, not necessarily because they are the most equipped but because they bear the least amount of risk of being penalized and facing negative repercussions.

> Courage is the most important of all the virtues, because without courage you can't practice any other virtue consistently. You can practice any virtue erratically, but nothing consistently without courage.
> —Maya Angelou[15]

---

*Harm can occur even in the physical absence of a targeted community. For example, just because there isn't a queer person present in the room doesn't mean it isn't harmful when a homophobic joke is made.

Note that the approach toward intervention is different when *you* are the one experiencing harm or are the direct target of harm. When you experience harm—whether it is a subtle microaggression at work or school or a physical threat on the street—your survival reaction will likely take over in an attempt to keep you safe. This may look different depending on the situation and the person, but my experiences working with survivors of racial- and gender-based violence tell me that it can often look like freezing, dissociating, or even appeasing the person who caused harm in the moment. I occasionally get messages from people who have been victims of racial and sexual violence who regret their immediate reaction or lack thereof: "I just didn't know what to do." "I froze." "I feel so ashamed." "I wish I could have stood up for myself." To this, I say unequivocally: *It wasn't your fault.* It is perfectly normal and understandable for you to freeze up and not know what to say or do immediately, even when you've practiced all of the above tips. You may experience shock and confusion and even question whether what you experienced was "actually" harmful. You may question whether you'd be overreacting by addressing what just happened or feel flustered while trying to reground yourself. When you've been the target of violence, it is important to remember that it is not your responsibility to address the harm or educate the person who harmed you—and removing yourself immediately from the unsafe situation or disengaging from the person or people *is* an act of resistance. So release yourself from any sense of guilt, shame, or inadequacy for the times you were unable to defend yourself the way you should have been protected. *It wasn't your fault.*

THE POWER OF THE SECOND COURAGEOUS

In my years of both attending and facilitating countless bystander trainings, I've observed a pattern of incomplete conversations that deserves more attention. People often focus on learning how to intervene when they first observe harm, but they rarely prepare themselves for what happens *after* the initial intervention. In order to understand why toxic cultures so often go unchallenged, and therefore unchanged, we ought to examine not only the barriers that prevent the initial intervention but also the *aftermath* of someone's first courageous act of defiance. In other words, we can't overlook what happens after someone *does* intervene.

Think about this common scenario: you're in a meeting, and someone makes a racist or sexist joke or uses offensive terminology. A courageous soul intervenes, using the tactics they learned in a bystander training. Everyone shifts in their seats; the air thickens with an awkward tension. Most of us want to imagine the scene ending here, with the offender apologizing sheepishly, "You're right. My bad." But for too many of us who have actually been in these situations, we know the scene *rarely* plays out this way.

The first punch to toxic culture will often be met by a counterpunch from the power source that sounds like this: "Oh, stop being so sensitive. It's just a joke," or "Come on, lighten up," followed by a few chuckles in the room. The moment will quickly pass, and the group will move on to a different topic, with everyone desperately wanting to forget the momentary discomfort, leaving that first courageous person behind. And perhaps more importantly, the quick dismissal of the first courageous will signal to the rest of the people in the room to abandon future attempts to shake the status quo. This further reinforces the permissive culture in which insidious forms of oppression are allowed and dissenters chastised, stamping fear into everyone's memory. We all leave the meeting reminding ourselves to keep quiet.

How many times have you held back from intervening because you weren't sure if others were feeling the same way? How many times have you regretted not saying something because you were afraid of being the only party pooper breaking the social norm? How many times have you spoken up, only to find yourself standing alone in the fire, feeling let down by those you had trusted to have your back? Economist and political scientist Timur Kuran's study on *preference falsification*, or the act of misrepresenting one's true preference under perceived social pressures, shows just how frequently human beings act in ways that do not align with their true desires in order to gain social acceptance. This creates a distorted reality in which others make socially influenced decisions, so while we may all be thinking one way privately, we end up choosing to act in a way that maintains what we *perceive* to be more socially acceptable. (Like when one person declines to order dessert out of politeness, and everyone else says they don't want dessert either, when in reality we *all* want the damn dessert! But I digress.) Preference falsification can have massive social and political consequences, one of which is how our collective public lies contribute to "concealing political possibilities," according to Kuran. What's so powerful about the phenomenon, however, is that it shows we are often one minor event away from unlocking the flood-gate of truths about vastly disliked, yet preserved norms, structures, policies, and systems that appear to be widely accepted on the surface but in reality are vulnerable to a sudden collapse. Kuran reveals that "when the support of a policy, tradition, or regime is largely contrived, a minor event may activate a bandwagon that generates massive yet unanticipated change."[16] And in moments of collective and silent complicity, when the first courageous person is followed by what I call the *second courageous*, they have, together, the power to tip the scale and reveal opportunities for revolutionary change.

Sideliners who watch the first courageous without also jumping into the arena have an irritating habit of engaging in what I call *delayed camarade-rie*—a display of performative sympathy by a bystander who enthusiastically expresses their awe and gratitude to the risk-taker in a completely risk-free setting after the critical opportunity for harm intervention has passed. How many times have you heard or given these sentiments after the fact: "Hey, what you did in the meeting was really brave and inspiring!" "I totally agree with what you said back there." What the first courageous needs is solidarity in real time, not appreciation afterward. The repeated experience of observing harm and violence go unaddressed, or witnessing the first courageous be left to fend for themselves, has a lasting impact on our collective psyche. Such experiences compound our fear, making us feel alone in the struggle. It fast-tracks us to lose faith in our vision for change while making us less likely to intervene when we observe harm experienced by others. We may develop resentment and cynicism over time, which can be poisonous to ourselves and the movement. Instead, we need to learn to show up when it actually matters, instead of waiting for a time when there is no real risk associated with jumping into the fray. Instead of being a sideliner to the first courageous, be the second courageous who doubles down on the intervention *in* the moment, when your support will have the greatest impact.

> *Every moment is an organizing opportunity, every person a potential activist, every minute a chance to change the world.*
> —Dolores Huerta[17]

Imagine the same meeting scene, but with someone else joining in shortly after the sneer and chuckles of others: "Hey, cut it out." "Yeah, she's right." "I didn't find it funny, either." Even if there is no apology or acknowledgment from the person who caused harm, the addition of the second courageous will magnify the impact of the intervention and amplify the integrity of the first challenger. By affirming the validity of the first, you send a message of reassurance and solidarity not only to that one brave person but also to everyone else taking note. And maybe next time, someone else will try on the role of the first courageous, knowing they can count on the support of others. This is how we begin to truly shift the permissive culture that allows for misogyny, homophobia, transphobia, racism, ableism, ageism, and other forms of oppression to fester.

THERE IS NO SINGLE-HERO MOVEMENT

We can only truly practice courage when we are afraid.
—Mia Mingus[18]

CONTENT NOTE: *sexual assault*

In 2017, I quit my director-level job at a fast-growing tech company not long after this headline appeared in the news: "CEO sued by ex-employee for alleged sexually suggestive assault."[19] The said ex-employee was my coworker and dear friend Bea, whose immediate shock and trauma I witnessed that summer evening at a company offsite. I remember knocking on her cabin door, my heart pounding after having run across the compound when I heard she was "in trouble." Upon seeing the devastation on her face, my survivor's gut preempted her words. I had seen her cry before but not like this. Memories of my own trauma flooded my body—I knew all too well that she was going to be forced to relive this moment for the rest of her life.

The CEO refused to take accountability for what happened, and the company attempted to cover up the incident.[20] I remember Bea's trembles and disbelief when the HR department portrayed the incident as her own made-up nightmare. After contemplating a mountain of risks—endangering her professional reputation and ability to get hired in the future, losing thousands of dollars and months of time on the lawsuit, and compromising her and her family's privacy, which included her two-year-old son—Bea decided to sue. As expected, the legal battle was arduous and harrowing, as the company did not hesitate to use their resources and powerful connections to intimidate and silence Bea every step of the way.

Anytime someone decides to speak out against injustice, no matter how small of an act, it is courageous. When someone who has limited power decides to take direct action against those in positions of power by punching upward, it requires daring levels of audacity and conviction beyond momentary courage. In our battle for justice, those in favor of maintaining the status quo will not hesitate to throw their full weight to asphyxiate anything that threatens their power. And it is the righteous duty of those in proximity to the audacious to stand with them in solidarity, if not to push for change then to soothe the pain from the inevitable blowback—because there is *always* blowback. The first courageous will almost always be cast away as an "anomaly," "the difficult one," "the troublemaker," "the squeaky wheel." Without the second domino toppling with the first courageous, the trail of change is extremely difficult to accomplish.

And the second domino is not necessarily safe from the blowbacks, either. After I provided evidence backing Bea's claims, the company delayed my promised promotion. And when I quit without signing a nondisclosure agreement, I received threats from the CEO's attorney. I walked away from the job without a plan. For the first time in thirteen years, I had no source of income, and the thought of not being able to pay my bills or support my mom haunted me. It was a scary move, but the possibility of looking back at this moment and regretting my complicity scared me even more. Being a second courageous was a jarring experience, albeit a freeing one and one that came with material consequences. Make no mistake, being committed to the lifelong work of social justice is not cost-free, even as the *second* courageous.

The vast majority of my ex-coworkers chose to stay at the company despite their knowledge of the incident. Out of eighty-something people, only three people quit, including me, Bea, and Marissa, the company's only Black woman, whose lived experiences had given her the knowledge and understanding of the power of solidarity. The rest decided it wasn't the right time or the right reason for them to leave. Instead, they said:

"I understand why you're quitting. I'm so sorry about what happened to her; I hope she feels better soon."

"I'm trying to buy a house, so I really can't change jobs right now."

"I'm not sure where I want to go next."

"I think I'm just going to stick it out."

"I'd rather not get involved."

"My lawyer advised me to stay quiet for now."

My coworkers had too much to lose. And *I get it*. It is *hard* to give up something we've worked so hard for or risk our well-being and that of our loved ones. It might even feel unfair that we would have to give up something when we believe we weren't responsible for the harm. But the truth is my coworkers' inaction served as tacit approval of the CEO who had perpetuated harm with impunity while diminishing the gravity of the harm, which apparently was awful but not awful enough to warrant a bigger uproar. When we are part of the same system that continues to cause harm and violence, at some point, our inaction and unwillingness to give up our position of relative privilege *will* blur the line of complicity. Given everyone's different contexts and the contradictions we all live with, I do not have the moral authority to say that the people who decided to stay were in the wrong. *But* I want those who stayed to know that while their actions may not have been *wrong*, they were also not *harmless*.

I often wonder what would have happened if half the company had threatened to quit. Or what would have happened if some of them, short of quitting, had raised hell inside the company and organized to hold its leaders accountable while advocating for policy and culture change. The real power of the second courageous is being the *link* that carries the ripple toward sustainable change and away from the intoxicating status quo. Three brave women of color made a statement, but we did not create a movement at the company. We needed five, ten, fifteen, twenty more "second courageous" people to do that. With the domino ending after the third, the ripple toward change halted and the water swung back into equilibrium of inertia. Only now, there were three fewer wheels that squeaked.

The real power of the #MeToo movement was not in the "Me" but in the many "Toos" that followed. It was in the ripple effect of thousands of second courageous coming forward, inspiring others to believe in their power to drown out the noise of toxic naysayers. Let me clarify: the second courageous is not a singular person. It is not an identity given based on a sequence of events. Rather, the second courageous is a role we all get to play to create the domino effect, each of us claiming our power to inspire the next domino. A real movement is never about the bravest voice; a movement happens when a critical mass takes on the responsibility to carry on the momentum of the wave. It's jumping into the arena so the person already in the fight doesn't hurt alone. It's signaling to the rest of the world that they, too, can muster up the courage to act because *we have their back*. The second courageous is a role for *everyone, anytime* we witness the brave going against the giant.

You may not always be in the position to be the first courageous—maybe you didn't spot the harm as quickly as someone else did or maybe your fear made you hesitate—but you have a second chance to realign yourself to your values when someone else decides to take the first step. If you're not the first courageous, be the second courageous in full knowing that you, too, will be risking something. Be the second courageous because your solidarity *matters* and because you can tip the scale of power in moments that truly count. Be the link between the first and the rest of us waiting to jump in when the tide turns.

> There is no silver bullet, no one person, no one way. It is literally going to take us all doing all that we can at capacity to move the needle just a little bit. Let's work together. Let's heal together. And if you all are ready to do that work along with me, I can only leave you with these two words. Me, too.
> —Tarana Burke[21]

CHAPTER 11

KNOW WHAT YOU'RE WILLING
TO GIVE UP

Would it be fair to measure our commitment to equity and justice by our willingness to sacrifice what is important to us? Instead of asking, "What can I do to achieve equity and justice?" what if we asked, "What am I willing to give up to achieve equity and justice?" How would our answers differ, if at all?

One of the most important questions I ask C-suite leaders before they make any public commitments to DEI is this: "What are you willing to trade off in order to build a more diverse, equitable, and inclusive organization?" Having honest and upfront conversations around trade-offs is incredibly important for building a sustainable DEI strategy, and yet, many organizations dive into the to-dos before grappling with different tensions inherent in the work of disrupting the status quo, setting themselves up to fail and disappoint their teams in the near future. Whether we're an organization or an individual, being able to anticipate, name, and make different trade-offs helps pressure-test our commitment beyond our good intentions while preparing us for the challenge-zone where unexpected demands for sacrifice cause many to give up the journey.

These trade-offs can come in a variety of forms: they can be measurable, like money ("Am I willing to pay more money to purchase the same product from a small local business instead of big corporations?") or time ("Am I willing to spend my time volunteering on a Saturday?"), or immeasurable, like reputation ("Am I willing to risk my professional reputation or social standing by calling out my boss?"), power ("Am I willing to give up my decision-making power or my seat at the table to make room for marginalized people?"), ego or pride ("Am I willing to admit I was wrong or be called out publicly?"), safety

("Am I willing to put my body on the line at protests or intervene when I witness someone being harassed in public?"), comfort ("Am I willing to interrupt harmful jokes in a social setting?"), or sentimental traditions and customs we hold dear ("Am I willing to let go of racist sports team mascots, gender-reveal parties, or childhood memorabilia like Dr. Seuss, etc.?").

Trade-offs are an essential part of prioritization, and prioritization is an essential part of achieving the goals we say are important to us. Companies make trade-offs all the time, like when they decide to prioritize speed to market over getting all of their features perfectly fine-tuned, or when they decide to delay international expansion in order to focus on their current market engagement. And yet, when it comes to the work of achieving equity and justice, so many of us seem to believe our good hearts alone will help us achieve the feel-good outcomes advertised in grandiose, premature public diversity statements or social media posts, while underestimating the trade-offs required to make them come true. Outside of the organizational setting, we observe self-proclaimed antiracist parents in the supposed progressive state of California vote against affirmative action because they fear it might reduce *their* children's chances of being admitted to college,[1] or homeowners with liberal political yard signs vote against measures that would allow homeless shelters and affordable housing units to be built in their neighborhoods because they don't want their house values to plummet (referred to colloquially as a NIMBY—not in my backyard). Doing the work is not just about increasing our awareness through self-education; the real work begins through our deliberate and intentional choices that enable us to apply what we've learned into action every single day, which often requires us to make difficult trade-offs in service of equity and justice.

BEING HONEST WITH OURSELVES

Unfortunately, it is not unusual to find ourselves avoiding such trade-offs even when we say we are committed to the work. Despite the well-known best practice of including an image description or alt text* when posting

---

Alt text, short for *alternative text*, refers to written descriptions of nontext elements on webpages, such as an image. Alt text allows these elements to be accessed by people using screen readers.

images online, I often encounter equity advocates forgoing such a practice, rendering that piece of art, photo, or infographic inaccessible. I am guilty of this too, and I use my own justifications to make myself feel less guilty: "What are the chances someone who is blind is following me?" "Is this image really that important for me to describe?" "I'll do it next time." These excuses reveal the trade-off I am not willing to make in the moment—and my decision to skip the effort of making my content more accessible is a direct violation of my proclaimed values and an outcome of my prioritizing convenience and efficiency over inclusion and equitable access. Similarly, every time I decide to host an event without an ASL (American Sign Language) interpreter or closed captioning, every time I decide to promote an event being held in a location that is not wheelchair accessible, every time I decide to skip asking about people's accessibility needs, I am actively deciding to not give up my time or money at the expense of the disabled community and my own values. In these moments of willful complicity, I have to be honest about the harm I cause without dressing myself as an "ally."

Being clear about the necessary trade-offs early on and communicating honestly what we are willing or not willing to give up help set better expectations while minimizing unintended harm. I have come to hold a perspective that has not always been widely celebrated, which is that I would rather have organizations and their leaders be honest about their lack of desire to prioritize DEI or social justice than virtue signal to marginalized people that they are committed to keeping them safe and empowered. Too often, organizational leaders promise a grand, yet ambiguous vision for diversity and inclusion but find themselves unable to deliver on it because the trade-offs they eventually face feel too costly, leading to massive cognitive dissonance that could have been avoided. Coinbase, a cryptocurrency trading platform based in San Francisco, is a crude example of this honest approach. In 2020, its CEO, Brian Armstrong, published a controversial blog post stating that Coinbase was a "mission-focused company" and wouldn't be engaging in social activism because it "creates internal division," which distracts the company from its intentionally narrow focus of "creating infrastructure for the cryptoeconomy." Armstrong further clarified that if some of the current employees disagreed with this approach, they could work with their manager who would "help them get to a better place" that was not Coinbase.[2] Although I did not agree with his tragically underdeveloped logic, I found his transparency refreshing and helpful. His drawing a clear line in the sand sent an important message to those inside and outside the company to make informed decisions around how to engage with Coinbase.

In the end, both Coinbase and companies that make performative, and ultimately empty, promises will cause harm through their inaction, which contributes directly to upholding the status quo reinforcing systems of oppression. However, in the case of the latter, harm takes on a much more insidious, subtle, and lasting undertone, where the seductive message of hope and its opposing reality produce a blatant disconnect that gaslights and exploits marginalized people and their earnest support and labor. Companies—and indeed individuals—that subscribe to virtue signaling, hoping to disingenuously benefit from their gift-wrapped, empty gestures, end up causing harm in a more deceitful way.

The unfortunate reality is that white supremacy culture discourages transparency and accountability, which makes radical honesty even more challenging to practice inside our current systems. At one executive workshop I was facilitating at a national nonprofit organization, the leadership team spent over three hours trying to agree on the right and "legally safe" way for the leaders of the organization to acknowledge that their recent layoffs disproportionately impacted their Black employees. Though the team agreed that the way they had handled the layoff was problematic, they were hung up on the idea that if they were to even *hint* at the idea of being racially biased, consciously or unconsciously, they would face legal actions. In *admitting* their mistakes, they would be taking a major legal risk, which exposed the inherently adversarial predicament our systems have put us in that makes practicing principled accountability—or simply doing the right thing—that much more challenging.

I've had to make many decisions that tested my commitment to this work, from turning down a six-figure check from a company that wanted to use my company as a mere marketing tool to risking my reputation and ability to be hired by calling out powerful tech leaders publicly. But the uncomfortable truth is that I've not always succeeded in sacrificing the things that are important to me in order to stay in integrity. Money has been a source of deep trauma for me and my family, and when it comes to staying in alignment with my values, sacrifices that threaten my financial security are especially terrifying. My dad went through bankruptcy twice, both times due to systemic failures (the 2008 subprime mortgage crisis when he was a realtor, for example) that rendered the most vulnerable populations even more deprived. In 2009, he awoke one morning to the sound of a tow truck and watched strangers confiscate his car, with his belongings still in it, because he had not been able to make his car payment. The first house he bought after years of backbreaking labor was foreclosed and taken by the bank, along with his last sliver of pride. Though my dad has been able to claw himself out of bankruptcy over the last decade, the ease and security he has always yearned for remains elusive. For so long I thought money was the one way I could restore, or buy back, my dad's dignity, and achieving the financial stability my family has never had in the United States has been my lifelong chase. When my partner and I decided to purchase our first home, all of these traumas were kicked up to the surface, haunting me for weeks. "What if we can't pay the mortgage?" "What if we end up going bankrupt?" "How am I going to keep supporting my family?" "What makes me think I deserve to own a house?"

While comparing different lenders for the mortgage loan, we were offered an incredible deal through a personal connection at a major financial institution. Going into the process, I had crossed off that bank out of principle, knowing their atrocious history of racism, discrimination, and lack of accountability for the harm they've caused. All of a sudden, I found myself deeply troubled by the choice in front of us and also by my indecision. I found myself negotiating with myself, and I agonized for days (which, of course, delayed our escrow and made the sellers very unhappy) over whether I was going to stick to my proclaimed values or take the better deal. Against my moral compass, I took the deal. Instead of feeling pride for what I had finally accomplished after years of nonstop grinding, I signed the paperwork feeling disgusted with myself for trading in my values for fifty thousand dollars, which I would be saving over the next thirty years.

Despite my proclaimed values, there continue to be times when I am unable or simply unwilling to make sacrifices. I share my stories of when I failed to stay principled not to ask for forgiveness or absolution but to illustrate how staying in alignment with our values is much more complex than a simplified, morally upright sound bite. Clearly, I am not above betraying my proclaimed values for self-interest, sometimes out of necessity, sometimes out of my unhealed wounds, and other times out of desire, but regardless of the reasons, our choices demand we be honest about our complicity and commit to practicing accountability in material ways. Being truthful is the first step toward understanding what gets in the way of living our values, and only then can we begin to repair the harm caused by our compromised choices. This honest reflection also helps to ensure we set ourselves up to make decisions that are better aligned with our values in the future. In addition to exploring what values-aligned wealth building and redistribution look like for me, actively working through my money traumas, which hold me back from living out my values, has been a critical part of my accountability practice and has helped me make future decisions in a more grounded way rather than from a place of scarcity and fear. While these actions do not absolve me of my fifty-thousand-dollar decision, they serve to remind me of the importance of being honest about my choices and what they represent, as well as my ongoing need to interrogate my complicity in upholding systems that I denounce.

In order to stay in alignment with our proclaimed values, we will be met with countless opportunities to truthfully ask ourselves what we are and are not willing to sacrifice to be the person we say we want to be. Our commitment to equity and justice will be tested and measured by our willingness to give up our privileges and comfort in moments that require them to tip the scale of injustice. It won't always be easy (it rarely is) and we are not aiming for perfection, but in this practiced grappling to remain in integrity and to be accountable when we fall short, we sharpen our ability to stay principled.

THE DISPROPORTIONATE WEIGHT OF SACRIFICE
ON MARGINALIZED PEOPLE

Trade-offs are being made, voluntarily and involuntarily, by marginalized people on a daily basis and in a disproportionate way compared to those in positions of more power and privilege. Marginalized people are forced to sacrifice higher stakes—their dignity, safety, comfort, culture, authenticity, wellness, and humanity—while navigating toxic spaces in order to survive. While we, people of relative privileges in different contexts, may fret about the inconvenient consequences of the trade-offs we're being asked to make, so many marginalized people are penalized and punished for simply existing outside the norm of white supremacy. As a stark example, we may decide it's not worth the discomfort to challenge a homophobic joke at a family dinner table; meanwhile, many queer and trans people in my life do not get to contemplate such a decision as they've been estranged from their family of origin* due to their family members' homophobia and transphobia. In a more nuanced example, there is often an implicit and, at times, explicit expectation placed on already marginalized people to shoulder additional risks and sacrifices that are not often expected, to the same degree, of their more privileged counterparts navigating in the same systems. While marginalized people bear the disproportionate burden of risk and repercussions in a system that rewards allegiance to the status quo—for example, women and people of color are penalized and scrutinized for promoting diversity at work, while white men do not face the same negative repercussions[3]—when it comes to equity and justice, marginalized people still continue to play a dominant role in speaking up against injustice, intervening when there is harm, and risking their own safety to advocate for change. Meanwhile, those with more privileges and power tend to take a back seat despite being less likely to face negative consequences when *they* take risks. When my company was just starting out, why were the vast majority of our early clients women of color, predominantly Black women in mid- to senior-level positions who took a chance on our social justice–based approach to corporate diversity trainings; and why did white women HR leaders, often in higher positions, reject our proposals as too "radical" for their majority white men corporate audience? Why are marginalized people, who have far less power and far more to lose, the ones who always take on the burden of these risks first? And why, when they fail to take on even more sacrifices, do they bear the brunt of the harshest criticisms?

Yes, we always have a choice to stay as closely aligned to our values as possible. But before asking marginalized people to stay pure and become martyrs to maintain their right to hold others accountable, let's not ignore nuance and the context of power, history, and trauma, while examining the systemic forces that drive people to pick and choose between terrible

---

*By *family of origin* I mean the family unit in which we were raised (e.g., biological family, adoptive family, legal guardians, different caregivers, etc.), as opposed to a *chosen family*, which refers to people we have consciously chosen to be our support system based on our own definition of "family" and associated values.

options. It is disconcerting to observe marginalized people be ruthlessly criticized for the times they choose incremental comfort over scarcity or momentary safety over penalty by the same people who are quick to celebrate privileged white executives for the mere display of bare minimum cultural competence. This type of disproportionate scrutiny and criticism seems to target Black women most noticeably, both inside the field of DEI as well as in the public arena. And similar to my experience, I know many marginalized people for whom the decision to work inside for-profit institutions came with a painful cost either way: walk away from an opportunity as a matter of principle that could help them and their family get out of debt, or take the opportunity and live in crushing shame and self-punishment that come from believing they've betrayed their values and their communities. It's a lose-lose binary trap set up meticulously by oppressive systems and our problematic assumptions about what constitutes moral purity.

To be clear, echoing the messages in Chapter 6, The Double-Edged Sword of Representation, I'm not calling to absolve any and all harms caused by marginalized people or asking to extend grace to marginalized people who are egregiously complicit in perpetuating oppression. What I *am* noting is the importance of considering nuance and context, questioning the broader conditions that create false dichotomies, and pointing out the pattern of behaviors that place inequitable expectations on certain groups while continuing to privilege others. Depending on their identities and context, sometimes people on the margins may *not* be able to give up something—whether it's staying in toxic workplaces for the paycheck, immigrant visa, or health insurance; shopping at Walmart or Amazon to save money; or accepting grants and funding from problematic institutions—not because they don't desire to but because that something might mean *everything* to their ability to survive. Often marginalized people find themselves in exhausting mental and emotional battles to balance survival and integrity, while others who are more privileged don't need to "sell out" to put food on their table or cross the picket line to keep their futures intact. That is the kind of abundance I wish all marginalized people could taste.

While we stay steadfastly committed to the work of securing equity and justice for all, the fact is we all live in varied contexts and with different needs, with many of us trying to navigate this messy and deeply flawed world as best as we could. Systems of oppression, by design, manifest in ways that make many trade-offs difficult and even impossible, especially for already marginalized people. Part of the unrelenting tension in this work is being able to hold with care these complexities and contradictions at the same time without losing sight of one another's inherent humanity, and always aiming our most fiery anger at the violent systems that have created only bad and worse options. While we do our very best to live our lives according to our values and with accountability, we need to resist the tempting path of dehumanizing, shaming, and blaming marginalized people for prioritizing their survival over the impossible standard of moral perfection while living in an exploitative society. We can be disciplined without obliterating our humanity. We can, and should, hold ourselves and one another accountable when we've deviated from our values and still put earnest effort toward reducing the harm created out of our choices. And we can, and must, continue to demand more sacrifice from those in positions of power while always working in solidarity to dismantle oppressive systems.

> Being oppressed means the absence of choices.
> —bell hooks[4]

REBALANCING THE BURDEN OF SACRIFICE

Working to achieve equity in the kinds of sacrifices marginalized people are asked to make, compared to those with more power and privilege, is not about giving marginalized people a free pass out of making tough decisions to stay in alignment. Rather, it's about redistributing the disproportionate amount of sacrifice placed on their shoulders when they have not been afforded as many opportunities or resources in the first place and shifting the weight to those with relative privileges who can alleviate the burden. I'm asking us to sacrifice our comfort for others' safety, our politeness for others' dignity, and our maximum profitability for others' livelihoods free of exploitation. We also have the opportunity to proactively create conditions that lessen the negative repercussions for the marginalized, making it easier for everyone to do the right thing. When more people, and people with more privileges, move in solidarity to share this burden and risks, our necessary sacrifices become more equitably distributed and our chances of succeeding enhanced.

One year, I was invited to speak at a prestigious conference targeting HR professionals. Though it was an unpaid engagement, I jumped at the opportunity to be a part of an event that would be advertised to thousands of industry leaders. Two weeks before the event, I let out an audible curse word as I scrolled through the photos of the other conference speakers on their website. Out of twenty-some speakers, I was the only person of color. Aggravated, I emailed the conference organizer asking them to correct the situation by promptly hiring additional speakers of color and shared that I would not be a part of the event otherwise. The organizer replied with a virtual shrug, stating there was just no time to make any changes and that they would do better next year. So, I emailed two of the white speakers I knew personally and solicited support. Without putting additional labor on me, they took the baton and reached out to the white conference organizer, explained the urgency and applied pressure, contacted a group of Black and brown speakers, and, in the end, convinced the conference to hire a Black speaker. Though I didn't consider this a real "win," given the last-minute scrambling and the danger of tokenization, I appreciated the two white speakers who were willing to put their professional reputation and opportunities on the line to push for change, while enabling me to keep my seat at a table that was already limited in diversity. If my ultimatum had gone unaddressed, my stepping away from the conference would have been another lose-lose situation for everyone involved—me for losing a platform to amplify my company's important work and the conference attendees for missing out on a valuable and different perspective, ultimately resulting in no real change.

In 2014, Indigenous Action Media published "Accomplices Not Allies: Abolishing the Ally Industrial Complex. An Indigenous Perspective." Highlighting how the concept of allyship has been commodified and "rendered ineffective and meaningless," the authors proposed the idea of an *accomplice,* or a person who helps another commit a crime: "But we need to know who has our backs, or more appropriately: who is with us, at our sides? The risks of an ally who provides support or solidarity (usually on a temporary basis) in a fight are much different than that of an accomplice. When we fight back or forward, together, becoming complicit in a struggle towards liberation, we are accomplices. Abolishing allyship can occur through the criminalization of support and solidarity."[5]

The accomplice framework challenges the morality of the legal system: just because a practice is legal and lawful does not mean it is moral or just. To achieve equity, sometimes unjust laws must be broken, and those who break these laws, no matter how morally correct, risk being criminalized by design. For example in the United States, chattel slavery and racial segregation were both legal *and* unjust, and one had to actively engage in the illegal act of defying unjust laws to fight for justice. The accomplice framework asks people to go beyond being a mere supporter to being a coconspirator, challenging those committed to collective liberation to shoulder the same kinds of risks marginalized people face, including being disproportionately criminalized and punished for fighting for justice in a supremacist society. An example of applying this framework to real life is when white people and others with relative privilege, understanding the risks of physical harm and arrests shouldered by Black and brown protesters, strategize to form human barricades at BLM protests and directly confront the police. In an effort to not dilute the original intent of the framework, I only use the term *accomplice* or *coconspirator* in the context of fighting unjust and oppressive legal systems that come with material risks (e.g., criminalization, incarceration, physical safety, etc.).

As noted by Indigenous Action Media, true accompliceship is often limited to the sphere of direct actions, like risking arrest and safety during the Dakota Access Pipeline protests, which resulted in over 480 arrests[6] and 300 injuries.[7] Nonetheless, I believe these clarifying messages around sharing risks, challenging the notion of risk-free support, and divesting from the harmful system's definition of justice in favor of *real* justice and safety for the most marginalized are critical lessons for us to keep in mind as we journey toward change in different spheres.

DON'T FORGET THE UPSIDE

Though I've been preaching the importance of sacrifice, it is critical we don't just focus on what we're giving up in our quest for justice as there is so much to gain from our trade-offs that make these decisions worthwhile. For every trade-off we make, there are upsides we may not be thinking about.

Nobel Prize–winning psychologist and economist Daniel Kahneman and his associate Amos Tversky were the first to identify the economic principle of *loss aversion*, the human tendency to prefer avoiding losses over acquiring equivalent gains ("it's better to *not lose* five dollars than to find five dollars"). Kahneman states it succinctly: "The response to losses is stronger than the response to corresponding gains."[8] Our inherent resistance to loss makes it difficult for us "predictably irrational" humans, as behavioral economist Dan Ariely would say,[9] to agree to a trade-off, especially when we aren't made aware of potential gains. Each time I press the organizational leaders I work with to identify what sacrifices they are willing to make as a requirement for building a more equitable and diverse organization, I also pose these complementary questions, which can apply to all of us individually too: What are the *upsides* (it can be as concrete as "fewer lawsuits" or as abstract as "better employee engagement" or, for individuals, reduced violence, resilient relationships, community engagement, etc.)? What upsides are we potentially undervaluing? What do we gain when we stay in alignment with our values, both in the short term and long term? How can we make these gains explicit and known across the organization or in our personal lives? And I remind us: inclusive and equitable solutions that prioritize the needs of the most marginalized always end up benefiting *all* people.

I remain hopeful as I observe people making trade-offs small and big in their decision-making in favor of equity and justice: executive teams that acknowledge and fix existing pay gaps despite being advised to keep quiet by their legal team; ad agencies that dedicate additional time and resources to redo entire campaigns because the original lacked authentic representation of marginalized people; young people who have access to wealth or class privilege mobilizing to equitably redistribute wealth, land, and power through organizations like Resource Generation.[10] I've also observed people working together in solidarity to use whatever power and privilege they have to push back against oppressive systems while risking their own livelihood—from employees coalescing power to strike against inequitable working conditions to courageous individuals whistleblowing on unethical practices and others rallying to protect them. When risks are shared and more of us lock arms in favor of our collective liberation, the risks themselves become less risky.

When we take risks and willingly give up our access, resources, privileges, safety, comfort, status, ego, and power in service of equity and justice, we are not only remaining in integrity with ourselves, we are also opening ourselves up for the possibility of deeper and more genuine connections marked by our shared commitment to justice, freedom, and healing. Purposeful and deliberate choice making is a lifelong practice that enables us to become closer to who we say we want to be every day—and that is a pretty compelling upside, if you ask me.

CHAPTER 12

HOLD TRAUMA WITH CARE

Audre Lorde's now famous line, "Caring for myself is not self-indulgence, it is self-preservation, and that is an act of political warfare," is often quoted without the context from which it emerged. The quote, from *A Burst of Light*, was written when Lorde was battling cancer for the second time, and she underscores the importance of survival as an act of resistance for marginalized people in the face of ongoing battles against racism, sexism, and heterosexism. She wrote, "Racism. Cancer. In both cases, to win the aggressor must conquer, but the resisters need only survive."[1] Her caring for herself to survive and heal was an act of political resistance in a society that did not, and continues not to, value the lives, dignity, or healing of Black women and other oppressed people.

In short: self-care is not about bath bombs or yoga retreats. This stripping of context—specifically, the history and context of trauma—is a dangerous pattern of white supremacy, which occurs all around us. It is dangerous because without frequent reminders of the sheer weight and vastness of the trauma marginalized people carry, it becomes easy to forget exactly what it is that we are, and have been, fighting for. When we forget to acknowledge the decades' and centuries' worth of systemic violence that have been committed against marginalized people, it becomes all too convenient for us to put the onus of healing on individuals using the now-commodified rhetoric of self-care, rather than exposing and targeting the conditions that created such disparate pain in the first place. Acknowledging the omnipresence of prolonged and repeated trauma—both at the individual and systemic levels—is critical to avoiding reductive analyses and myopic solutions.

At the interpersonal level, obtuse responses to trauma can sound like gaslighting, tone policing, or spiritual bypassing, often coming from those typically insulated from the impacts of sustained trauma. At the systemic level, policies devoid of the historical context of legacies of systemic oppression can emerge, while those seeking to right historical wrongs are challenged with false narratives of meritocracy and the troubling assumption of a level playing field, as illustrated in Chapter 5, The Only Constant Is Context. In many heated debates where multiple parties don't seem to see eye to eye, I've found there's often gravely varying levels of understanding and calculations about the weight of historical and present-day traumas held by individuals and different marginalized communities. And if left unaddressed, this widening disparity can exacerbate existing inequities and cycles of harm over generations and across communities, while prohibiting us from being able to move forward together.

UNDERSTANDING THE CONTEXT OF TRAUMA

CONTENT NOTE: *stories about corporal punishment, descriptions of racial trauma from chattel slavery and genocide, mentions of sexual violence, intimate partner violence*

Before immigrating to the United States, I attended a Korean Catholic elementary school for six years where I experienced public shaming and corporal punishment as the primary tool for motivation. Fear ruled my daily drive to complete my homework as I was terrified of both the physical pain and humiliation of getting beaten by the teacher in front of the class. Whether it was forgetting to bring art supplies, getting a bad grade on an exam, or mistakenly turning in an assignment without your name, reasons for different punitive consequences varied depending on the teacher you had. Some would hit your palms with a ruler, some would force you into a stress position for an entire class period, such as kneeling in front of the class with arms raised or maintaining a push-up position, and some would yell at you, calling you stupid and lazy or, the worst, scolding you had "brought shame onto your whole family." Memorable pain was the point, cemented through public shaming, which reminded other kids to never, ever mess up. "I'm hitting you because I love you," some people used to say, including my own mother who occasionally spanked me and my sister whenever we fought, almost always while crying along with us. Meanwhile in the United States, stories of Asian people's strict discipline and cutthroat focus on academic achievements permeate through caricatured depictions of Tiger Moms and studious Asian students who never dare to defy the rules. Many white people, feigning genuine concern for Asian youth, sometimes ask, "Why are Asian parents so strict?" "How can they treat their children like that?" What I feel seeping through their questions are traces of moral superiority, and I'm in awe at how easily white people tend to forget the brutality of their own ancestors' hands.

In early 2021, South Korea became the sixty-second country to ban corporal punishment against children.[2] The pressure to prohibit school beatings had been building since the early 2000s when students, now with an increasing access to camera phones, began filming and sharing scenes of violent beatings inside classrooms. Banning corporal punishment in schools and at large has been a contentious topic among Koreans, with many conservative Koreans arguing it is an integral part of our culture, a tradition rooted in our deep veneration for educators, elders, discipline, and hard work, while others argue it is time to outgrow such practices that terrorize youth who are already living under immense pressure to achieve in a highly competitive and demanding society. Although the use of corporal punishment in Korean schools is believed to have begun in the tenth century with the adoption of Tang dynasty China's Confucianism-based education system, some Korean scholars show that extreme cases of such practices mimic what Koreans endured during the Japanese colonization of Korea. According to Hanshin University professor Soon-Won Kang, "corporal punishment during the colonial period was especially harsh since students faced whipping if they expressed an interest in learning about Korean culture. Though Korea returned to a more Western-style education system following Japanese colonization, the resulting ideological commitment to capitalism led to unprecedented competition among students."[3]

In his book *My Grandmother's Hands*, author and trauma expert Resmaa Menakem warns of our tendency to mistake unhealed trauma retention as culture: "And if [unhealed trauma] gets transmitted and compounded through multiple families and generations, it can start to look like culture. But it isn't culture. It's a traumatic retention that has lost its context over time."[4] How many times have I watched unruly white children run around in a restaurant and joked, "It's because they don't get beaten," instead of asking myself, *Who taught* us *to hit like that?* Menakem, while emphasizing the importance of mending the Black heart and body, implores we do not lose the context: "The term *whupping* is a slightly sanitized version of *whipping*, which for centuries was a standard practice in America. Overseers on plantations routinely whipped Black bodies, both to punish them and to control them."[5]

The explicit connections drawn by Menakem between the legacy of white violence, the unhealed traumas of Black people, and the generational retention and reincarnation of such traumas were an epiphany for me. It put into perspective just how often we, as a global society, create stories divorced from the full context, creating dangerous realities in which the roots and perpetrators of mass violence go unnamed while the victims of unhealed traumas become the sole responsible party for the pain experienced today. With this newfound knowledge of seeing trauma in context and interrogating the why, I am now reevaluating a number of trauma retentions that many have dubbed as our "culture" through a critical lens of the vast and lasting legacies of mass violence committed against my people.

According to the American Psychological Association (APA), *trauma* is defined as "an emotional response to a terrible event like an accident, rape or natural disaster."[6] Immediate reactions of shock and denial are commonplace, and longer-term reactions to trauma include "unpredictable emotions, flashbacks, strained relationships, and even physical symptoms like headaches or nausea." Traumas can result from a variety of sources, for example, a one-time event like a car accident with lingering psychological and physical impacts. For this conversation, however, I'll focus on traumas resulting from the pervasive systemic and interpersonal oppressions perpetrated against marginalized social identities. Numerous studies have illustrated the undeniable impact of *racial trauma*, also known as race-based traumatic stress (RBTS), which is defined as "mental and emotional injury caused by encounters with racial bias and ethnic discrimination, racism, and/or hate crimes."[7] Though not all incidents of racism or racial bias are experienced as traumatic, all racial traumas result from different forms of racist violence. These studies have also proven that the negative symptoms of long-term racial trauma are not limited to our emotional and mental health but can also go on to cause serious physical illnesses, making both the reduction of trauma sources as well as healing from historical traumas urgent and paramount.

However, the current state of our society does not provide adequate conditions for oppressed people to prioritize their healing, let alone stop experiencing the violence that created the trauma in the first place. Take, for example, accessing talk therapy: finding people of color mental health professionals is unreasonably difficult, as is finding ones whose approaches are truly trauma informed and socially conscious. Then there is the issue of health insurance: many still lack it, which makes accessing therapy incredibly difficult; even if you have insurance, most insurance carriers do not cover therapy. Finding time for therapy, especially if your job has inflexible working hours or if you depend on hourly pay, can be difficult, as most therapists do not work outside the standard business hours. Some may be in a position where it is unsafe to access therapy, whether due to situations involving intimate partner violence or toxic family dynamics. Stigma around mental health issues still exists in many people of color communities, including my own Asian community, which is three times less likely to seek mental health services than white people.[8] And some may not trust the institutions that offer mental health services out of fear of being pathologized, criminalized, reported, dismissed, or gaslighted.

Even if we actively work toward healing, the same forms of violence, which remain embedded in our systems, become roadblocks and present ongoing opportunities for trauma. So long as the conditions that enabled our trauma do not change, we risk being retraumatized at such a frequency and intensity that doesn't allow for our wounds to ever fully heal. The incorporation of this broader systemic analysis is one reason why I appreciate the definition of trauma from Staci K. Haines, cofounder of Generative Somatics and author of *The Politics of Trauma*: "[Trauma is] an experience, series of experiences, and/or impacts from social conditions that break or betray our inherent need for safety, belonging, and dignity." She goes on further to deliberately name *systemic trauma* as "the repeated, ongoing violation, exploitation, dismissal of, and/or deprivation of groups of people."[9] If the traditional approach to trauma, which focuses on *individuals*, asks, "How can I heal?" the systemic approach to trauma asks, "Why is there so much trauma to heal from in the first place?"* When we connect the dots between

---

*These questions and the language of systemic trauma were introduced to me by Amanda Machado, an incredible writer, facilitator, and friend whom I had the honor of collaborating with via Awaken.

individual traumas and the conditions that birthed and perpetuate them, we can start to grasp the reality that individual self-care is not enough for us to bring about real, sustainable change that can nurture collective healing.

Another important concept is *historical trauma,* or "cumulative emotional and psychological wounding over the lifespan and across generations, emanating from massive group trauma experiences."[10] The term was first conceptualized and coined in the 1980s by Maria Yellow Horse Brave Heart, a Native American social worker and mental health expert who studied the lasting effects of the psychological and emotional traumas of genocide, colonization, displacement, and assimilation within generations of the Lakota communities. In an article published in 2000, Brave Heart describes a range of historical trauma responses, including depression, anger, suicidal ideation, low self-esteem, psychosomatic illnesses, and more, which together are "the constellation of features in reaction to this trauma."[11] Brave Heart's scholarship over the years suggests that while the study began with specific examples and impacts observed within the Lakota communities, similar implications and patterns exist across all massively traumatized and oppressed populations, where unresolved grief passes down through generations.

In our quest toward collective healing, we must first examine the historical legacies and systemic manifestations of trauma. By always engaging in the practice of contextualizing the pain of historically oppressed people, we can understand the conditions in which they are called to heal, and extend the scope of our solutions to encompass the disruption of violent patterns. And we must also resist the temptation of seeing ourselves as innocent bystanders to others' traumas by critically examining our roles in the larger systems, interrogating how we may have aided or benefited from violent conditions such as generational poverty, segregation, and mass incarceration that continue to traumatize, and instead choose to become active participants in shaping conditions that can heal.

> *Historical unresolved grief is the associated affect that accompanies historical trauma response.*
> —Maria Yellow Horse Brave Heart[12]

WHEN OUR TRAUMAS COLLIDE

CONTENT NOTE: *assault, descriptions of anti-Black racism*

A few years ago, my mom was assaulted and robbed at night by a Black man in San Francisco. He struck her head hard, making her fall to the concrete pavement; the fall injured her leg, causing it to bleed. He ripped my mom's handbag out of her clenched hands, which had her favorite pair of sunglasses and her month's rent in cash. The incident left her bruised physically and emotionally, and it took a lot of courage for her to walk outside again. A few days later, she noticed a Black man walking toward her on the same side of the street. As her body remembered the horror from the recent attack, her survival reaction told her to flee. When she crossed the street, the Black man noticed her sudden move and confronted her: "Why did you cross the street? I'm not dangerous!" She was mortified and called me to tell me what had happened. That day, two people's traumas collided, against the backdrop of white supremacy culture.

My mom's instinctive response to flee is one of the five common survival reactions inherent in all humans according to Haines: fight, flight, freeze, appease, and dissociate. These reactions are natural protective mechanisms that help keep us safe, but sometimes they can be deployed indiscriminately, with our brains unable to distinguish a real threat from a perceived threat. "Usually once we have been hurt or endangered," Haines explains, "our automatic defenses generalize and assume the harm will come again. When this happens, we can't 'put down the defense' to see trustworthy, good people and situations. It feels more like we are waiting for the next bad thing to happen. . . . These survival reactions can then create suffering and breakdowns, mistrust and disconnection. We can mis-assess safety, love, dignity, and others' actions."[13] Given the context, my mom's survival reaction was understandable. Yet, her immediate harboring of overgeneralized fear toward all Black men, assisted by existing, ubiquitous anti-Black stereotypes (if her attacker had been a white woman, would she fear all white women? I think not), if left unaddressed, could continue to harm others and her.

The Black man's reaction to my mom's behavior was also understandable and valid. We know that microaggressions, such as the one my mom enacted, are commonly experienced by Black and brown people, whom white supremacy culture likes to portray as "threatening" or "dangerous." Left to proliferate, these tropes pave the way to legitimize police brutality against Black and brown people, justify targeted overcriminalization and mass incarceration, and accelerate the school-to-prison pipeline that disproportionately impacts Black and brown youth who are overpoliced and underbelieved. While I don't have a good answer for what my mom should have done instead in that moment, what I do know is that different and equally valid realities are clashing around us all the time, with one's trauma response triggering another's and every hurt soul yearning for safety and understanding.

Whether direct or vicarious, none of us is immune to the impacts of systemic and interpersonal violence happening all around us. For example, white supremacist delusion doesn't just harm people of color; it robs white people of their humanity too. The "ultimate irony of white-body supremacy," Resmaa Menakem says, is the ways in which white Americans have been allowed to "avoid developing the full range of necessary skills for navigating adulthood . . . in the name of protecting and serving" them, which has ultimately made many of them "more vulnerable to trauma and caused them to feel more fragile and threatened."[14] My experience working with countless white executive leaders validates this. I've witnessed that, beneath their surface-level confidence, many white leaders harbor deep-seated fears, shame, and insecurities about their own abilities and worthiness as measured by their internalized standards of white supremacy, which tells them they are supposed to be superior, dominant, and almighty. This internal dissonance often manifests in frightening levels of rage, entitlement, and a desire to conquer—money, people, power—as well as their inability to be in right relationships to self, their lineage, and the people in their lives.*

The footprint of violence is always much larger than it seems.

---

*A stark difference, however, is how society often rewards white people's trauma reactions while criminalizing that of marginalized people's.

THE DANGERS OF DIRTY PAIN

Pain is important: how we evade it, how we succumb to it, how we deal with it, how we transcend it.
—Audre Lorde[15]

CONTENT NOTE: *stories about anti-Asian racism*

In acceptance and commitment therapy (ACT), *clean pain* is thought of as the pain we feel when something terrible happens to us.[16] Meanwhile, dirty pain, according to Resmaa Menakem, is the "pain of avoidance, blame, or denial." Dirty pain is when hurt people "respond from their most wounded parts, become cruel or violent, or physically or emotionally run away," which in turn can create even more dirty pain for themselves and those around them.[17] Whether through internalized oppression or the weaponizing of our pain, the by-product of unhealed trauma is that we sometimes become complicit in perpetuating cycles of oppression ourselves, often to obtain relative positions of power, privilege, and safety, however conditional and temporary they may be.

As a new immigrant, I was an obvious target of anti-Asian racism and xenophobia. My first week at an American middle school, two white boys came up to me during lunchtime. Before I could practice my rehearsed introduction, one of the boys held up a banana in my face and said, "Do you know what this is? It's called BUHHHH-NAHHH-NAHHHHH!" I stood there, humiliated, with no words to fight back. Every day thereafter that I spent refusing to speak Korean and listening to my favorite Korean music was my protest for survival. I fought to rid myself of my Korean accent and to assimilate, which included distancing myself from other Korean immigrants and appeasing white kids. I frequently allowed myself to be the subject of laughter among my new white American "friends," who enjoyed making me say words that were particularly challenging to pronounce and then parroted the way I sounded. I ached for their acceptance, no matter how artificial, even if it came at the expense of my own dignity. And eventually, I started to believe it was actually working, except what I was feeling wasn't their genuine acceptance but my own self-hatred, which deluded me into believing that by alienating my people I was becoming more like my white friends. One day, as my white friends and I walked past a group of Korean kids sitting on the floor eating lunch and laughing loudly, I felt ashamed of their brazenness but also insecure, thinking those Korean kids were talking about me behind my back. *They can't* stand *that I speak better English than them,* I simply told myself as I walked away, wondering what they were laughing about.

> The system perpetuates itself by turning the victims into victimizers
> and everyone becomes complicit in this system of oppression.
> —Timur Kuran[18]

The dangerous effects of this internalization of oppression, aided by generations of uninterrupted cycles of socialization, can be observed on various fronts. Even those with privileged social identities, though they don't experience the same magnitude of systemic oppressions or traumas, experience alienation and hurt, and their unhealed wounds can have an even more damning impact on society when wielded with their social power and privilege, along with an active desire to perpetuate systemic oppressions to remain in positions of power. Like when men who have experienced bullying and emasculation turn their anger into toxic masculinity, with accompanying controlling behaviors that degrade and endanger marginalized genders. Or when some white activists refuse to acknowledge their white privilege by *only* owning their marginalized identities and taking center stage instead of centering activists of color at the intersections of those margins and racism. And this collective pain transfer continues to cycle through our bodies and is injected into others', creating more tentacles through which we uphold oppressive systems.

What I have come to understand is that my unprocessed hurt makes me that much more susceptible to the lure of white supremacy and capitalist culture, which whispers to me that I, too, can gain a slice of safety, belonging, and abundance, if only I continue to believe I am better than, worthier than, and more deserving than those whom society has taught us to hate, deplore, and marginalize. Stuck in a mindless loop of trauma transfer, it is easy to become a fierce protector of oppressive social stratification and structures while faithfully believing I am better off so long as I'm not at the bottom of the ladder. But while my trauma can *explain* my instinctive shortcutting to repeat the same brutality that hurt me, it cannot absolve me from accountability. As Menakem reminds us, a statement like "I had been traumatized" is a "call to heal, not to cause harm."[19] Though he addresses this specifically to white readers, I find this message pertinent to me, too.

The need for collective healing is daunting—and yet it is critical. Despite these oppressive systems and the unfairness of it all—but also because of it— all of us need to fight for our healing because the loss of our own humanity and joy is too great a cost.

CREATING CONDITIONS TO HEAL

*Healing makes room for us to fight in the places where it's necessary
and love in the places we long to.*
—Prentis Hemphill[20]

CONTENT NOTE: *a story about rape*

When I was raped in college by my ex-boyfriend, I had an out-of-body experience. Once I realized fighting was futile and the violation inevitable, my soul left my body, and I watched myself from above my dorm room bed. I felt numb the entire time. For years, I did not tell anyone about what had happened except for one other person. I don't think it was shame that prevented me from talking about it; I think it was a prolonged survival reaction protecting me by denying what had happened for as long as I could, until my dirty pain got so filthy I had to vomit it out. The sense of lacking control over my own body had already been a pattern in my life that had begun years before, from my experience growing up in a punishing education system that beat my ten-year-old body to moving to America where I suddenly lost my ability to communicate, along with any agency to define myself on my own terms. I no longer saw myself as a heroine with boundless possibilities but as someone barely hanging on, trying to survive the daily indignities. I relied on my survival reactions of appeasing and dissociating frequently to let those moments pass without being consumed or defined by them.

Oh, but how these unmetabolized dirty pains have a way of catching up to you. My past experiences have shaped the way I have lived most of my adult life, in fierce protection of my sense of control and dignity that had been taken away from me one too many times. When my collaborators do not communicate changes proactively, I am quick to assume they do not respect me. When my boundaries are unintentionally crossed, I wall up and vow to never trust anyone ever again. At the first sign of interpersonal risk, my body dysregulates and my mind readies for battle, or I prematurely abandon my post before I get left behind. And when good things come my way, I am first skeptical and then rush to prepare for the worst-case scenario in an attempt to control my disappointment. My hypervigilance and skepticism have set me up to get hurt, over and over.

In a society where women of color are continually disrespected, disbelieved, exploited, and mistreated, my survival reactions often *do* keep me safe—they help me to draw firm boundaries, flee toxic dynamics, and address harm directly. My spidey senses have gotten me out of numerous dangerous situations that could have harmed me physically. But I've also had to acknowledge when they've gone into overdrive, clouding my discernment and ultimately pushing away opportunities to connect, heal, and recognize safety with people who genuinely desire my wellness.

Luckily, over the years I've been able to discern which types of conditions are most likely to exacerbate my trauma reactions and which make me feel more at ease. I'm starting to understand the types of relationships that allow me to be vulnerable and which ones make me feel guarded. And in this ongoing process of identifying the common traits of both trauma-informed cultures and traumatizing ones, it has become evident to me that despite the pervasive presence of systemic oppressions, there still exist opportunities for us to work toward creating conditions that can support one another's healing in parallel. While not exhaustive, here are some ways we can begin to cultivate a culture in which all of us can be seen and feel held:

- **Restore agency and respect boundaries.** In any interpersonal or organizational setting, exercise the habit of proactively asking for permission and consent before diving into demands, sharing, or questioning. This is especially important when it involves sharing or exposing our or others' traumas. Providing options and honoring people's choices help create a culture of mutual respect, agency, and healthy boundaries.

- **Practice holding space.** Holding space means "being physically, mentally, and emotionally present for someone."[21] We can do this by practicing active listening through which we seek to fully understand without doubting, projecting, problem-solving, or centering ourselves ("Oh, I know exactly what you mean!" *No, you probably don't*).
- **Acknowledge the validity and truth inherent in marginalized people's reactions.** Remember, though we may analyze or experience things differently based on our identities and context, each person's emotions are *always* valid and true. Especially when someone is sharing their experiences of harm, believe them and reassure them that you believe them. When we begin to intellectualize and debate someone else's lived experience, even with the best of intentions of trying to make them feel better, we inadvertently participate in the creation of a victim-blaming culture in which survivors are gaslighted and required to convince others of their lived realities (e.g., "Are you sure that's what happened?" "I don't think that's what they meant").
- **Contextualize through history.** Understanding different types of historical traumas within marginalized communities is an important step to being able to contextualize our current situations. Learn about the untold histories of traumas endured by oppressed people, and practice broadening the scope of how we make sense of individual and interpersonal actions in our lives. If you are white, do this while also learning about your related intergenerational ancestral legacy: What role did you and your ancestors play in upholding, benefiting from, and/or opposing systems that mass-traumatized people of color?
- **Avoid glorifying overcoming systemic trauma or fawning over marginalized people's resilience.** Though well-intentioned, statements like "You're so strong!" or "I could never be like you!" can reduce trauma to an individual experience and place responsibility for overcoming it solely on the individual, thereby raising expectations for the marginalized and absolving the rest of us and systems from responsibility. Instead, let's get in the habit of asking ourselves: "What can I/we do so that marginalized people do not have to continuously be resilient?" "What can I/we contribute to aid in others' healing?" Acknowledge the unfair burden of overcoming inequity-induced

traumas that is placed on marginalized people (e.g., "I am really sorry you had to experience that." "That must have been incredibly challenging. Is there anything I can do to support you?").

- **For people with organizational power, institutionalize care.** Go beyond interpersonal support to advancing organizational changes such as providing access to mental health care and ensuring there is no penalty for actually accessing it. Working to disrupt white supremacy culture means building a culture of care and equity, which includes equitable pay, humane working conditions, balanced work hours, unbiased hiring and promotions, transparent and clear expectations, and inclusive team dynamics that center the needs of the most marginalized.

It's worth underscoring the importance of never faulting people for their trauma or their unhealed trauma. As my therapist reminds me regularly, we can only truly understand our *own* pain and no one else's. We do not get to interpret, judge, or control others' pain or their expressions of it; we can only be responsible for ours. That means we do not get to decide what should or should not trigger someone, or be the judge of what is or is not a "real" threat or what is clean or dirty pain, or how fast or slow someone's healing process should be. So when I write about the significance of our collective healing, it is *not* a call for us to demand others to heal but rather an invitation for you and me to go inward to individually examine our own hurt places with a lens of compassionate criticality and accountability, while also seeing the broader footprints of systemic trauma that have left so many people hurting over and over. I hope you keep this in mind as you read the rest of this chapter.

WE DESERVE TO HEAL

One of the things that I really want to impress upon people in the world is that healing is possible. We define what resilience looks like.
—Tarana Burke[22]

I believe that our decision to begin our own healing beyond today's commodified version of self-care is more urgent than ever. Healing is not only vital for our own reclamation, it is also a pathway to building a principled, compassionate, and resilient solidarity movement, an inseparable part of social justice work.

Remaining in our unhealed trauma robs us of our ability to practice discernment. It prohibits us from being at ease, and we get stuck in an elevated state of high alert, which takes a toll over time. It fractures our relationships and denies us the ability to trust, hope, dream, and connect. It eats our movement alive from the inside. Exploiting our unhealed trauma is one of the greatest weapons of our oppressors. And it takes diligence, proactive accountability, and deep and difficult self-work supported by our community to halt its proliferation. For me, the work has also included my realizing and accepting the hard-to-believe truth that I *deserve* to heal, despite my unshakable feeling of unworthiness this oppressive system has tattooed in my mind.

We have the opportunity to find a way to heal—for our own sake and for our movement, for our ancestors and our future generations. While we are not responsible for the violence that harmed us, carrying our trauma with gentleness, care, and discernment is a choice we have control over.

Though my healing journey has been just as messy as my traumas, it has played a critical role in helping me grow as a person and as an activist committed to the social justice movement. Here are some of the lessons I've learned during my ever-continuing journey, specifically geared toward people of color and those who are subjected to recurring systemic traumas.* I hope you take what is useful for you and try them on:

- **Be clear about what you are and are not responsible for.** We are not responsible for the violence that traumatized us. We are also not responsible for educating others on our traumas by explaining, excavating, or otherwise making them palatable. What we *are* responsible for is our own reckoning and how we choose to heal.

---

*If you are white or identify as someone who has not been subjected to recurring systemic traumas, I hope you'll be able to glean from the following list how you can show up to lessen the burden on marginalized people. This list is not to be weaponized against others ("Go heal yourself!") or shared to rush others' healing.

- **Seek to understand your traumas, including intergenerational and ancestral traumas, in a way that feels safe and within *your* control.** If you are able to, seek professional support (e.g., socially conscious therapists, healers, somatic coaches, etc.) to guide your exploration.

- **Practice naming and honoring your feelings.** It is vital that we honor our truths and validate our pain by not gaslighting, minimizing, or diminishing ourselves. We can do this on our own through practices such as journaling or in the presence of people we deem safe.

- **Set and respect your boundaries.** One of my favorite quotes on boundaries comes from writer, embodiment coach, and facilitator Prentis Hemphill: "Boundaries are the distance at which I can love you and me simultaneously."[23] We set boundaries not to push people away but to pull the right people closer to us. Understanding, communicating, and respecting our needs to feel safe are critical practices to our healing journey and to build trust with others. "I'm not ready to talk about that, can we change the subject?" "I need some space to think about it. I will come back to you."

- **Surround yourself with people who are willing to hold your pain with care *and* who support you to stay in integrity.** This allows us to be vulnerable while practicing discernment, and helps us process our hurt without making decisions from our most hurt place.

- **Understand your activators (or triggers, hot buttons, etc.) that are likely to set off survival reactions.** Learning about our activators can help us to proactively manage our experiences and to reflect when we are triggered. When I find myself feeling activated, I try to slow down by using these guiding questions: What is happening? Am I in danger? Is this my survival reaction? Where does it hurt? Why? What do I need to feel safe? Then I practice setting boundaries and making requests to have my unmet needs met. We won't always have the capacity to name our needs or a clear path forward in moments of activation, and that's OK. We can allow ourselves time to process the hurt and de-escalate first.

- **Pay close attention to the body and practice building somatic awareness.** We cannot "best practice" our way out of human trauma; our traumas won't heal from our intellectual analysis. Healing requires us to reconnect with our bodies and to trust the way our body responds to our environments. We can learn a lot by being curious about how traumas reside in our bodies and engaging in physical practices* that help them move through and out of it.

- **Develop coping strategies informed by ancestral values and resilience.** Inherent in every historically oppressed community is incredible resilience and sacred traditions. Brave Heart, in her study around *transcending* trauma, emphasizes the possibility of healing through returning to traditional values and intergenerational support.[25]
- **Find communities of people who understand or share your trauma and engage in collective action.** As we understand our traumas in the context of systemic oppression, collaborating with others to create social change can be incredibly empowering and fulfilling.

> *Healing is for ourselves and for others. Sometimes we start healing through collective action. Sometimes healing leads us to collective action. This interdependence of healing and social action, of loving internally and externally, is affirming of life. Yours and ours.*
> —Staci K. Haines[26]

Like everything else, healing is not a linear, clean, or complete process; sometimes it will feel like we are taking two steps forward and three steps back. Healing requires us to hold our trauma with care, to be intentional and gentle with ourselves while we remember our context and history. For all of us to truly heal, we must go beyond self-care at the individual level to transformation at the systemic and collective level. We need to create conditions and systems that allow for the most wounded to heal, without requiring them to make more sacrifices or risk being further traumatized, while we grow our capacity to tenderly hold both the complexity and vastness of our collective pain without evading, denying, diminishing, solving, or over-intellectualizing, especially when our hurt parts inevitably collide.

I write to you not from a "healed" place but from a place of continuously fighting for my healing. Slowly but surely, I'm finding healing with people who create a mutually consensual space for me to express my hurt unfiltered,

---

*Resmaa Menakem's *My Grandmother's Hands* includes a number of body practices you can follow in each chapter.[24]

no matter how disproportionate it feels to the perceived or actual threat in front of me. Their caring spirits who hold and rock me gently to remind me that I am safe, I am worthy, that whatever I feel is valid, seen, and justified, given my past and present unmet needs. And in this volatile yet safe place, in community with people I love and trust, I return to my values and extend myself grace to practice both self-soothing and accountability. I recognize that my battle is, and will always be, with the oppressive conditions and systems that create violence and trauma.

Choosing to heal is a radical act of courage and love—a choice to love ourselves and our community in defiance of the systems that want us to do otherwise. The practice of healing is perhaps the most difficult but rewarding and purposeful part of this work; enabling the collective healing of the most marginalized, perhaps, *is* the entire point. Against all odds, I hope we choose to heal.

> *The journey will be longer than you imagined, trauma will find you again and again. Do not become the ones who hurt you. Stay tender with your power. Never fight to injure, fight to uplift. Fight because you know that in this life, you deserve safety, joy, and freedom. Fight because it is your life. Not anyone else's. I did it, I am here. Looking back, all the ones who doubted or hurt or nearly conquered me faded away, and I am the only one standing. So now, the time has come. I dust myself off, and go on.*
> —Chanel Miller[27]

CHAPTER 13

CREATING OUR OWN
LIBERATORY TOOLS

CONTENT NOTE: *This chapter unpacks the March 16, 2021, Atlanta massage parlor shooting and contains a number of potentially activating topics, including but not limited to mass shooting, misogyny, sexual violence, rape, murder, US imperialism, anti-Asian violence, police violence, and war crimes.*

In the midst of our journey, it is easy to become distant *studiers* of pain and forget the very real human impacts of oppression that are at the foundation of all of this work. I'm guilty of this too, and sometimes a little bit of desensitization even feels like a necessary defense mechanism amid an onslaught of atrocities. But there are certain types of events that rupture what you thought was your toughened heart, unlocking a flood of tucked-away feelings to remind you of the real cost of oppressive violence.

The March 16, 2021, Atlanta massage parlor shooting was one such event that blew open the tightly enclosed jar of suppressed memories of my twenty-something years living in America as an Asian woman, specifically a Korean woman. Koreans say our people have a lot of rage. I grew up listening to my grandmother describe us as "한 맺힌 민족": the people with *haan*. The Korean word *haan* describes a complex mix of emotions, including deep intergenerational sorrow, grief, and resentment. Generations of mass trauma and resistance course through our blood, marked by colonization, imperialism, multiple wars, and a split nation with permanently separated families. I grew up in a family that was loud, with everyone's voices multiple octaves louder than what is socially acceptable, where we laughed loudly, argued loudly, and spoke in matching hyperbole. And yet, in America, our passionate, fiery, and sad people are expected to be the model minority—quiet, apolitical, timid, grateful, and somehow always apologetic. It is an unnatural predicament for my people—it was for me, and my parents, anyway. Taming the fire inherent within, quieting the ancestral rage, some of us kill parts of ourselves to give what's left of us a fighting chance at survival. We call that, I suppose, *assimilation.*

As I frantically searched for more details about the eight victims in the Atlanta shooting, six of whom were Asian women, the voices of white men I'd encountered throughout my life spoke through the photo of the shooter, their words like shards of glass, cutting open old wounds.

Memories from waitressing at a Japanese restaurant near a navy base, inebriated older white men calling me over: "Hey cutie, can you pour me a sake?" "Here, drink this! Come on, don't be a bitch!" "What are you doing after your shift?" *Three massage parlors.*

Memories of too many bad dates that could have ended worse: "I've never had a Korean before." "I bet your pussy is tighter than white chicks'." "Me love you long time!" *Eight killed.*

Memories of white men coworkers and bosses rubbing my shoulders at happy hours, their alcohol breath and glazed eyes scanning my body for comfort and entertainment. "My wife is Asian." *Appeared to be women of Asian descent.*[1]

Memories of my first, and abusive, relationship with a white man: the yelling when I didn't pick up his phone calls, the condescension when I offered my perspective, the name calling—*slut, cunt, bitch*—when he thought I was leaving him, the "talk to me in Korean while I'm fucking you." *Motive, unknown.*

I've lived my entire life in America under the gaze of white men who see me as an exotic fuck or a loyal, selfless workhorse. Each time I deviate from their expectations, I am punished and immediately relegated to being a perpetual foreigner or a bitch. And though the mainstream white media seemed to lack the nuance, the perspective, and the simple vocabulary to identify the massacre for what it was—a targeted attack on Asian women massage workers—I didn't need to rely on their reporting to understand what had happened.

In the days following, I read about the four Korean victims' use of English nicknames while working, which made tracking down their relatives challenging. I briefly thought about my own nickname, *Michelle*, which my toddler self had chosen after seeing a young blond girl called by the same name during a visit to the United States, and how it has somehow become my entire identity detached from my now-distant life in Korea. And then I thought about the grave injustice of drawing comparisons to the victims while I sat in my cozy living room decked out in West Elm furniture and fiddle-leaf plants, my privileges shielding me from the kind of violence these women faced in their deaths and in their lifetimes.

I've grappled a lot over the best way to honor the eight lives lost in Atlanta, and I'm still not sure I have the right answers. What feels important is remembering—all of their lives, legacies, and the context in all of its complexities—and doing whatever I can in my lifetime to root out the violence that killed them. It feels important that this atrocity be remembered not as an isolated incident tied to one monstrous white man but rather as an event that was made possible through multiple forces of violence that made these women vulnerable. And I want to seek justice by imploring that we each see ourselves as being part of the ecosystem responsible for countering those oppressive forces and for building safer futures for the most marginalized among us.

CONTEXTUALIZING THE VIOLENCE

Understanding the full scope of white male supremacy violence through a historically contextualized, intersectional, and global lens is imperative to our dismantling it, as any omission in our understanding will fuel its proliferation in the shadows as we fall into false equivalences and flattened narratives. For example, the shooting required an analysis of the interplay among race, gender, and class, at minimum, with ample historical and current context, to understand the various factors that had paved the way to making such extreme violence against these Asian women possible and to properly capture the particular vulnerability they faced at the intersection of multiple marginalized identities.

The shooting was more than an "anti-Asian hate" incident; it was also about the unique oppression faced by these Asian women who experienced fetishization and criminalization due to their work, with its roots dating back centuries to the Page Act of 1875, the first restrictive immigration law in the United States that effectively banned the entry of Chinese women (and practically all East Asian women) under a generalized presumption that they would engage in prostitution or immigrate for "lewd and immoral purposes."[2] The law, which has had multiple enduring impacts on an already Sinophobic, racist society—from hypersexualizing Asian women to criminalizing sex work and inflaming the racist rhetoric of the yellow peril, which portrayed East Asians as an existential and moral threat to the Western world—eventually paved the way for the Chinese Exclusion Act of 1882, which prohibited all Chinese people from entering the United States while simultaneously excluding Chinese people already here from obtaining US citizenship, continuing the motion of a long history and legacy of anti-Asian rhetoric in the country.[3]

In addition to the act of violence itself, patterns of white supremacy culture were replicated from the very moment the incident was publicized, as we saw the police, the media, and the legal system's coordinated dance, practiced to perfection over the years: from law enforcement being the arbiter of what is and isn't considered racialized and gendered violence and their refusal to designate the incident as a hate crime; to mainstream white media's immediate humanization of the white man perpetrator as being troubled and loved by his grandparents while invisibilizing the victims; to the butchering of the victims' names and their dignity with it; to the casual and widespread denigration of low-wage massage parlor workers and sex workers;* to the systems' failure to capture the necessary nuance, context, and multilayered nature of the situation.

While the Atlanta shooter's white male rage, entitlement, and violence failed to see these women's humanity beyond their objectification, the media enacted another violence, first by failing to describe the event as being racialized and anti-Asian and then by spending their early hours piecing together a story of the life of the shooter instead of the lives of the victims. In less than twenty-four hours, a narrative emerged from the police, with the captain of Cherokee County Sheriff's Office sharing the shooter's testimony,

---

*In case it requires clarifying: not all massage workers are sex workers. *And* it is important to acknowledge that this often-made association, coupled with the stigmatization of sex work, makes both massage workers and sex workers a frequent target of criminalization and violence regardless of their actual work.

during which he added, describing the shooter, "Yesterday was a really bad day for him, and this is what he did."[4]

The mainstream white media's inadequacy and unjust reporting continued beyond its prompt humanization of the white perpetrator when multiple news outlets shared the names of the victims with an embarrassing level of cultural incompetence, once again following the pattern of white supremacy culture in which any deviation from the standard of whiteness is seen as less than and therefore prone to careless and perpetual denigration. The published list included names that were misspelled and misarranged, with the last names of some placed as their first, and others' first names cut in half and part of it abbreviated as an initialed middle name.[5] It was clear that many journalists had no knowledge of the victims' cultural naming conventions, nor had they taken the steps to acquire such key and easily attainable knowledge as part of their reporting process. The culture of urgency in the newsroom also demanded that we mourn under a strict time line: they hastily published these incorrect names even when some of the victims' families had not given consent,[6] once again robbing them of their agency and dignity. The rushed amplification of these botched names by the media, corporations, and well-intentioned individuals rang especially hollow, coming on the heels of a yearlong silence on escalating anti-Asian violence.

It's hard to say if Asian women have ever truly been safe in this country, or even in their homelands, since Asian women, and really all women of color, have been targets of white supremacy and patriarchal violence throughout history and today beyond US borders. Koreans are no strangers to the legacy of colonization, war, and US imperialism, where our women have been dehumanized, exploited, raped, and killed as weapons of war at the hands of multiple abusers, from the Imperial Japanese Army and our own government to the US military. Between the 1950s and 1980s, an estimated one million Korean women, many of them coerced,* were "caught up in a state-controlled prostitution industry that was blessed at the highest levels by the U.S. military."[8] The gruesome rape and murder of 윤금이, Yun Geum-I, a

---

*While it's important to clarify this within this particular historical context, it's important to not conflate sex work and trafficking. Conflating consensual sex work with coerced trafficking can lead to further criminalization of sex workers while reducing their access to critical resources and control over their work.[7]

twenty-six-year-old military camptown sex worker in Dongducheon, South Korea, by a white GI in 1992[9] still haunts the souls of many Koreans, and countless accounts of military sexual violence pervade the Asia-Pacific region, which has the highest number of US military troops outside the US mainland, concentrated in Japan, Hawaii, South Korea, and Guam.[10] Our understanding of the Atlanta massacre, and the solutions we put forth, would be incomplete without the dots being connected to the Asian and Pacific Islander women abroad who continue to be direct targets or "temptations," in the words of the Atlanta shooter,[11] of the white male supremacist and imperialist gaze that seeks to conquer, violate, and exploit them. The violence here continues there, and it has been happening for decades at a scale many cannot fathom.

> Women like me were the biggest sacrifice for my country's alliance with the Americans. Looking back, I think my body was not mine, but the government's and the US military's.
> —"Jeon"*

THE TOOLS OF WHITE SUPREMACY: POLICING

> For we have, built into all of us, old blueprints of expectation and response, old structures of oppression, and these must be altered at the same time as we alter the living conditions which are a result of those structures. For the master's tools will never dismantle the master's house.
> —Audre Lorde[13]

Though the Asian community hurt collectively, when it came to our vision toward accountability, justice, and healing from this trauma, there were

---

*In a 2015 Politico article, David Vine tells the story of "Jeon": "One of the sex workers, who would identify herself to a reporter only as 'Jeon,' moved to a camptown in 1956 as an 18-year-old war orphan. Within a few years, she became pregnant, but she gave up her son for adoption in the United States, where she hoped he would have a better life. In 2008, now a U.S. soldier, he returned to find her. Jeon was surviving on public assistance and selling things from the trash. She refused his help and said he should forget about her. 'I failed as a mother,' Jeon says. 'I have no right to depend on him now.'"[12]

fierce disagreements across a wide spectrum. Following the early police briefings, there was an immediate pushback to the police's refusal to call the event a hate crime. Many Asian people were outraged, rightfully so, by the police and the media's gaslighting of an entire community traumatized by the racist, misogynistic, and classist violence. Some had already been calling for more police involvement to combat the recurring anti-Asian street violence that had been escalating over the past few months. A number of Asian celebrities offered monetary incentives to aid in the arrest of perpetrators of violence, while some politicians urged the police to create special hate crimes task force units. The same influencers who had posted #BlackLivesMatter and marched to defund the police less than a year ago were now calling for increased police surveillance and budgets, which for some served as an unwelcome reality check that brought down any surface-level facade of interracial, or even intracommunity, solidarity, exposing its wobbly foundation fraught with unresolved tensions and oppressive patterns. In less than two weeks after the Atlanta shooting, the NYPD announced its creation of a special Asian Hate Crimes Task Force and boasted its deployment of undercover officers to the streets in plain clothes to "add layers of enforcement."[14]

White supremacy is masterful at drawing silos and disconnecting the dots that unite us, especially in the moments we need it the most. It was clear that for some, the attacks on Asian elders and the Atlanta shooting were not seen as linked to the ongoing movement toward defunding the police and prison abolition, nor were they seen as by-products of the shared root of white supremacy upheld by the very systems these people turned to for justice. Traumatized and angered by the continuing violence, many on the internet called for the harshest and most punitive sentencing to hold the attackers accountable: *Death penalty! Lock them up for life!* White supremacy culture is obsessed with punishment and vengeance, and under its spell we thirst for the blood of our supposed enemy while forgetting the dangerous traps we create for those most impacted by the weapon we wield—undocumented Asians, queer and trans Asians, poor Asians, disabled Asians, criminalized and incarcerated Asians, Asians in survival work, Sikh and Muslim Asians, and Black and brown Asians, who are disproportionately targeted and harmed by the police. By endowing more power to a system that has never hesitated to deport, assault, criminalize, and kill the most vulnerable among us, we successfully extract our tears to oil the machine that will go on to build bigger cages—more criminalization, harsher sentencing, packed prisons—that will eventually house more of us too.

When we are cornered and desperate, we have been trained to grab the tools of white supremacy for immediate relief, believing it is the only medicine to heal our hurt before discerning whether it is poison concocted to maim us. And within the confines of the current paradigm, some of us continue to expect justice to come from the same institution that has never prioritized our humanity. But we must not forget that the very construct of crime designations is a by-product of a system that enforces white supremacist "criteria" to determine who should be criminalized and who should be protected, or that so many of our own have been victims of the inherently white supremacist police institution, rooted in a long history of anti-Blackness, slavery, and capitalism.

Countering the calls for more policing were voices of longtime AAPI organizers and abolitionists, who urged the community to remember the footprint of police violence within our own communities. Dr. Connie Wun, cofounder of AAPI Women Lead, urged us to remember Tommy Le,[15] a Vietnamese American high school student who was shot in the back by police and killed while holding a pen, hours before his graduation.[16] And Christian Hall, a nineteen-year-old Chinese American teen, and Angelo Quinto, a thirty-year-old Filipino navy veteran, whose mental health crises just months before the Atlanta massacre had served as their death sentence when the cops arrived.[17] Red Canary Song, a grassroots coalition working to support Asian massage workers and sex workers that was founded after Yang Song, a thirty-eight-year-old Chinese massage worker in New York, was killed during a police raid in 2017 after enduring police sexual violence and threats of criminalization,[18] released a statement denouncing the calls for increased policing, noting that "policing has never kept sex workers or massage workers or immigrants safe." The statement was cosigned by over three hundred multiracial organizations, including a large number of progressive AAPI-led organizations.[19] Some, including activist and journalist Helen Zia and professor and filmmaker Renee Tajima-Peña, revived the memory of Vincent Chin, a Chinese American man who was targeted and beaten to death by two white men, whose life, in the eyes of the American legal system, was worth no more than three thousand dollars and whose murder was charged as manslaughter with no jail time because the system chose to believe the two white men's empty words over their actions.[20] Amid my own efforts to redirect people to seek alternative solutions to keep us safe, I received a handful of messages from people who raised questions, using examples from the times when the legal system had supposedly advocated on behalf of Asians. But we must not be so tunnel-visioned as to believe the justice system is on "our side" by citing the deeply troubling examples of Soon Ja Du's five-hundred-dollar fine for killing fifteen-year-old Black teen Latasha Harlins[21] or Peter Liang's eight hundred hours of community service for the death of Akai Gurley,[22] and conflating the white supremacist system's disregard for Black lives as its valuing of ours.

Four days after the massacre, when piecemeal findings about the victims were beginning to emerge, I spotted a detail buried in a *Washington Post* article that nonchalantly mentioned Mario González, a Mexican man and husband of Delaina Ashley Yaun, one of the victims, who was "mistakenly" arrested and handcuffed for hours while his wife lay dying.[23] I frantically searched for more information, except there were no other reports investigating what had happened besides Mundo Hispánico, a Spanish-language news outlet in the United States, which interviewed González in Spanish, in which he shared how he had kept asking his detainers, "Where is my wife? Where is my wife?" He showed his bruised wrists from the handcuffs and said he did not know why the cops had treated him so badly: "Maybe because I'm Mexican, I don't know."[24]

The renewed calls for policing for the safety of a select few only served to advance white supremacy's agenda while marking those most vulnerable to it as expendable, creating yet another crack in the collective liberation movement with our initials next to it, cosigned by our oppressors holding our trembling hands. The handprints of white supremacy continue to be everywhere, even in our responses to it.

LETTING GO OF THE MASTER'S TOOLS

Grace Lee Boggs, during a conversation with Dr. Angela Davis at UC Berkeley, talked about what she calls "visionary organizing," urging us to "*reimagine everything*." She explained, "We have to see every crisis as both a danger and an opportunity. It's a danger because it does so much damage to our lives, to our institutions, to all that we have expected, but it's also an opportunity for us to become creative."[25] The Atlanta shooting served as yet another painful reminder that we cannot attain justice or healing using the same weapons that harmed us in the first place, whether it is our instinctive allying with the systems that do not keep us safe, or our operating inside of a punitive justice framework rooted in anti-Blackness. Instead, we need to put down the master's tools and reimagine new liberatory tools envisioned through the lens of those most marginalized among us, tools that can help us arrive at our ultimate vision of justice and freedom for *all*.

It is important to understand that the Atlanta shooting did not happen in a vacuum. It did not happen because one bad white man woke up one morning and decided to shoot up three massage parlors; that would be an overly reductive yet convenient narrative of white supremacy that distances us from the heinous murders. Instead, we need to understand violence and its long buildup in context and see ourselves playing an active role in it: How have we, as a society and as individuals, been complicit in perpetuating racialized, gendered, and classed violence against working-class Asian women in our daily lives, whether through erasure, reinforcing biased narratives, or being a bystander to different levels of harm? How have we benefited from systems that rely on the oppression of Asian people, immigrants, women, low-wage migrant workers, sex workers, and all marginalized people, and what have we done to actively disrupt them? How have we been part of the conditions that gave birth to this attack, and what must we shift—in ourselves, with one another, and in every sphere of influence we find ourselves in, from our workplace to school, family, church, neighborhood, and more—to ensure this type of violence never happens again? How could we center and support the needs of the survivors, not only those directly impacted by the massacre but also those who have been, and continue to be, impacted by the same systems of oppression? We each have a role in this work. And we must take the work of transforming ourselves and our relationships seriously to transform the world because our transformation *is* part of the liberatory tools we need to dismantle all forms of oppression. By replacing the master's tools, we can begin our process of reimagining and becoming the solutions that can keep us safe, for good.

In honor of the eight victims, and in honor of their memory, let us commit to protecting each other and loving each other while we are

still here, not only in these moments of crisis, but in all the quiet,
unseen, and humble moments that constitute our lives.
—Hyejin Shim[26]

Transformative justice (TJ) is one such framework that has helped me reimagine and redefine my role in the broader justice movement. TJ, as defined by Mia Mingus, is "a political framework and approach for responding to violence, harm, and abuse. At its most basic, it seeks to respond to violence without creating more violence and/or engaging in harm reduction to lessen the violence."[27] According to Mingus, transformative justice responses do not rely on the state, such as police and prisons, and TJ does not reinforce oppressive norms or vigilantism. Instead, it actively focuses on "cultivating things we know prevent violence such as healing, accountability, resilience, and safety for all involved."[28] Foundational to the work of abolition and transformative justice is the question posed by scholar and prison abolition activist Dr. Ruth Wilson Gilmore: "What are the conditions under which it is more likely that people will resort to using violence and harm to solve problems?"[29] Rooted in these teachings of abolitionist leaders, I learned, and am continuing to learn,* the importance of broadening the lens of accountability beyond the individual perpetrator of harm in order to invite *all* of us to reflect on our own complicity in the larger systems, cultures, and behaviors that allow for such harm to occur. It is increasingly important that we think beyond the good-bad or victim-perpetrator binary and to take accountability for our everyday small and big actions to help eliminate the violence at its root.

In thinking about transformative justice, I often reflect on my three-year-long abusive relationship and how my life, as well as his, would have turned out differently if he had been in community with people who cared for him, helped him practice accountability, and tended to his hurt so he could stop hurting me. Had the smaller incidents of harm not been allowed to fester in isolation to be turned into abuse, maybe they would not have escalated to his ultimate exertion of power over me through rape after our final breakup.

---

*I encourage everyone to continue their own education by learning from those who have been practicing TJ and leading the abolition movement for years, like Mariame Kaba, Dr. Ruth Wilson Gilmore, Dr. Angela Davis, Shira Hassan, Dr. Mimi Kim, Mia Mingus, adrienne maree brown, Derecka Purnell, Dr. Connie Wun, and many more, and support the work of BIPOC-led grassroots organizations and abolitionists.

I wonder how things would have turned out differently if instead of cops, mental health workers showed up to respond to his cry for help. Maybe they would've noticed my pain, too. In the end, I believe he was both perpetrator *and* victim of white heteropatriarchy, and though I do not absolve him of the pain he inflicted on me through choice, I now extend the scope of responsibility to the broader white male supremacist society and rape culture that incubated him.

Despite Grace Lee Boggs's call to "reimagine everything," I'm often struck by my own limitations to reimagine and dream beyond what I've been told is possible within the current paradigm. When movement leaders call for the abolition of prisons and defunding of the police, most people's initial reaction is panic because the alternative seems unfathomable. I, too, couldn't imagine life without police—my imagination often stopped at the hypothetical nightmares of "dangerous people" running wild and wreaking havoc on our "orderly" society. But the truth is I've met plenty of dangerous people in my life whose violence was never criminalized but rather protected, while nearly two hundred thousand innocent people, the majority of them Black and brown, remain unjustly incarcerated as a result of wrongful conviction.[30] And though the United States incarcerates more people than any other nation in the world,[31] we are far from being free of violence or the safest country. Without an alternate vision, we have a tough time letting go of what's not serving us, and many can't imagine and tangibly describe a society without the carceral system at the center of it. But what if we can? What if our goal went beyond reforming oppressive systems incrementally to transforming them entirely, with radical reimagining? What if *all of it*— not just piecemeal—was *possible*? And what if they are being done already?

> Just as we hear calls today for more humane policing, people then called for a more humane slavery.
> —Dr. Angela Davis[32]

Reimagining alternative futures that are more just, equitable, and safe is possible, and we are not starting from scratch. Black- and Indigenous-led grassroots organizations, abolition movement leaders, and multiracial and intersectional coalitions of organizers across the country have already been paving the way to reimagine what our society, relationships, and safety could look like. Those most impacted by the unjust systems have been leading the work of building community-based safety solutions, as exemplified by the Anti Police-Terror Project in Oakland, which launched MH First, the city's first nonpolice response to mental health crises.[33] The website Don't Call The Police catalogs a number of similar efforts currently available all across the country.[34] To combat enduring anti-Asian violence, grassroots organizers and community organizations came together to model the "we keep us safe" mantra in real time: Oakland Chinatown Coalition, a coalition of twenty different Chinatown nonprofits, associations, and individuals, swiftly brought together a diverse group of volunteers to engage in dialogue and actions to keep Oakland Chinatown safe, through initiatives like the Chinatown Ambassadors Program and recruiting volunteers to stroll the neighborhood and accompany elders.[35] In an effort to track and respond to incidences of violence, the Asian Pacific Planning and Policy Council (A3PCON), Chinese for Affirmative Action (CAA), and the Asian American Studies Department of San Francisco State University launched the Stop AAPI Hate reporting website independent of law enforcement[36] and created online forms accessible in more than ten different Asian languages to encourage wide participation and disaggregated data.

In lieu of any material support from the police or the government, countless GoFundMe pages were launched to support the survivors of violence and victims' families. A "How Do I Talk to Asian Elders about Anti-Asian Violence?" guide was launched on social media and translated by individuals across the diaspora into Chinese, Tagalog, Indonesian, Hmong, Vietnamese, Japanese, Korean, Bisaya, and more.[37] Youth activists organized rallies and vigils across the country, and healers and therapists hosted virtual safe spaces for people to process their emotions. Donation-based self-defense classes were conducted by street medics and martial artists, and thousands of people participated in bystander trainings to build capacity to intervene. People of all races came together to check in on their colleagues, friends, and neighbors, and committed to deepening their bonds beyond this moment of crisis.

Meanwhile, two months after the Atlanta shooting, against the backdrop of overwhelming cross-racial solidarity and local organizing against more policing, Oakland's white woman mayor released a new budget proposal to increase police spending over the next two years, nearly doubling the funds budgeted for police overtime pay.[38] The mayor had already drawn criticism for attempting to pit Black and Asian communities against each other by blaming the increased anti-Asian violence on the defund the police movement.[39] As I read about her proposed budget, the Democrat mayor's cheerful video message to the AAPI community a couple of months earlier rang in my head: "We will fight for you. You are welcome here."[40] It is not enough to rely solely on those in positions of power within white supremacist systems to fight on our behalf and to "welcome" us—we need to demand and create safety for ourselves. We simply cannot wait for their awakening because it may never come.

> It's up to us to reimagine the alternatives and not just to protest against them and expect them to do better.
> —Grace Lee Boggs[41]

HEALING TOGETHER

Exactly a week after the Atlanta shooting, local organizers hosted a vigil in Oakland's Madison Park where grief-stricken people gathered to mourn, remember, and console in community.* As soon as I reached the park, I smelled a fire burning in a portable fire pit situated next to the speakers, where I spotted the familiar faces of leaders in our community, many of them Asian women. The crowd reflected the diversity of our AAPI diaspora, as well as our solidarity network made up of people of all races, all ready to link arms and heal through collective action.

The organizers of the event sought to center Korean and Chinese women, reflecting the ethnicities of the six women who were killed in the shooting, four of whom were Korean and two Chinese. There were ASL, Korean, and Chinese interpreters, and the moderator of the event was a Korean woman, liz suk, a longtime community organizer and activist in Oakland and the ex-

---

*Oakland Rising's blog entry entitled "#LoveOurPeople: Oakland to Atlanta Vigil" lists a number of organizations that helped make the event possible in addition to those I mention in this chapter. They include Asian Pacific Environmental Network, East Bay Alliance for a Sustainable Economy, Ella Baker Center, Causa Justa: Just Cause, Communities United for Restorative Youth Justice, Mujeres Unidas y Activas, Parent Voices Oakland, Bay Rising, Good Good Eatz, and more. The blog post also includes a recap and performance videos from the event. See https://oaklandrising.org/reflections-from-the-atlanta-to-oakland-vigil/.

ecutive director of Oakland Rising. My dearest friend Michelle "Mush" Lee, a Korean American spoken-word poet, put on a passionate performance that simultaneously softened our hearts and lit a fire in our guts. Cat Brooks, "the people's mayor of Oakland" and cofounder of the Anti Police-Terror Project, spoke of the importance of Black and Asian solidarity and reminded us "they are coming for us because *we are winning. Together.*" A beautiful altar was set up for the victims, decorated with fresh flowers, candles, letters, photos, and items with cultural significance, from incense sticks burning in a sand-filled copper bowl to a plate of Korean pears with their tops cut off, just like how my family prepares them for 제사, a memorial ceremony for the ancestors. People knelt before the altar and prayed.

At one point, the volunteer Korean interpreter had difficulty translating one of the English speeches into Korean. The speech had deviated from the originally prepared one, leaving her to translate nuanced sentences live without any support. She apologized to the audience in Korean, and she asked if anyone in the audience could speak Korean to be able to interpret live. No one came forward, and she stood staring at the unusable notes she had prepared. Her back looked lonely. Without much thought, I walked over. "I'm not that good, but maybe we can help each other and figure it out?" So there we stood together, taking turns with the mic, skipping over too many words but somehow piecing things together, one roughly translated word at a time in our quest to connect our elders in the audience to the present moment. There were so many words I did not know how to translate—*Defund the police? Climate change? Collective liberation?!*—but with her help and ample grace from the audience, we managed to get through the rest of the program, with each other side by side.

When 이음새 Ieumsae,* a collective of queer and trans Korean 풍물 folk drummers, began to drum, I felt my body reverberate to their beats. "Our

---

*From Dohee Lee's website: "Ieumsae is a collective of Korean drummers living in the Bay Area. As Koreans in diaspora, playing together is a powerful spiritual and political act. Through drumming, we are able to connect with and reclaim our cultures and identities and uphold the legacy of resistance of Pungmul drummers, who were a constant presence during the political uprisings in Korea to end military dictatorship. As Korean immigrants, feminists, queer folks, trans folks, mixed race folks, and adoptees, we take our drumming into the streets and alongside our comrades—bringing energy, rhythm, and solidarity to people resisting police violence, war, and imperialism in the US and abroad."

dancing releases the grief of our ancestors. Their spirits want to speak! So you have to use your body! Shake your body! Stomp your feet!" said Dohee Lee, a Korean-born artist leading the crew, who proceeded to sing the traditional 판소리, belting out different sounds of grief, sorrow, and longing—the sound of *haan*. So we obliged. We moved toward the center of the park, forming multiple concentric circles and blending with the drummers, with children running around in the center laughing and dancing with glee. As we moved our bodies to the gregarious drumming, we let our anguish be heard through our stomping, our rage felt through the heat of our clapping palms, our pain expressed through the shaking of our bodies. We howled and shouted, we cried, and we laughed. We dared to return to communal joy in a moment of such profound tragedy and trauma, and we sought solace in one another's presence in a time of prolonged distance. As I stomped my feet and clapped my hands over and over, I felt the presence of my grandparents and great-grandparents, their spirits holding me, caressing my pain, reminding me of who I am, who we are, who we've always been: warriors, survivors, dreamers, healers. I let my pent-up grief expel out of my chest into the windy, crisp air, hoping to give relief to my ancestors' sorrow so they could welcome and guide the new spirits to their rightful places of peace. And in this collective, embodied mourning, I began to find my ground again.

When the drumming was over, a Black woman who had been dancing next to me looked over and whispered, "I don't know you, but you are my sister."

The very last activity was lighting and flying the sky lantern. It was a particularly windy day, so it was a challenge to light the fuel cell. After a bit of struggle, the lantern floated into the sky but then quickly plunged downward with a strong gust of wind. Everyone gasped audibly and my toes curled, thinking the lantern was going to crash and burn out. But as if they had heard our desperate need for symbolic reassurance and hope, our ancestors' unyielding spirits intervened and swept the lantern off the ground, and it flew up and up, farther into the blue sky, into the arms of the eight beloved souls. I felt my jaw soften as I let out a sigh of relief with a smile underneath my mask. *Thank you, Grandma, Grandpa.*

PART 4

MOVING TOGETHER

CHAPTER 14

OWN YOUR SPACE

We have to shake things up and focus less on a lot of pontification,
analysis, right now. Focus less on that and focus more on
instrumental ways for us to act. Find ways to act and find ways to act
with numbers and together. What actions can we take?
—Mariame Kaba[1]

As critical social justice frameworks, language, and thoughts become more accessible and "mainstream," I feel a sense of both hope and caution, stemming from my fear of these ideas being used as mere concepts upon which people pontificate, as Mariame Kaba so astutely points out, falling into the trap of intellectualizing without real action. I've observed this pattern repeat over and over inside organizations that obsess over "knowing the right things to say" but without the spirit of accountability, their leaders insisting on "data-driven" analyses of inequities but rarely investing real efforts to create safer conditions and equitable structures. I see unconscious bias trainings being used as an interesting thought exercise but rarely not tied to naming centuries-old systemic oppressions that are working at full throttle today, and I hear about people forming book clubs to unpack dense texts yet stopping at thought-provoking conversations without any real community engagement.

This chapter is my plea for you to take everything you've learned to *act*.

Survival is not an academic skill.
—Audre Lorde[2]

TRY ANYWAY

For two years, my team and I facilitated a yearlong equity education program at a prestigious executive MBA program. Given the makeup of these students—current executives at established companies from all over the world—we believed the impact of our work would be tenfold. Our hope was that these executive leaders would take their learning back to their respective organizations and build more diverse, equitable, and inclusive workplaces that would benefit thousands. At Awaken, we always end each workshop with a commitment exercise, where we ask each participant to commit to one tangible action to take back to their organization in the next thirty days, and a closing circle where we share our commitments aloud and assign an accountability partner. During one of the workshops, when a participant committed to normalizing the practice of sharing and asking for people's gender pronouns in their organization, a white man participant responded, "Ha, that would never work at my company. That's a California thing." A handful of other students laughed and nodded in agreement. "Oh, definitely not at my company either. They'd think I'm nuts." I looked at the commentator and asked, as earnestly as possible, "Have you tried?"

Even before we begin the work, there are endless reasons for us to not even try, to believe all of this is futile and that we should live our precious lives focused on making the most of what we've got today. Every single day, I am showered with doubts, cynicism, and hesitations that sound like this:

"We're never going to get rid of _____ (racism, capitalism, police, prisons, etc.), so why even try?"

"People in my life don't care about this stuff at all."

"I don't have any power at my organization to create change."

And these feelings, often rooted in fear, intrude everywhere in our lives: many are uncomfortable broaching "political" conversations during family or social gatherings, fearing they will be cast aside as difficult or annoying, and some feel as though it's "not their place" to challenge other people's points of view or behaviors, no matter how problematic. Some feel so overwhelmed and powerless by the sheer magnitude of the battle that they dissociate and leave the work to "braver people." Throwing in the towel and returning to the status quo might feel like a seductive option amid relentless criticisms to do better and do more, not only for people with immense privileges but also for those constantly disappointed by the endless cycle of performative virtue-signaling and broken promises. Living in a society that constantly tells us *nothing will ever be enough*, there are days I, too, feel demoralized, crushed by the weight of forces so much greater than me and depleted by the repeating patterns of violence. Some days, I mentally check out and distract myself by mindlessly scrolling through Netflix or watching silly TikTok videos. But even in the midst of self-induced numbness, or in times of necessary rest, I remember that many others do not have the luxury of checking out of the fight completely even when they are tired and that I, too, cannot afford to remain idle indefinitely because my loved ones' survival, and my own, depend on it.

While some days it may feel impossible to make a dent inside an enormous system ruled by powerful, seemingly apathetic people, remember that the resistance movement for liberation has persevered through generations, continually rewriting history and righting injustices, and that the movement has never ended but is continuing right here, right now, led by visionary Black, Indigenous, and people of color organizers and change agents who are powerful in their principles, courage, and community. While the defenders of the status quo will want us to believe the fight is futile, repelling this cynicism and continuously reclaiming our collective power to reimagine what is possible is a political act of resistance that has proven to be the only way we agitate systems of oppression. As Dr. Angela Davis said, "You have to act as if it were possible to radically transform the world. And you have to do it all the time."[3] So how could we *not* try? Remembering generations of this work that have brought us to where we are today, we must refuse to believe the lies told by the oppressive systems that change is impossible and unworthy of our best efforts.

Try. *Especially* if you have relative privilege and power. Try, knowing people may ridicule you for your "idealism," knowing you will face backlash, knowing you may not get it "right" the first time, knowing you are afraid. Try by refusing to be satisfied with the unjust realities of today and reject the false dichotomy of bad and worse choices so often presented to us as the only options. Try with audacity, and dare to dream bigger. Let us try and try again. And again.

There is no shortage of entry points for you to become activated, politicized, and engaged because there is no shortage of injustices surrounding us to get you enraged. Queer and trans people can still be legally fired and refused services in most states because of their sexual orientation and gender identity. Refugees and children of immigrants are still being held in cages and deported. Mass incarceration hasn't slowed, and companies continue to exploit incarcerated people for cheap labor. Sex work is still criminalized, as is poverty, while it remains legal for politicians to surgically disenfranchise people of color of their right to vote. The school-to-prison pipeline is robbing Black and brown young people of their youth and their future, while legacy admissions and racist standardized tests privilege rich white kids. Indigenous peoples still don't have their land back, and Indigenous women and girls go missing and murdered without much public outcry. Black people still haven't been paid reparations, and the legacy of redlining still lives on. Black and Indigenous mothers and infants are still dying at a disproportionately high rate. Asians in America are getting beaten, stabbed, and killed, while our families and Pacific Islander siblings abroad battle US imperialism and military occupations. Kids in schools are still doing drills in preparation for possible mass shootings, and politicians are still sending empty "thoughts and prayers." Millions still suffer from mental health challenges without adequate community or systemic support, and our health "care" system still prioritizes profit over people's livelihoods. Food deserts still exist, and environmental racism is real. And at every site of injustice, there are people who are already doing the work, who have been resisting, dismantling, rebuilding for years. Join them. Listen and follow their lead.

BEGIN AT YOUR FRONTLINE

As my dear friend and mentor Kalaya'an Mendoza recently reminded me, "The frontline is not just the streets. The frontline is wherever you are doing the work." We each have our own frontline that requires us to bring urgency and earnest effort, consistently and over time. And you don't have to do it alone. If you are serious about the work of creating a more just world, then gather your people—two, five, seven, ten, however many you can gather—and commit to achieving something together. Pick an issue and go deep. You can start small by first engaging in conversations and then checking out volunteer opportunities at local grassroots or nonprofit organizations together. You can participate in reading groups that lead to actionable steps. You can gather your neighbors and create a plan to keep one another safe and divest from the police. You can organize with your coworkers to demand equitable and inclusive working conditions, with marginalized people in seats of power. You can gather your family members to become politically engaged. Get imaginative, get creative, get activated.

We are becoming quite skilled at holding people in positions of power accountable publicly. But how can we hold *ourselves* accountable on a daily basis, recognizing that we, too, have the power to change and, perhaps more importantly, to harm? When designing workshop curricula, my team and I make it a point to ensure that we illustrate the ways oppression manifests at all layers of our society—from the personal sphere to interpersonal to organizational to systemic—to show the inextricable connections between systemic oppression and its manifestations within each of us, illustrating how our innermost thoughts and beliefs drive our behaviors, which then drive the decisions that influence policies and structures that impact our entire society, ultimately ensuring that the cycle of oppression endures. At the same time, illuminating such connections reveals that we each have real power and opportunities to disrupt the cycle at all levels. Every decision we make in our lives matters, and these decisions can either exacerbate the very disparities we claim we want to solve, or we can make conscious choices that halt the chain reaction of the status quo.

So we have to constantly ask ourselves: How are we doing *our* part to ensure we're not adding to the snowballing inequity? How are *we* breaking that domino effect from right where we are? I hope the following noncomprehensive list of ideas on how to engage at different spheres of influence will inspire you to continue your change journey:

• **Personal sphere.** This sphere is all about the internal, intrapersonal work. We cannot do meaningful work unless we are constantly engaging in our own work of understanding ourselves, reflecting on our actions, building awareness, practicing accountability, evaluating and reevaluating our whys, and unlearning harmful patterns.

Sample actions:
  – Explore your social identities (e.g., race, gender, class, age, citizenship status, etc.) and locate yourself within larger systems of oppression; identify how you benefit from, perpetuate, or are harmed by systems of oppression (Chapter 3, Wake Up to Your Hidden Stories).

- Interrogate your beliefs, worldviews, and narratives about yourself and others and set out to intentionally disrupt harmful patterns and unlearn beliefs rooted in stereotypes or falsehoods of supremacy (Chapter 4, Unlearning White Supremacy). While Harvard's Implicit Association Test[4] is one way you may learn about your implicit biases, there are a myriad of ways you can spot your own biases by intentionally practicing mindfulness and critical inquiry every single day.

- Continue to educate yourself. Research shows counterstereotypic training is one way to rewire our brains to replace harmful stereotypes with different associations.[5] Given that we learn best when new information is presented through stories, immerse yourself in counterstereotypic narratives by reading books, watching movies, and listening to podcasts by marginalized people sharing diverse stories. Demand more of untold stories, including concealed histories, from institutions that have historically devalued and invisibilized them (Chapter 6, The Double-Edged Sword of Representation).

- Practice self-management to regulate your emotional responses when you are called out, and trust your ability to learn from mistakes and to do better (Chapter 8, Permission to Be Called Out). Get to know your own triggers and get curious about what hurt parts of you may need tending to (Chapter 12, Hold Trauma with Care).

- Come back to your why often and continue to deepen your understanding. As your context shifts, reevaluate your commitment to this journey (Chapter 2, Know Your Why).

• **Interpersonal sphere.** At this level, our work is relational and focuses on interrupting harm when we observe or experience it, and working with one another to prevent harm from occurring. We empower ourselves through education and capacity building in order to work effectively across differences, nurture resilient relationships, and support one another in practicing accountability.

Sample actions:

- Intervene when you observe harmful behaviors, for example, harmful jokes, tone policing, gaslighting, credit taking, stereotyping, interrupting, whitesplaining or mansplaining, harassment, bullying, physical harm, and more (Chapter 10, Disrupt the Pattern).

- When called out or called in for causing harm, practice accountability by apologizing, reflecting, repairing, and ensuring changed behavior (Chapter 8, Permission to Be Called Out).
- Learn how to hold space for other people in ways that are supportive. Build your active listening skills, which can help validate and affirm someone who may be going through a challenging time or experiencing harm (Chapter 12, Hold Trauma with Care).
- Share your access and resources with marginalized people; participate in mutual aids, information transparency, and network and platform sharing. Equitable redistribution of resources is justice work (Chapter 3, Wake Up to Your Hidden Stories; Chapter 11, Know What You're Willing to Give Up).
- Proactively invite people to learn with you, and educate people in your circle on all things anti-oppression (Chapter 10, Disrupt the Pattern).

• **Organizational sphere.** Whether it's the workplace, school, neighborhood association, place of worship, or a volunteer group, organizational-level work must seek to create cultures, processes, and policies that build equity and inclusion at scale. Those in positions of power must be engaged in creating sustainable change that permeates throughout the organization, and each person, especially those in management, has a role to play in ensuring there are values alignment and integrity in how organizational norms are developed, enforced, and managed, and how power is distributed (Chapter 4, Unlearning White Supremacy; Chapter 10, Disrupt the Pattern).

Sample actions:
- Conduct an equity audit to examine levels of access and equity across all areas of the organization: how you recruit, onboard, pay, include, empower, benefit, marginalize, promote, or fire members of the organization. Review organizational policies, values, and informal rules that may perpetuate patterns and characteristics of systemic oppression and disrupt them by intentionally rewriting them.
- Implement procedural interventions that act as guardrails and help to create conditions that will result in more equitable outcomes, rather

than solely relying on individual goodwill or willpower. For example, rather than relying on people's individual judgment and sense of fairness, create standardized criteria and deliberation processes for hiring and making promotion decisions; develop meeting protocols to intentionally set engagement norms (e.g., no interruptions, use "I" statements, etc.); formalize and rotate "office housework," which includes commonplace culture building (e.g., mentoring activities, planning social events, etc.) or administrative work (e.g., scheduling, note-taking, etc.) that is important but undervalued, so it doesn't fall disproportionately on women of color.[6]

- Intentionally build a culture of psychological safety in which interpersonal risks are not only welcome but normalized and where marginalized people are able to challenge the status quo without facing negative repercussions. Engage in critical dialogues and education as a team to cultivate a shared language and set of values rooted in equity and justice.

- No organization exists in a vacuum. Discuss the organization's impact on its surrounding local communities. Build relationships with community stakeholders and identify opportunities to support their needs. Invest in community organizations and programs that create access and opportunities to learn (e.g., paid internship, mentorship, or apprenticeship opportunities for marginalized communities, especially young people).

- If you are not in a position of power to enact policy changes, organize with other coworkers and community members to demand it. Write letters, boycott, strike, walk out, unionize. Call for diverse representation at all levels of the organization and build grassroots power to root out organizational inequities. Demand concrete actions to advance equity from organizations you purchase from, invest in, donate to, live in proximity to, subscribe to, or have simply come to know.

• **Systemic sphere.** Actions happening within other spheres of influence in aggregate will help push for changes at the systemic level. At this level, we are pushing for systems-wide (e.g., legal system, education system, economic system, etc.) reform through policy change, foundational disruption or uprooting, and reimagining new systems that center the most marginalized.

- Get involved in local politics. Pay attention to local grassroots efforts in passing progressive ballot measures, making budget demands, and electing progressive candidates. Attend public meetings and put pressure on elected officials to listen to the demands of their marginalized constituents. Participate in protests, boycotts, and other actions that call for change that can positively impact different communities at scale. Vote oppressive people out of office.
- Leverage the power of coalitions. Strategic coalition building through which multiple organizing bodies come together in solidarity to make a demand (e.g., multiracial coalition of organizations coendorsing a bill, multiple school boards working together to push for curricula change, etc.) can be an incredibly effective tool for change.
- Continue to learn from grassroots organizers and visionary leaders who have been working to reimagine and create alternative futures without oppressive systems. For example, seek to better understand the prison industrial complex abolition movement, which I believe is one of the most urgent and critical battles of our generation.

We encounter countless opportunities every day to make decisions that align with who we say we are. And the ripple effect of each of our principled decisions will help topple unjust norms and wake those around us to pay attention to these details that keep the violent machines going. We all have so much power to influence change. When the thought of centuries of systemic oppression feels like too high a mountain to climb, and everything feels too big and too hard compared to your smallness in front of them, look to your immediate surroundings to identify choices you can control and find people who might already be doing it. Start within yourself and let your work spread outward into your home, your neighborhood, and your community. And don't lose sight of the interconnectedness of our frontlines that map to all systems of oppression—from our bedroom to the church, from our kitchen to the schools, from our backyard to Congress, from our streets to the workplace, from our neighborhoods to the prison industrial complex—that can also transform into sites of liberation. If we each own our corner of the fight and push our frontlines while working toward the direction of revolutionary change across all systems, I believe that we can, and will, win.

*Within each one of us there is some piece of humanness that knows
we are not being served by the machine which orchestrates crisis
after crisis and is grinding all our futures into dust. If we are to keep
the enormity of the forces aligned against us from establishing a false
hierarchy of oppression, we must school ourselves to recognize that
any attack against Blacks, any attack against women, is an attack
against all of us who recognize that our interests are not being served
by the systems we support.*

—Audre Lorde[7]

CHAPTER 15

FIND JOY IN COMMUNITY

It's not activism. It's the work of being more fully alive.
—Janaya Khan[1]

CONTENT NOTE: *depression, suicidal ideation*

A few years ago, when depression engulfed me whole into the kind of darkness I had never thought could exist within me, the thought of not existing in the world briefly crossed my mind. How freeing that must feel. How the dark clouds I brought with me everywhere would no longer be a burden to others, or to this world, which didn't seem too concerned about me anyway. I was disinterested in everything and anything that once gave me joy, and my days were filled with perfunctory, empty gestures that met the bare minimum requirements for my survival: wake up, brush my teeth, skip the shower today (and yesterday), answer emails (often lying in bed), shut my stomach up with a few nibbles, try to not be too anxious about my future, sleep. I had nothing to look forward to. I brute-forced my way through getting my tasks done, relying on pure discipline that had become ingrained in me as the only way to survive in a world that demanded I never rest. I had no emotional capacity or physical energy to meet my friends. Socializing became too heavy, and I felt guilty that I didn't even have the gift of attention left for those who cared for me. My entire life, my sense of self-worth had been defined by my ability to serve others, so just like that, believing I had nothing to offer, I became acutely self-conscious that my presence would feel like an unwanted weight on those who deserved more than my gloom. Lost and ashamed, I felt utterly unworthy of existing.

But for some odd reason, people still lingered. With no expectation of anything in return, my friends met me in my empty world and kept me company.

They kept checking in, even when I didn't have the wherewithal to respond, to remind me, *We're still here.* Without trying to solve me, they simply sat next to me and welcomed my numbness to be cowitnessed. Though it was my battle, my people caught me in their net as I was falling deeper into a hole and showed me that though it was dark, I was not alone, that I could stretch out my arms to find that they were all surrounding me, ready to hold my hand while I found my ground again. What my loving, endlessly kind community taught me was that I did not have to *do* anything to be worthy—of love, care, respect, dignity, and life—nor did I have to earn my worth by giving something back in exchange. I was worthy for simply being. I *am* worthy for simply being.

And everyone else is, too.

We live in a world that is filled with messages that question our inherent worth as human beings and systems that tell us we are undeserving. We are told we need to contribute to society to garner respect; we need to have money to be allowed wellness. We need to look, sound, and appeal to the ideals of whiteness to belong. We need to have credentialed paperwork to legitimize our existence, whether to be deemed "legal" on stolen land, or to certify our intelligence. We need to have bodies that match the medical picture-book definition of "normal" (e.g., able bodied, cisgender, neurotypical, etc.) or risk being ostracized, pathologized, criminalized, and precluded from accessing safety and resources. We need to labor endlessly to earn ourselves and our loved ones shelter, food, and a future that is maybe, hopefully, slightly easier than our current reality.

But to live is our birthright.

To live with our most basic human needs met, without having to suffer violence and exploitation, should not feel like an outrageous demand.

So every day, I return to what is innate wisdom in all of us yet so easily forgotten: that each of us is worthy of living our lives fully and with unabashed joy, dignity, safety, and freedom—not because we've *earned* it but because we exist. In fierce protection of this truth, I commit to resisting and dismantling oppressive forces that say otherwise.

RESILIENT RELATIONSHIPS: THE FOUNDATION OF OUR MOVEMENT

Movements are born of critical connections rather than critical mass.
—Grace Lee Boggs[2]

Resilient relationships are the most underrated social justice strategy, yet also the most powerful and enduring one. I know this to be true because the most impactful changes I've ever made were cocreated in community built on resilient relationships, and I've also been part of short-lived dreams that couldn't extend beyond our inability to trust one another. As adrienne maree brown said, "the strength of our movement is in the strength of our relationships, which could only be measured by their depth."[3] How we show up for one another matters just as much as what we set out to accomplish together because we practice what we seek to accomplish inside our relationships, and "what we practice at the small scale sets the patterns for the whole system."[4] Our unrelenting care for each other is what makes possible the most just, loving, and equitable paths toward our collective liberation. I believe these goals are one and the same: resilient relationships and community care are foundational values, and they *are* the movement. And the journey we take alongside one another—the why and the how, the reasons for and process through which we realize our common vision together—matters. So, no, we cannot build a movement that bulldozes toward change using the tools of white supremacy while leaving behind a trail of traumatized marginalized bodies. Or a movement that prioritizes a hyperintellectualized battle of analyses over the actual lives affected by the very violence being analyzed. There is room for all of us so long as there is genuine care and commitment to do right by each other beyond performative unity or mirrored dynamics of oppression.

> *The kind of change we are after is cellular as well as institutional, is personal and intimate, is collective as well as cultural. We are making love synonymous with justice.*
> —Prentis Hemphill[5]

From my experience working with countless people in varying stages of their social justice journey, however, I've come to learn that these types of values-aligned relationships are strikingly rare in most people's lives. The repeated pattern of loneliness among us is profoundly troublesome, and it is most pronounced among those who are in the beginning stages of their journey: "I don't know who to talk to about this." "I have no one to process with." "My family and friends don't want to engage." As people try to make sense of their newfound awareness, many experience isolation and disappointment from realizing their immediate network of family and friends is "not quite there yet." Some are met with the sobering realization that most of their friendships have been superficial and transactional, rather than deeply rooted in caring for each other's full humanity. This makes continuing both self-education and behavioral change much more difficult because our surroundings can make or break our paths to long-term transformation. Some may struggle to continue the journey alone and give up on the work altogether, while others may feel the urge to cut off their longtime ties with their friends and family at the first sign of a challenge. And when a crisis occurs, those without an existing values-aligned support network often end up suffering alone, while their well-intentioned acquaintances, coworkers, and "brunch friends" fail to safely hold space for their pain.

The good news is it is never too late to begin nurturing our existing relationships and to forge new ones. Opportunities to engage more deeply are everywhere, as are possibilities for new relationship constellations. In the age of social media, I urge people to get offline and connect with people in real time, whether in person or virtually. Let's bring back the art of connecting over coffee, meeting at local rallies, and picking up our phones to call one another. Authentic relationships aren't built over Instagram comments or witty one-liner tweets, and as a certified mediator, I would especially discourage trying to tackle interpersonal conflict through social media DMs ☺. Many relationships are tossed when conflicts occur without an opportunity to repair. Conflict is hard, and accountability is harder; we will fumble, and it will be messy, awkward, and uncomfortable. But they also offer us opportunities to build deeper trust while practicing what we value. Let's expand our capacity to work through conflict and tension with principle and with ample compassion. It is also helpful to discern which relationships we want to continue investing in and which ones we need to take a break from based on our needs: "Is this a relationship I want to nurture and commit to making work despite the discomfort of conflict? Or is this relationship so harmful and unsafe to me that I need to break away from it (for now or for good)?"

I feel immense tenderness when I think about my relationship with my dad. There were years when we didn't speak, and I wondered if we would ever be in each other's lives again. I'm glad we have found our way back to each other despite the unspeakable, painful conflicts and harm we've endured and inflicted on each other. Slowly, we have been rebuilding, and though society has taught him he need not express his emotions—because he's a man, because he's Korean, because he's an immigrant, because, be- cause—we are (un)learning together and practicing showing love. I guess Lao Tzu was right—"From caring comes courage."

We should all be more intentional about the relationships in our lives, not only because they are the fulcrum of our movement but also because, simply, we need each other. I have received so much from the people in my life, so much more than I could have ever asked for, and so much more than I will ever feel like I deserve. These people are the reason why I am here, meeting you. People whose wounds, though different in their shapes and origins, al- lowed for pathways to resilient connection and healing. The gratitude I feel is enormous and overwhelming, and I use it to ground myself to keep my promises to this work and to them. So check in with the people you love to see how they are *really* doing. Tell them, in all the ways you can, that you love them dearly. *Thinking about you. Have you eaten? I love you, friend. I love you, family. Thank you for existing.* We need to hear and read these words often. And in this world filled with incessant violence, hate, cynicism, and rage, I hope we remember that our joy is revolutionary. I hope you find many mo- ments of joy, levity, and loving connection with your community. Amid all the challenges, these moments help us remember why we do this, together.

I LOVE YOU MORE THAN THEY HATE US

Although we may want the same thing—equity, justice, and liberation for all—we will not always be on the same page. And as we battle toward change, we will be faced with the difficult work of redeeming one another when we veer off our promises or fall short of expectations. Perhaps one of the most daunting tasks in front of us is achieving real alignment among ourselves amid all of our imperfections, contradictions, and hypocrisies, and pulling each other in closer when it's easiest to let go.

I am often reminded of my grassroots organizing days as a student ac- tivist. Although we did not always agree on the tactics, we knew we were *always* on the same side and that the *real* enemies were the systems of op- pression that held all of us down. No matter how intense our internal battles got, when it came time to show up for each other, we could always count on us. We would shout, yell, and scream at each other for taking approaches that were too accommodating or too radical, but at the end of the day, we knew that we were all we had, and that we loved each other as fiercely as we argued. As my dear friend and award-winning poet Terisa Siagatonu wrote, "Our children will wonder what we did to ensure their survival and I want to be able to say, *we came for systems more than we came for each other*. We chose to be in complexity instead of simply in community."[6]

> Sometimes there are no easily available, set answers. You have to work through contradictions.
> —Dr. Angela Davis[7]

When a peaceful BLM protest I was at turned violent, with the riot cops deploying tear gas and throwing flash-bangs into a crowd of vulnerable protesters, including children and the elderly, I was shaken. On the phone with my 오빠, *kuya*, and lifelong activist Kalaya'an Mendoza, I sobbed in rage, "How could they be so cruel?"

I will never forget what he said: "I love you more than they hate us."

I love you more than they hate us.

Of course, I am angry. I've *been* angry for a long time. And I am furious that I have to fear for my loved ones' safety, especially in this very moment when anti-Asian violence is everywhere I look, and our elders, so many of whom have survived wars, poverty, colonization, and imperialism, are being attacked and murdered in the streets. But what has kept me going all these years isn't anger or fear. What keeps me going, what quiets my fear, what drives me to action is and has always been *us*. It is our love for one another—not hate against our enemy—that grounds us, fuels us, unites us, and sustains us.

> Anger is useful to help clarify our differences, but in the long run, strength that is bred by anger alone is a blind force which cannot create the future. It can only demolish the past. Such strength does not focus upon what lies ahead, but upon what lies behind, upon what created it—hatred. And hatred is a deathwish for the hated, not a lifewish for anything else.
> —Audre Lorde[8]

When I think of the word *activism*, I feel the warmth of community. Like feeling the sunshine on my face through a window that delivers a summer breeze, as I lie down in the middle of my grandparents' living room, with my grandpa quietly flipping through his newspaper and my grandma working on her newest fashion piece using her heirloom sewing machine. Activism smells like soiled sweat after an evening of marching side by side, or flavored markers used on flip chart papers to write community agreements, or cheap Costco pizza and even cheaper wine that we shared while laughing, crying, and dreaming. Activism feels like being moved in unexpected ways, witnessing people's hardened hearts soften as they take a leap of faith to share their stories, even with a shaky voice. Activism reminds me of the many faces that have carried me through the darkest of times, people who teach me to get back up and breathe amid the fight, reminding me to protect my tenderness even, and especially, when it is the hardest to do so.

It's the faces of my high school teachers and counselors who gave me money to pay for health insurance and a microwave to take to college. It's the Asian woman doctor who paid enough attention to spot my depression when I was on the brink of losing myself. It's my friends who reminded me, at the lowest point in my depression, that I did not need to give or do anything to deserve their love and care. It's all the times I have felt protected by frontline street medics who risked their lives and livelihoods to care for protesters confronting police brutality. It's the silent "You got this?" and "I got you" looks exchanged with my cofacilitators during workshops in front of curious faces. It's the random "love tap" texts and unexpected food and boba drops from my Awaken and Bay Area chosen family. It's my dysfunctional biological family, with all of our collective and individual brokenness, who still manages to love abundantly with a sense of humor. It's the gentle trauma-informed care I received from other women of color survivors of sexual violence. It's my partner's warm reassurance when I'm afraid, "You're the most courageous person I know," and his reminding me that I am deserving of love, unconditionally. It's the hundreds of caring messages I received—from my close friends to strangers from the internet—in the wake of the Atlanta massage parlor shooting. It's the queer and trans young people, my dearest Campers, whose joy, courage, and resilience changed me forever.

Remembering these tender moments of connection, deep kinship, and healing through being seen by each other's mirrored pain . . . *this* is what keeps me going. I work for them. I show up for them. I remember them. And in our battle for collective liberation, I am reminded that we can access joy, right here, right now. We can nurture freedom right here in front of us, within us, with each other as we work to dismantle oppressive systems.

A few years ago, I had the honor of attending Ericka Huggins's lecture at UC Berkeley's annual Empowering Womxn of Color Conference in 2017. In her signature soothing yet incisive tone, she recalled the time when she and Bobby Seale were targeted and arrested on conspiracy charges in 1969, merely four months after her daughter's birth and her husband John Huggins's murder. She was imprisoned for two years, including time in solitary confinement, while awaiting trial separated from her newborn daughter. She talked about her daily routine while in prison, which involved disciplined spiritual practices like yoga and meditation and being allowed to spend limited time outside, always accompanied by a state prison guard. I remember her saying that one day, while standing outside, she looked up at the sunny sky. Smiling gently, she said to the prison guard, "Isn't that beautiful?" He looked back at her, and replied, "Yeah, it is." After a brief pause, Ericka continued to her audience, "There we were, looking at the sky together."

Then she said the words that have grounded my work ever since: "We always need to look for a window of connection, not because we want to change them, but because *we* need to be able to believe in humanity again."[9]

> The stories of goodness always stick to my heart. I have to carry them around with me right now. Are you carrying good stories around with you? If you're not . . . take a few seconds and grab one. A story from your life that is full of goodness and love. Got it? Don't let it go.
> —Ericka Huggins[10]

FINAL PROMISES

The work requires each of us to wake up over and over, meet each morning with our hearts and souls aligned to our greater calling. We are always waking up to new and continuing calls to action, relationships, ideas, futures, and possibilities. Welcome it, embrace it, go pursue it.

As you journey toward transformation—within yourself and in the world—make yourself these promises:

Promise to be honest. Be honest about your why, your values, your stories, your fears, your unhealed wounds, your needs, your hopes, your sacrifices. Be honest about what you are willing or unwilling to give up. Be honest about who you are and who you want to be. Be honest when you are out of integrity.

Promise to be accountable. Be accountable to your words, your actions, your harm, your spaces, your people, and your power. Be accountable to your own learning and growth. Be accountable to repairing the harm you've caused. Be accountable to the movement and the people you care about. Be accountable for your own healing, and support others to do the same.

And finally, promise to be human. This work, like our own complex and beautiful humanity, *will* get messy. Strive for progress, not perfection. Be vulnerable, authentic, compassionate, and forgiving—to others but also to yourself. Welcome new folks who need to be caught up, called in, or showed the way to be part of the movement. Share your notes. Recognize that this is trauma work, healing work, relationship work. Never forget that this work, ultimately, is about human lives.

You're wide awake now. Can you feel the steadiness of your heartbeat? The rumbling in your belly? The fiery thoughts in your head? The aching in your soul that searches for healing and togetherness? Our continuous dreaming passes down through the generations, and we are always beginning anew. Thank you for being here, and staying.

Here is to being more alive, together.

ACKNOWLEDGMENTS

I grew up hearing my mom constantly say, "We have so many people to thank. So many people we're indebted to for the rest of our lives. You can never forget them." She often reminded me of how my uncle slipped money into her pocket to help pay for my diapers, and how my other uncle showed up at my elementary school's family sports day to run a sprint race in place of my absentee dad, who at the time was thousands of miles away. So many people have filled different holes in my life to protect my heart from being drained of tenderness. I could write a whole book on People I Need to Thank, but for now, I dedicate the next few paragraphs to those who have made this book, and the person behind it, possible.

Writing this book has been one of the most challenging and purposeful experiences of my life, and so many people's care went into making it come to life. Kimberley Lim, thank you for bearing witness to the rawest parts of my writing process without judgment, and for your unrelenting compassion. You helped me cut through the noise of my insecurities and self-doubt and emerge with more clarity in each rewrite. Renée Sedliar, thank you for kicking open the door and allowing my truth to exist without being shushed. I was able to write honestly and show up with courage because you had my back every step of the way. Thank you for building trust with me, and for trusting me. Your grace and care throughout the process, not only for the book but also for my well-being, meant the world to me. Lynn Johnston, our first conversation allowed me to dream about a future that I thought was so much further away from my reality. Thank you for finding me, showing me the way, and advocating for me. You understood and believed in my vision long before anyone else—it was your yes that led to so many other yeses. Thank you.

Thank you Na Kim for the beautiful book cover that encapsulates so much and thank you Mandy (Amanda) Kain for your flexibility and helping my vision come true. Thank you to the broader Hachette team for working under an incredibly tight timeline and making everything come together, including Alison Dalafave, Julianne Lewis, Michelle Aielli, Michael Barrs, and many others who worked tirelessly behind the scenes. Thank you Christine Marra and team for your attention to detail and helping us cross the finish line.

When people ask me what my superpower is, I say it's surrounding myself with good people. Somehow life has gifted me with the privilege of finding and connecting with incredible human beings whom I call my friends, my support network, and my chosen family.

To my Awaken family—thank you. Thank you for your trust, the community we've built, and for making this challenging journey so incredibly worthwhile. We always say we have the best team, but really, we have *the best team*. Liz Van Lente, thank you. Thank you for being daring enough to take this wild ride, for being by my side through the toughest of times, for being my rock and an incredible friend, and for allowing me spaciousness to write even in the midst of your own transition. Thank you Christine Wang for holding space for me when I was shaken and for allowing me to be human, always. Cindy Joseph, if I hit the best seller's list, it's because of the T-shirt you gave me and the many affirmations you share with me each time we connect. Serian Strauss, thank you for your gentle strength, and for our unforgettable Tokyo trip (among many others) where we shifted hearts and minds. Thank you Kimi Mojica for teaching me so much, including how to listen deeply for people's real needs and the necessary art of acknowledging goodness in everyone. Thank you Joel Brown for your brilliance, your love taps, and your groundedness. Thank you to my cofounder, Bea Kim, for our incredible journey together—with you by my side, I was able to take the biggest leap of faith in my life. Thank you for being my friend, my life coach, and for helping me dream ten times bigger. Thank you to every single facilitator and every partner who helped make an impact, including our early clients. The world is better because of all your commitment to this work.

Kenny Gong, I love how our friendship has evolved over the years as we grew in different ways, each pivotal moment marked by countless heartfelt conversations and boba trips. Thank you for supporting me every step of the way, including reading my manuscript in its infancy and giving me invaluable feedback, and for *Bird by Bird*. Eunice Kwon, thank you for always making me laugh and reminding me of the journey I've been on whenever

I feel shaky. You help me find my ground again, and your random banchan drops fuel my soul and belly. Thank you so much for lending me your time, perspective, and insight during my writing process, and reading my drafts multiple times. Stacy Parson, I love us and how we exist in the grays, just like our conversations that are often filled with complexities and nuance. Thank you for always making me feel so seen, held, and understood, and for helping me to stay in integrity with discernment. To all my amazing friends and mentors who encouraged me to keep going, keep writing, keep dreaming—thank you. I love y'all so much and I hope I did you proud.

A lot happened during my writing period. From the COVID-19 pandemic to a global Black Lives Matter uprising to Stop AAPI Hate to my grandmother's passing . . . it has been an intense time filled with rage, grief, and exhaustion. Michelle Mush Lee, Katrina Jones, Karla Monterroso, Lisa Lee, Laura I. Gómez, Brooklyn Wright, Kristen Brillantes, the EHB crew, WhatsApp DEI squad, Main Stacks oldies, and everyone mentioned above—thank you for helping me get through some of the toughest parts of the journey. To everyone who reached out with words of love and solidarity amidst the onslaught of anti-Asian violence and following the Atlanta shooting, thank you. During this time, I found tremendous hope and grounding re-membering my roots and those who built my foundation. Thank you YALI organizers, especially Steph Lee and Kalaya'an Mendoza, for being my first guides in this movement and helping me grow into a fiery youth activist. Thank you Billy Curtis and GenEq for being my refuge in college, and my QSA and QYLC squad for some of the best memories of causing good trouble. Samantha Paras, my roommate of ten years, thank you for never once making me feel like a burden when we lived together. You have no idea how much your generosity meant to me when I no longer had a steady income. Thank you to countless activists and movement leaders who are on the front-lines doing the hard work of organizing and envisioning. Thank you educators and facilitators building bridges to different possibilities every day, and thank you healers and artists who help us tap into our humanity. Thank you to everyone whose courageous work inspires others to take righteous risks.

To my therapist, thank you for supporting me learn, unlearn, and heal. Thank you for your compassionate reminders about my strength and for helping me to not betray myself. Thanks to you and our untangling, I am learning how to be more gentle with myself.

Mom, Dad, thank you for loving me the best way you know how. Thank you for all the sacrifices you've made, even the ones that I will never fully know. Thank you for your resilience and for your willingness to change with me. I love you both so much, and it scares me to death to think about one day being without you. Let's make more memories. Amy, my little sis, sometimes I think you have a much stronger heart than I do, but also a deeply soft one. Despite our tiffs, I love you, I'm proud of you, and I will always be here for you. Thank you for being the daughter that Mom and Dad go to to complain about my unresponsiveness. Ahjoomma, I know being a stepmom has not always been easy—I may not express it often, but I am grateful for you and all that you do for everyone in our family.

To Grandma and Grandpa, thank you for raising me. I love you, I thank you, and I miss you . . . so much. You would have been the first ones to receive this book. Thank you ancestors for looking after me. I feel your presence more and more, and I become less afraid.

Amrit, my person, my partner, my home. I learn what safety feels like with you. Your love heals the most wounded parts of me, and I am so grateful to be in this life as us. Thank you for keeping me grounded and being patient, especially when I am stuck in the dark. Let's never stop redefining love and life for ourselves and giving the middle finger to the confining expectations of the world. They always underestimate us, and we're good at proving them wrong. I love you.

Thank you to everyone who has ever supported me and my work—from old friends to new ones, from social media friends to my neighbors, from old colleagues to new collaborators—I believe we all cross paths for a reason and that every connection is sacred. Thank you for rooting for me.

To every single person trying their best in this very moment: thank you. Thank you for existing, and thank you for not giving up.

NOTES

AN INVITATION

1. adrienne maree brown, *We Will Not Cancel Us: And Other Dreams of Transformative Justice* (Chico, CA: AK Press, 2020).

2. Audre Lorde, "Age, Race, Class, and Sex: Women Redefining Difference," in *Sister Outsider: Essays and Speeches* (Berkeley, CA: Crossing Press, 1984), 114–123.

3. Lorde, "Learning from the 60s," in *Sister Outsider*, 134–144.

4. Grace Lee Boggs, *The Next American Revolution* (Berkeley: University of California Press, 2012).

1. WHEN "GOOD PEOPLE" CAUSE HARM

1. Elliot Aronson, *The Social Animal* (New York: Palgrave Macmillan, 1984).

2. Michael Tomasello, "The Ultra-Social Animal," *European Journal of Social Psychology* 44, no. 3 (2014): 187–194, www.ncbi.nlm.nih.gov/pmc/articles/PMC4302252/.

3. The Anti-Oppression Network, "Allyship," accessed May 6, 2021, https://the antioppressionnetwork.com/allyship/.

4. Ijeoma Oluo, *So You Want to Talk About Race* (New York: Seal Press, 2018).

2. KNOW YOUR WHY

1. Sandy E. James et al., *The Report of the 2015 U.S. Transgender Survey* (Washington, DC: National Center for Transgender Equality, December 2016), https://trans equality.org/sites/default/files/docs/usts/USTS-Full-Report-Dec17.pdf.

2. Madeleine Roberts, "New CDC Data Shows LGBTQ Youth Are More Likely to Be Bullied Than Straight Cisgender Youth," Human Rights Campaign, August 26, 2020, www.hrc.org/news/new-cdc-data-shows-lgbtq-youth-are-more-likely-to-be -bullied-than-straight-cisgender-youth.

3. Roberts, "New CDC Data Shows LGBTQ Youth Are More Likely to Be Bullied Than Straight Cisgender Youth."

4. Stephen T. Russell, Amanda M. Pollitt, Gu Li, and Arnold H. Grossman, "Chosen Name Use Is Linked to Reduced Depressive Symptoms, Suicidal Ideation,

and Suicidal Behavior Among Transgender Youth," *Journal of Adolescent Health* 63, no. 4 (October 2018): P503–505, https://doi.org/10.1016/j.jadohealth.2018.02.003.

5. HRC, "A National Epidemic: Fatal Anti-Transgender Violence in the United States in 2019," Human Rights Campaign, November 2019, www.hrc.org/resources /a-national-epidemic-fatal-anti-trans-violence-in-the-united-states-in-2019.

6. David Rock and Heidi Grant, "Why Diverse Teams Are Smarter," *Harvard Business Review*, November 4, 2016, https://hbr.org/2016/11/why-diverse-teams-are -smarter.

7. Kate Rooney and Yasmin Khorram, "Tech Companies Say They Value Diversity, but Reports Show Little Change in Last Six Years," CNBC, June 12, 2020, www .cnbc.com/2020/06/12/six-years-into-diversity-reports-big-tech-has-made-little -progress.html.

8. Rohini Anand and Mary-Francis Winters, "A Retrospective View of Corporate Diversity Training from 1864 to the Present," *Academy of Management Learning & Education* 7, no. 3 (September 2008): P356–P372, https://ideas.wharton.upenn .edu/wp-content/uploads/2018/07/Anand-Winters-2008.pdf.

9. Joanna Barsh, Sandra Nudelman, and Lareina Yee, "Lessons from the Leading Edge of Gender Diversity," McKinsey & Company, April 1, 2013, www.mckinsey .com/business-functions/organization/our-insights/lessons-from-the-leading-edge -of-gender-diversity.

10. MZ. Many Names, "Attributing Words," U.S. Against Equine Slaughter, November 3, 2008, http://unnecessaryevils.blogspot.com/2008/11/attributing-words .html.

11. Audre Lorde, "Learning from the 60s," in *Sister Outsider: Essays and Speeches* (Berkeley, CA: Crossing Press, 1984), 134–144.

12. Resmaa Menakem, *My Grandmother's Hands: Racialized Trauma and the Pathway to Mending Our Hearts and Bodies* (Las Vegas: Central Recovery Press, 2017).

3. WAKE UP TO YOUR HIDDEN STORIES

1. Ellen D. Wu, *The Color of Success: Asian Americans and the Origins of the Model Minority* (Princeton, NJ: Princeton University Press, 2015).

2. Lucas Waldron and Brenda Medina, "When Transgender Travelers Walk into Scanners, Invasive Searches Sometimes Wait on the Other Side," ProPublica, August 26, 2019, www.propublica.org/article/tsa-transgender-travelers-scanners-invasive -searches-often-wait-on-the-other-side.

3. Ericka Huggins, "Spiritual Activism and Social Justice," Central Oregon Community College, April 9, 2020, YouTube video, 1:16:24, https://youtu.be/5wx-gh _Ektw.

4. Joseph Stromberg, "The Forgotten History of How Automakers Invented the

Crime of 'Jaywalking,'" Vox, November 4, 2015, www.vox.com/2015/1/15/7551873/jay
walking-history.

5. Gersh Kuntzman, "'Jaywalking While Black': Final 2019 Numbers Show Race-Based NYPD Crackdown Continues," Streetsblog NYC, January 27, 2020, https://nyc.streetsblog.org/2020/01/27/jaywalking-while-black-final-2019-numbers-show-race-based-nypd-crackdown-continues/.

6. Rebekah Riess, Jamiel Lynch, and Jennifer Henderson, "Tulsa Police Release Body Cam Video of Officers Handcuffing Black Teenagers for Jaywalking," CNN, June 11, 2020, www.cnn.com/2020/06/11/us/tulsa-police-handcuff-teenagers-jay walking/index.html.

7. Everton Gayle, "What Happened When a Worker Took Google to Task over Pay," Euronews, July 22, 2015, www.euronews.com/2015/07/22/google-worker-fights-back-over-equal-pay.

4. UNLEARNING WHITE SUPREMACY

1. "White supremacy," Merriam-Webster's, accessed May 11, 2021, www.merriam-webster.com/dictionary/white%20supremacy.

2. Sonya Renee Taylor (@sonyareneetaylor), "White Folks Are Out of Balance aka I'm Not Your Black Oracle," Instagram post, June 27, 2020, www.instagram.com/tv/CB779XDAbsr/?hl=en.

3. Frances Lee Ansley, "Stirring the Ashes: Race, Class and the Future of Civil Rights Scholarship," Cornell Law Review 74, no. 6 (1989), https://scholarship.law.cornell.edu/clr/vol74/iss6/1.

4. Elizabeth Chuck and Haimy Assefa, "She Hoped to Shine a Light on Maternal Mortality Among Native Americans. Instead, She Became a Statistic of It," NBC News, February 8, 2020, www.nbcnews.com/news/us-news/she-hoped-shine-light-maternal-mortality-among-native-americans-instead-n1131951.

5. Xingyu Zhang et al., "Racial and Ethnic Disparities in Emergency Department Care and Health Outcomes Among Children in the United States," Frontiers in Pediatrics 7 (December 19, 2019), https://doi.org/10.3389/fped.2019.00525.

6. Mariame Kaba, "So You're Thinking About Becoming an Abolitionist," Medium, October 30, 2020, https://level.medium.com/so-youre-thinking-about-becoming-an-abolitionist-a436f8e31894.

7. Ezekiel Edwards, Will Bunting, and Lynda Garcia, "The War on Marijuana in Black and White," American Civil Liberties Union, June 2013, www.aclu.org/files/assets/1114413-mj-report-rfs-rel1.pdf.

8. The Sentencing Project, Report to the United Nations on Racial Disparities in the U.S. Criminal Justice System, The Sentencing Project: Research and Advocacy for Reform, April 19, 2018, www.sentencingproject.org/publications/un-report-on-racial-disparities/.

9. Marc Mauer, "Addressing Racial Disparities in Incarceration," *Prison Journal* 91, no. 3 (August 2011): 87S–88S, https://doi.org/10.1177/0032885511415227; NAACP, "Criminal Justice Fact Sheet," https://naacp.org/resources/criminal-justice -fact-sheet.

10. Cathy Hu and Sino Esthappan, "Asian Americans and Pacific Islanders: A Missing Minority in Criminal Justice Data," Urban Wire, May 23, 2017, www.urban .org/urban-wire/asian-americans-and-pacific-islanders-missing-minority-criminal -justice-data.

11. Coalition for Juvenile Justice, "American Indian/Alaska Native Youth & Status Offense Disparities: A Call for Tribal Initiatives, Coordination & Federal Funding," Tribal Law Policy Institute, accessed May 14, 2021, https://turtletalk.files.wordpress .com/2015/06/5e051a9-1707-4ffa-83d0-082b339f9ad4.pdf.

12. SPLC, "SPLC report: U.S. Education on American Slavery Sorely Lacking," Southern Poverty Law Center, January 31, 2018, www.splcenter.org/news/2018/01/31 /splc-report-us-education-american-slavery-sorely-lacking.

13. Joy Buolamwini and Timnit Gebru, "Gender Shades: Intersectional Accuracy Disparities in Commercial Gender Classification," *Proceedings of Machine Learning Research* 81 (2018): 77–91, http://proceedings.mlr.press/v81/buolamwini18a.html.

14. Guy Birchall and Tom Michael, "Chinese Users Claim iPhone X Face Recognition Can't Tell Them Apart," December 20, 2017, *Sun* (London), www.thesun.co .uk/news/5182512/chinese-users-claim-iphonex-face-recognition-cant-tell-them-apart/.

15. Julia Angwin, Jeff Larson, Surya Mattu, and Lauren Kirchner, "Machine Bias," Pro Publica, May 23, 2016, www.propublica.org/article/machine-bias-risk -assessments-in-criminal-sentencing.

16. Junia Howell and Elizabeth Korver-Glenn, "The Increasing Effect of Neighborhood Racial Composition on Housing Values, 1980–2015," *Social Problems*, September 4, 2020, https://doi.org/10.1093/socpro/spaa033.

17. ArcGIS, "Invasion of America," accessed May 4, 2021, http://invasionof america.ehistory.org/.

18. PowWows.com, "Native American Issues Today: Current Problems & Struggles 2020," November 6, 2020, www.powwows.com/issues-and-problems-facing -native-americans-today/;   and Dedrick Asante Muhammed, Rogelio Tec, and Kathy Ramirez, "Racial Wealth Snapshot: American Indians/Native Americans," National Community Reinvestment Coalition, November 18, 2019, https://ncrc.org /racial-wealth-snapshot-american-indians-native-americans/.

19. Richie Zweigenhaft, "Fortune 500 CEOs, 2000–2020: Still Male, Still White," The Society Pages, October 28, 2020, https://thesocietypages.org/specials/fortune -500-ceos-2000-2020-still-male-still-white/.

20. Denise Lu, Jon Huang, Ashwin Seshagiri, Haeyoun Park, and Troy Griggs, "Faces of Power: 80% Are White, Even as U.S. Becomes More Diverse," *New York Times*, September 9, 2020, www.nytimes.com/interactive/2020/09/09/us/powerful -people-race-us.html.

21. bell hooks and Gloria Steinem, "bell hooks: Transgression," Eugene Lang College, October 8, 2014, YouTube video, 1:45:29, published by The New School, www.youtube.com/watch?v=tkzOFvfWRn4.

22. Toni Morrison, quoted in *Guardian* (Manchester, UK), January 29, 1992, NotableQuotes, www.notable-quotes.com/m/morrison_toni.html.

23. bell hooks and Amalia Mesa-Bains, *Homegrown: Engaged Cultural Criticism* (New York: Routledge, 2018).

24. Tema Okun, "White Supremacy Culture," Dismantling Racism Works, accessed May 14, 2021, www.dismantlingracism.org/uploads/4/3/5/7/43579015/okun_-_white_sup_culture.pdf.

25. Mark Charles et al., "Time Perception Among Navajo American Indians and Its Relation to Academic Success," presented at the 119th Annual Convention of the American Psychological Association, August 4–7, 2011, https://wirelesshogan.com/time-perception/.

26. Katherine Anne Long, "New Amazon Data Shows Black, Latino and Female Employees Are Underrepresented in Best-Paid Jobs," *Seattle Times*, April 14, 2021, www.seattletimes.com/business/amazon/new-amazon-data-shows-black-latino-and-female-employees-are-underrepresented-in-best-paid-jobs/#:~:text=Among%20Amazon's%20entry%2Dlevel%20and,white%20workers%20made%20up%2047%25.

27. Michael Sainato, "'I'm Not a Robot': Amazon Workers Condemn Unsafe, Grueling Conditions at Warehouse," *Guardian* (Manchester, UK), February 5, 2020, www.theguardian.com/technology/2020/feb/05/amazon-workers-protest-unsafe-grueling-conditions-warehouse.

28. Marianne Bertrand and Sendhil Mullainathan, "Are Emily and Greg More Employable Than Lakisha and Jamal? A Field Experiment on Labor Market Discrimination," National Bureau of Economic Research, Working Paper 9873, July 2003, https://doi.org/10.3386/w9873.

29. Dina Gerdeman, "Minorities Who 'Whiten' Job Resumes Get More Interviews," Harvard Business School, May 17, 2017, https://hbswk.hbs.edu/item/minorities-who-whiten-job-resumes-get-more-interviews.

30. John Blake, "Why White Supremacy Is Actually Killing White People," CNN, July 17, 2020, www.cnn.com/2020/07/17/us/damon-young-race-reckoning-blake/index.html.

31. Tema Okun, "White Supremacy Culture Characteristics," White Supremacy Culture, first published 1999, updated 2021, www.whitesupremacyculture.info/characteristics.html.

32. Combahee River Collective, "The Combahee River Collective Statement," accessed May 17, 2021, https://americanstudies.yale.edu/sites/default/files/files/Keyword%20Coalition_Readings.pdf.

33. Hampshire College, "Disability Rights, Studies & Justice," Disability Justice, Library & Knowledge Commons: Resource Guides, Harold F. Johnson Library,

https://resourceguides.hampshire.edu/c.php?g=759682&p=5447794; and Patty
Berne, "Disability Justice," Sins Invalid: An Unashamed Claim to Beauty in the Face
of Invisibility, June 9, 2015, www.sinsinvalid.org/blog/disability-justice-a-working
-draft-by-patty-berne.

34. Ajitha Reddy, "The Eugenic Origins of IQ Testing: Implications for Post-
Atkins Litigation," *DePaul Law Review* 57, no. 3 (Spring 2008): 667, https://via
.library.depaul.edu/law-review/vol57/iss3/5.

35. Robert Paul Cabaj, "Working with LGBTQ Patients," American Psychiat-
ric Association, accessed June 21, 2021, www.psychiatry.org/psychiatrists/cultural
-competency/education/best-practice-highlights/working-with-lgbtq-patients.

36. 39 HRW, "New Health Guidelines Propel Transgender Rights," Human
Rights Watch, May 27, 2019, www.hrw.org/news/2019/05/27/new-health-guidelines
-propel-transgender-rights#.

37. HRC, "The Lies and Dangers of Efforts to Change Sexual Orientation or
Gender Identity," Human Rights Campaign, accessed June 21, 2021, www.hrc.org
/resources/the-lies-and-dangers-of-reparative-therapy.

38. The Trevor Project, "50 Bills, 50 States: Progress Map," updated June 15,
2021, www.thetrevorproject.org/get-involved/trevor-advocacy/50-bills-50-states
/progress-map/.

39. Cynthia Kraus, "Classifying Intersex in DSM-5: Critical Reflections on Gender Dysphoria," *Archives of Sexual Behavior* 44, no. 5 (May 2015): 1147–1163, https://
doi.org/10.1007/s10508-015-0550-0.

40. Kimberlé Crenshaw, "Demarginalizing the Intersection of Race and Sex:
A Black Feminist Critique of Antidiscrimination Doctrine, Feminist Theory and
Antiracist Politics," *University of Legal Forum* 1989, no. 8 (1989), https://chicago
unbound.uchicago.edu/uclf/vol1989/iss1/8/.

41. Kathy Steinmetz, "She Coined the Term 'Intersectionality' Over 30 Years
Ago. Here's What It Means to Her Today," *Time*, February 20, 2020, https://time
.com/5786710/kimberle-crenshaw-intersectionality/.

42. Moya Bailey, "Bio," accessed May 17, 2021, www.moyabailey.com/.

43. Dictionary.com, www.dictionary.com/browse/misogynoir.

44. Audre Lorde, "There Is No Hierarchy of Oppressions," in *Homophobia and
Education: How to Deal with Name Calling* (New York: Council on Interracial Books
for Children, 1983), 9.

45. Josh Margolin, "FYI Warns of Potential Surge in Hate Crimes Against Asian
Americans amid Coronavirus: Critics Say Rhetoric Has Fueled Ill Will," ABC
News, March 27, 2020, https://abcnews.go.com/US/fbi-warns-potential-surge-hate
-crimes-asian-americans/story?id=69831920.

46. Stop AAPI Hate, "National Report," May 6, 2021, https://stopaapihate.org
/national-report-through-march-2021/.

47. JuYeon Kim, "Report: Sam's Club Stabbing Suspect Thought Family Was

'Chinese Infecting People with Coronavirus,'" KXAN, April 8, 2020, www.kxan .com/news/crime/report-sams-club-stabbing-suspect-thought-family-was-chinese -infecting-people-with-coronavirus/.

48. Christina Capatides, "Bullies Attack Asian American Teen at School, Accusing Him of Having Coronavirus," CBS News, February, 24, 2020, www.cbsnews.com /news/coronavirus-bullies-attack-asian-teen-los-angeles-accusing-him-of-having -coronavirus/.

49. U.S. Against Equine Slaughter, "Attributing Words," November 3, 2008, http://unnecessaryevils.blogspot.com/2008/11/attributing-words.html.

50. Hyejin Shim, "Questions on (the Limits & Effects of) (Asian American) Allyship," Medium, August 22, 2017, https://medium.com/@persimmontree/questions -on-the-limits-effects-of-asian-american-allyship-bb545f019117.

51. Grace Lee, dir., *American Revolutionary: The Evolution of Grace Lee Boggs*, documentary, June 16, 2013, www.imdb.com/title/tt2385558/.

52. Brea Baker, "Stemming the Tide of Hate Towards the AAPI Community," Clubhouse panel, February 21, 2021, www.joinclubhouse.com/event/mWKkoWjD.

53. Ibram X. Kendi, *How to Be an Antiracist* (New York: One World, 2019).

5. THE ONLY CONSTANT IS CONTEXT

1. Kate Conger, "Exclusive: Here's the Full 10-Page Anti-Diversity Screed Circulating Internally at Google [Updated]," Gizmodo, August 5, 2017, https://gizmodo .com/exclusive-heres-the-full-10-page-anti-diversity-screed-1797564320/amp.

2. Matthew Panzarino, "Apple Diversity Head Denise Young Smith Apologizes for Controversial Choice of Words at Summit," TechCrunch, October 13, 2017, https://techcrunch.com/2017/10/13/apple-diversity-head-denise-young-smith -apologizes-for-controversial-choice-of-words-at-summit/.

3. Elliot Ackerman et al., "A Letter on Justice and Open Debate," *Harper's*, July 7, 2020, https://harpers.org/a-letter-on-justice-and-open-debate/.

4. Susan Scafidi, *Who Owns Culture?: Appropriation and Authenticity in American Law* (New Brunswick, NJ: Rutgers University Press, 2005).

5. The Mahjong Line, "Our Story," accessed May 17, 2021, https://themahjong line.com/pages/our-story.

6. Ijeoma Oluo, *Mediocre: The Dangerous Legacy of White Male America* (New York: Seal Press, 2018).

7. NUL, *State of Black America Unmasked: 2020 Executive Summary* (New York: The National Urban League, 2020), http://sobadev.iamempowered.com/sites/soba .iamempowered.com/files/NUL-SOBA-2020-ES-web.pdf.

8. John Eligon, "A Covid-19 Relief Fund Was Only for Black Residents. Then Came the Lawsuits," *New York Times*, January 3, 2021, www.nytimes.com/2021/01/03 /us/oregon-cares-fund-lawsuit.html.

9. Ibram X. Kendi, *How to Be an Antiracist* (New York: One World, 2019).

10. Dartmouth College, "Introduction to Power, Privilege, and Social Justice," Office of Pluralism and Leadership, 2021, https://students.dartmouth.edu/opal /education/introduction-power-privilege-and-social-justice.

11. John C. Turner and Penelope J. Oakes, "The Significance of the Social Identity Concept for Social Psychology with Reference to Individualism, Interactionism and Social Influence," *British Journal of Social Psychology* 25, no. 3 (September 1986), https://doi.org/10.1111/j.2044-8309.1986.tb00732.x.

12. Mary P. Follett. *Dynamic Administration: The Collected Papers of Mary Parker Follett*, ed. E. M. Fox and L. Urwick (London: Pitman Publishing, 1940).

13. Valerie Miller, Lisa VeneKlasen, Molly Reilly, and Cindy Clark, *Making Change Happen: Power; Concepts for Revisioning Power for Justice, Equality and Peace*, no. 3, Just Associates, 2006, www.justassociates.org/sites/justassociates.org /files/mch3_2011_final_0.pdf.

6. THE DOUBLE-EDGED SWORD OF REPRESENTATION

1. Cathy Park Hong, *Minor Feelings: An Asian American Reckoning* (New York: One World, 2020).

2. Darnell Hunt and Ana-Christina Ramón, "Hollywood Diversity Report 2020: A Tale of Two Hollywoods, Part 1: Film," UCLA College Social Sciences Institute for Research on Labor & Employment, February 2020, https://socialsciences .ucla.edu/wp-content/uploads/2020/02/UCLA-Hollywood-Diversity-Report -2020-Film-2-6-2020.pdf.

3. Danny Woodburn and Kristina Kopić, "The Ruderman White Paper on Employment of Actors with Disabilities in Television," Ruderman Family Foundation, July 2016, www.rudermanfoundation.org/wp-content/uploads/2016/07/TV-White -Paper_7-1-003.pdf.

4. Hong, *Minor Feelings*.

5. Anna Purna Kambhampaty, "In 1968, These Activists Coined the Term 'Asian American'—and Helped Shape Decades of Advocacy," *Time*, May 22, 2020, https:// time.com/5837805/asian-american-history/.

6. Andrew Yang, "Opinion: Andrew Yang: We Asian Americans Are Not the Virus, but We Can Be Part of the Cure," *Washington Post*, April 1, 2020, www .washingtonpost.com/opinions/2020/04/01/andrew-yang-coronavirus-discrimi nation/.

7. Narayan Liu, "Mulan: Disney Responds to Xinjiang Criticisms from British Politicians," Comic Book Resources, October 11, 2020, www.cbr.com/mulan -disney-xinjiang-criticisms-from-british-politicians/.

8. Bryan Wood, "What Is Happening with the Uighurs in China?" PBS NewsHour, 2019, www.pbs.org/newshour/features/uighurs/.

9. Michael Harriot, "The Privilege of White Individuality," The Root, October 5, 2017, www.theroot.com/the-privilege-of-white-individuality-1819184476.

10. Rakesh Kochhar and Anthony Cilluffo, "Income Inequality in the U.S. Is Rising Most Rapidly Among Asians," Pew Research Center, July 12, 2018, www .pewresearch.org/social-trends/2018/07/12/income-inequality-in-the-u-s-is-rising -most-rapidly-among-asians/.

11. Abby Budiman and Neil G. Ruiz, "Key Facts about Asian Americans, a Diverse and Growing Population," Pew Research Center, April 29, 2021, www.pewresearch .org/fact-tank/2021/04/29/key-facts-about-asian-americans/.

12. Buck Gee and Denise Peck, "Asian Americans Are the Least Likely Group in the U.S. to Be Promoted to Management," Harvard Business Review, May 31, 2018, https://hbr.org/2018/05/asian-americans-are-the-least-likely-group-in-the-u-s-to -be-promoted-to-management.

13. Karthick Ramakrishnan, Mai Do, and Sunny Shao, "State of Philanthropy Among Asian Americans and Pacific Islanders: Findings and Recommendations to Strengthen Visibility and Impact," AAPI Data, September 2020, https://aapidata .com/wp-content/uploads/2020/09/aapi-state-of-philanthropy-2020-report.pdf.

14. Grace Lee Boggs, Living for Change: An Autobiography (Minneapolis: University of Minnesota Press, 1998).

15. Erving Goffman, Stigma: Notes on the Management of Spoiled Identity (New York: Simon & Schuster, 1963), 102; and Kenji Yoshino, Covering: The Hidden Assault on Our Civil Rights (New York, Random House, 2007).

16. Courtney L. McCluney et al., "The Costs of Code-Switching," Harvard Business Review, November 15, 2019, https://hbr.org/2019/11/the-costs-of-codeswitching.

17. McCluney et al., "The Costs of Code-Switching."

18. Lean In, "What Being an 'Only' at Work Is Like," in Women in the Workplace 2018, LeanIn.org and McKinsey & Company, October 2018, https://leanin.org /women-in-the-workplace-report-2018/what-being-an-only-at-work-is-like.

7. CENTER THE MOST MARGINALIZED

1. bell hooks, Talking Back: Thinking Feminist, Thinking Black (New York: Routledge, 2015).

2. Angela Y. Davis and Elizabeth Martinez, "Coalition Building Among People of Color," discussion with Center for Cultural Studies, University of California, San Diego, 1993, https://culturalstudies.ucsc.edu/inscriptions/volume-7/angela-y-davis -elizabeth-martinez/.

3. Ange-Marie Hancock, Solidarity Politics for Millennials: A Guide to Ending the Oppression Olympics (New York, Palgrave Macmillan, 2013).

4. Sandra E. Garcia, "Where Did BIPOC Come From?" New York Times, June 17, 2020, www.nytimes.com/article/what-is-bipoc.html.

5. UNEP, "How Climate Change Disproportionately Impacts Those with Disabilities," UN Environment Programme, December 9, 2019, www.unep.org/news-and-stories/story/how-climate-change-disproportionately-impacts-those-dis abilities.

6. OECD, *Poverty and Climate Change: Reducing the Vulnerability of the Poor Through Adaptation*, Organisation for Economic Co-operation and Development, June 2003, www.oecd.org/env/cc/2502872.pdf.

7. Aneesh Patnaik, Jiahn Song, Alice Feng, and Crystal Ade, "Racial Disparities and Climate Change," Princeton Student Climate Initiative, August 15, 2020, https://psci.princeton.edu/tips/2020/8/15/racial-disparities-and-climate-change.

8. Brad Plumer and Nadja Popovich, "How Decades of Racist Housing Policy Left Neighborhoods Sweltering," *New York Times*, August 24, 2020, www.nytimes.com/interactive/2020/08/24/climate/racism-redlining-cities-global-warming.html?campaign_id=9&emc=edit_nn_20200824&instance_id=21556&nl=the-morning%C2%AEi_id=96909927%C2%A7ion_index=2%C2%A7ion_name=three_more_big_stories&segment_id=36808&te=1&user_id=ab7270241d0d903.

9. Tara Houska, "The Standing Rock Resistance and Our Fight for Indigenous Rights," TEDWomen 2017, November 2017, video, 10:55, www.ted.com/talks/tara_houska_the_standing_rock_resistance_and_our_fight_for_indigenous_rights/transcript?language=en#t-607194.

10. Talia Buford, "Indigenous Communities Are on the Front Lines of Climate Change," PBS Digital Studios, September 13, 2018, YouTube video, 6:11, published by Hot Mess, www.youtube.com/watch?v=xlGnve1cjOY.

11. Buford, "Indigenous Communities."

12. "Spotlight on Indigenous Activists," Lakota People's Law Project, December 10, 2019, https://lakotalaw.org/news/2019-12-10/spotlight-on-indigenous-activists.

13. Indya Moore (@indyamoore), "(Language Warning) Trans Awareness Week . . . ," Instagram post, November 17, 2020, www.instagram.com/tv/CHsviLvH68z/?hl=en.

14. Moore, "(Language Warning)."

15. Stefan Lembo Stolba, "Credit Card Debt in 2020: Balances Drop for the First Time in Eight Years," Experian, November 30, 2020, www.experian.com/blogs/ask-experian/state-of-credit-cards/.

16. Christine Sun Kim, "Access from the Start," TEDPartners, December 1, 2020, YouTube video, 3:45, www.youtube.com/watch?v=OwgbrWHTqZo.

17. Albert Shum et al., "Inclusive Microsoft Design," Microsoft Design, 2016, https://download.microsoft.com/download/B/0/D/B0D4BF87-09CE-4417-8F28-D60703D672ED/INCLUSIVE_TOOLKIT_MANUAL_FINAL.pdf.

18. Katelyn Cheng, "Deaf Culture: What Does 'D,' 'd,' and 'd/Deaf' Mean in the Deaf Community?" Start ASL, updated May 13, 2021, www.startasl.com/what-does-d-d-and-d-deaf-mean-in-the-deaf-community/.

19. A-i-Media, "The Difference Between d/Deaf and Hard-of-Hearing," www
.ai-media.tv/the-difference-between-d-deaf-and-hard-of-hearing-2/#.

20. Samantha Sauld, "7 Ways Captions and Transcripts Improve Video SEO,"
3Play Media, December 10, 2018, updated February 10, 2021, www.3playmedia.com
/blog/7-ways-video-transcripts-captions-improve-seo/.

21. Shum et al., "Inclusive Microsoft Design."

22. "Black Owned DEI Companies + Consultants Currently Accepting New
Corporate Clients!!!" Google Doc, updated March 24, 2021, https://docs.google.com
/spreadsheets/d/1giDIGTd5XvuCrP9n-Y70_NQPegvmcejdg8x3ypM5Iu4/.

23. bell hooks, "Choosing the Margin as a Space of Radical Openness," *Framework: The Journal of Cinema and Media* 36 (1989): 15–23.

8. PERMISSION TO BE CALLED OUT

1. Da'Shaun Harrison, "Committing Harm Is Not the Same as Being Abusive,"
dashaunharrison.com, February 11, 2020, https://dashaunharrison.com/committing
-harm-is-not-the-same-as-being-abusive/.

2. Franchesca Ramsey (chescaleigh), "Getting Called Out: How to Apologize,"
September 6, 2013, YouTube video, 8:36, www.youtube.com/watch?v=C8xJXKYL8pU.

3. Mia Mingus, "How to Give a Genuine Apology Part 2: The Apology—The
What and the How," Leaving Evidence, December 18, 2019, https://leavingevidence
.wordpress.com/2019/12/18/how-to-give-a-good-apology-part-2-the-apology-the
-what-and-the-how/.

4. Aaron Lazare, *On Apology* (New York: Oxford University Press, 2004).

5. Yohsuke Ohtsubo et al., "Costly Group Apology Communicates a Group's Sincere 'Intention,'" *Social Neuroscience* 15, no. 2 (November 23, 2019): 244–254, https://
doi.org/10.1080/17470919.2019.1697745.

6. Aaron Lazare, "You Call That an Apology," *Washington Post*, July 3, 2005, www
.washingtonpost.com/archive/opinions/2005/07/03/you-call-that-an-apology
/73d585c8-ec8c-48b4-b598-73c81a278861/.

7. Ornish Living, "The Science Behind Why Naming Our Feelings Makes Us Hap-
pier," HuffPost, May 15, 2015, updated December 6, 2017, www.huffpost.com/entry
/the-science-behind-why-na_b_7174164.

8. Gloria Willcox, "The Feeling Wheel," The Gottman Institute, accessed May
17, 2021, https://cdn.gottman.com/wp-content/uploads/2020/12/The-Gottman
-Institute_The-Feeling-Wheel_v2.pdf.

9. Geoffrey Roberts, "I Feel—Emotional Word Wheel—The Feel Wheel—Australian English," Imgur, March 5, 2015, https://imgur.com/tCWChf6.

10. Maya Angelou and bell hooks, "Angelou," *Shambhala Sun*, January 1998,
www.hartford-hwp.com/archives/45a/249.html#:~:text=For%20me%20forgive
ness%20and%20compassion,their%20capacity%20to%20be%20transformed%3F.

11. Mia Mingus, "Dreaming Accountability," Leaving Evidence, May 5, 2019, https://leavingevidence.wordpress.com/2019/05/05/dreaming-accountability -dreaming-a-returning-to-ourselves-and-each-other/.

12. Maya Angelou, tweet, August 12, 2018, https://twitter.com/DrMayaAngelou /status/1028663286512930817?s=20.

9. CHANGE THROUGH LANGUAGE

1. Noam Chomsky, "The Purpose of Education," Learning Without Frontiers Conference, February 1, 2012, YouTube video, 21:57, published by iwf, www.youtube .com/watch?v=DdNAUJWJNo8&t=261s.

2. Chester M. Pierce, Jean V. Carew, Diane Pierce-Gonzalez, and Deborah Wills, "An Experiment in Racism: TV Commercials," Education and Urban Society 10, no. 1 (November 1977): 66, https://doi.org/10.1177/001312457701000105.

3. Derald Wing Sue et al., "Racial Microaggressions in Everyday Life: Implications for Clinical Practice," American Psychologist 62, no. 4 (2007): 271–286, https:// doi.org/10.1037/0003-066X.62.4.271.

4. Lauren Michele Jackson, "We Need to Talk About Digital Blackface in Reaction GIFs," Teen Vogue, August 2, 2017, www.teenvogue.com/story/digital-blackface -reaction-gifs.

5. Lera Boroditsky, "Lost in Translation," Wall Street Journal, July 23, 2010, www .wsj.com/articles/SB10001424052748703467304575383131592767868.

6. Andrew Newberg and Mark Robert Waldman, Words Can Change Your Brain (New York: Plume, 2013).

7. "Voting Rights for African Americans," Library of Congress, accessed May 18, 2021, www.loc.gov/classroom-materials/elections/right-to-vote/voting-rights-for -african-americans/.

8. Lera Boroditsky "How Language Shapes the Way We Think," video, TED-Women 2017, November 2017, www.ted.com/talks/lera_boroditsky_how_language _shapes_the_way_we_think?language=en.

9. Caitlin M. Fausey and Lera Boroditsky, "Subtle Linguistic Cues Influence Perceived Blame and Financial Liability," Psychonomic Bulletin & Review 17, no. 5 (2010): 644–650, https://doi.org/10.3758/PBR.17.5.644.

10. Fausey and Boroditsky, "Subtle Linguistic Cues."

11. Kristen Harper, Renee Ryberg, and Deborah Temkin, "Black Students and Students with Disabilities Remain More Likely to Receive Out-of-School Suspensions, Despite Overall Declines," Child Trends, April 29, 2019, www.childtrends.org /publications/black-students-disabilities-out-of-school-suspensions.

12. Inti Pacheco and Stephani Stamm, "What CEOs Said About George Floyd's Death," Wall Street Journal, June 2, 2020, www.wsj.com/articles/what-executives -said-about-george-floyds-death-11591364538.

13. Nicholas Bogel-Burroughs and Vanessa Swales, "Prisoner with Coronavirus Dies After Giving Birth While on Ventilator," *New York Times*, April 29, 2020, updated June 16, 2020, www.nytimes.com/2020/04/29/us/coronavirus-inmate-death-andrea-circle-bear.html.

14. Sonya Renee Taylor, *The Body Is Not an Apology: The Power of Radical Self-Love* (San Francisco: Berrett-Koehler, 2018).

15. Noam Chomsky, "The Concept of Language," interview with Al Page, *Upon Reflection*, University of Washington, March 12, 2014, YouTube video, 27:43, published by UW Video, www.youtube.com/watch?v=hdUbIlwHRkY.

16. Interactive Constitution, "First Amendment: Freedom of Religion, Speech, Press, Assembly, and Petition," National Constitution Center, accessed May 18, 2021, https://constitutioncenter.org/interactive-constitution/amendment/amendment-i#:~:text=Congress%20shall%20make%20no%20law,for%20a%20redress%20of%20grievances.

17. Ibram X. Kendi, "We're Still Living and Dying in the Slaveholders' Republic," *Atlantic*, May 4, 2020, www.theatlantic.com/ideas/archive/2020/05/what-freedom-means-trump/611083/.

18. Donald Trump, "Meet the Press Transcript—August 9, 2015," interview with Chuck Todd, *Meet the Press*, NBC News, August 9, 2015, www.nbcnews.com/meet-the-press/meet-press-transcript-august-9-2015-n408516.

19. Phil Bump, "How 'Politically Correct' Moved from Commies to Culture and Back into Politics," *Washington Post*, December 17, 2015, www.washingtonpost.com/news/the-fix/wp/2015/12/17/the-interesting-evolution-of-political-correctness/.

20. Stephen T. Russell, Amanda M. Pollitt, Gu Li, and Arnold H. Grossman, "Chosen Name Use Is Linked to Reduced Depressive Symptoms, Suicidal Ideation, and Suicidal Behavior Among Transgender Youth," *Journal of Adolescent Health* 63, no. 4 (October 2018): P503–P505, https://doi.org/10.1016/j.jadohealth.2018.02.003.

21. Anna Purna Kambhampaty, "In 1968, These Activists Coined the Term 'Asian American'—and Helped Shape Decades of Advocacy," *Time*, May 22, 2020, https://time.com/5837805/asian-american-history/.

10. DISRUPT THE PATTERN

1. adrienne maree brown, *Emergent Strategy: Shaping Change, Changing Worlds* (Chico, CA: AK Press, 2017).

2. Joseph Epstein, "Is There a Doctor in the White House? Not If You Need an M.D.," *Wall Street Journal*, December 11, 2020, www.wsj.com/articles/is-there-a-doctor-in-the-white-house-not-if-you-need-an-m-d-11607727380.

3. Amy Diehl and Leanne Dzubinski, "We Need to Stop 'Untitling' and 'Uncredentialing' Professional Women," *Fast Company*, January 22, 2021, www.fastcompany.com/90596628/we-need-to-stop-untitling-and-uncredentialing-professional-women.

4. PayScale, "The State of the Gender Pay Gap in 2021," PayScale, accessed May 18, 2021, www.payscale.com/data/gender-pay-gap.

5. PayScale, "The State of the Gender Pay Gap."

6. Joan C. Williams, "The 5 Biases Pushing Women Out of STEM," *Harvard Business Review*, March 24, 2015, https://hbr.org/2015/03/the-5-biases-pushing-women-out-of-stem.

7. "How Often Are Women Interrupted by Men? Here's What the Research Says," Advisory Board, July 7, 2017, www.advisory.com/en/daily-briefing/2017/07/07/men-interrupting-women.

8. Mia Mingus, "The Four Parts of Accountability: How to Give a Genuine Apology Part 1," Leaving Evidence, December 18, 2019, https://leavingevidence.wordpress.com/2019/12/18/how-to-give-a-good-apology-part-1-the-four-parts-of-accountability/.

9. NiCole T. Buchanan, Isis H. Settles, Angela T. Hall, and Rachel C. O'Connor, "A Review of Organizational Strategies for Reducing Sexual Harassment: Insights from the U. S. Military," *Journal of Social Issues* 70, no. 4 (December 2014): 687–702, https://doi.org/10.1111/josi.12086.

10. Marianne Cooper, "The 3 Things That Make Organizations More Prone to Sexual Harassment," *Atlantic*, November 27, 2017, www.theatlantic.com/business/archive/2017/11/organizations-sexual-harassment/546707/.

11. Derald Wing Sue et al., "Racial Microaggressions in Everyday Life: Implications for Clinical Practice," *American Psychologist* 62, no. 4 (2007): 271–286, https://doi.org/10.1037/0003-066X.62.4.271.

12. Audre Lorde, "Learning from the 60s," in *Sister Outsider: Essays and Speeches* (Berkeley: Crossing Press, 1984), 134–144.

13. Chanel Miller, *Know My Name: A Memoir* (New York: Viking, 2019).

14. Sayumi Irey, "How Asian American Women Perceive and Move Toward Leadership Roles in Community Colleges: A Study of Insider Counter Narratives," PhD diss., University of Washington, July 2013, http://hdl.handle.net/1773/22898; and Cynthia Ganote, Tasha Souza, and Floyd Cheung, "Microaggressions and Microresistance: Supporting and Empowering Students," in *Diversity and Inclusion in the College Classroom* (Madison, WI: Magna, 2016).

15. Anne Ju, "Courage Is the Most Important Virtue, Says Writer and Civil Rights Activist Maya Angelou at Convocation," *Cornell Chronicle*, May 24, 2008, https://news.cornell.edu/stories/2008/05/courage-most-important-virtue-maya-angelou-tells-seniors.

16. Timur Kuran, *Private Truths, Public Lies: The Social Consequences of Preference Falsification* (Cambridge, MA: Harvard University Press, 1997).

17. Danielle Cohen, "International Women's Day: Women Who Inspire Our Work," The White House, March 8, 2016, https://obamawhitehouse.archives.gov/blog/2016/03/08/international-womens-day-3-women-who-inspire-us#:~:text

=For%20Dolores%2C%20%E2%80%9Cevery%20moment%20is,make%20the%20 world%20a%20more.

18. Mia Mingus, "Dreaming Accountability," Leaving Evidence, May 5, 2019, https://leavingevidence.wordpress.com/2019/05/05/dreaming-accountability -dreaming-a-returning-to-ourselves-and-each-other/.

19. Josh Constine, "BetterWorks and CEO Sued by Ex-Employee for Alleged Sexually Suggestive Assault," TechCrunch, July 14, 2017, https://techcrunch.com/2017 /07/14/betterworks-duggan-kim-assault-sexual-manner-lawsuit/.

20. Constine, "BetterWorks and CEO Sued."

21. Tarana Burke, "Inspiring Quotes from the Founder of Me Too," Lafayette College, accessed May 18, 2021, https://news.lafayette.edu/2018/09/19/inspiring-quotes -from-founder-of-me-too/.

11. KNOW WHAT YOU'RE WILLING TO GIVE UP

1. Jessica Wolf and Melissa Abraham, "Prop. 16 Failed in California. Why? And What's Next?" UCLA Newsroom, November 18, 2020, https://newsroom.ucla.edu /stories/prop-16-failed-in-california.

2. Brian Armstrong, "Coinbase Is a Mission Focused Company," The Coinbase Blog, September 27, 2020, https://blog.coinbase.com/coinbase-is-a-mission -focused-company-af882df8804.

3. Stefanie K. Johnson and David R. Hekman, "Women and Minorities Are Penalized for Promoting Diversity," Harvard Business Review, March 23, 2016, https:// hbr.org/2016/03/women-and-minorities-are-penalized-for-promoting-diversity.

4. bell hooks, Feminist Theory: From Margin to Center (New York: Routledge, 2015).

5. "Accomplices Not Allies: Abolishing the Ally Industrial Complex, an Indigenous Perspective," Indigenous Action Media, May 2, 2014, https://indigenousaction .org/wp-content/uploads/Accomplices-Not-Allies-print.pdf.

6. Sue Skalicky and Monica Davey, "Tension Between Police and Standing Rock Protesters Reaches Boiling Point," New York Times, October 28, 2016, www.nytimes .com/2016/10/29/us/dakota-access-pipeline-protest.html.

7. Derek Hawkins, "Activists and Police Trade Blame After Dakota Access Protester Severely Injured," Washington Post, November 22, 2016, www.washingtonpost .com/news/morning-mix/wp/2016/11/22/activists-and-police-trade-blame-after -dakota-access-protester-severely-injured/.

8. Daniel Kahneman and Amos Tversky, "Prospect Theory: An Analysis of Decision Under Risk," Econometrica 47, no. 2 (March 1979): 263–291, https://doi.org /10.2307/1914185.

9. Dan Ariely, Predictably Irrational: The Hidden Forces That Shape Our Decisions (New York: HarperCollins, 2009).

10. Resource Generation, accessed May 17, 2021, https://resourcegeneration.org/.

12. HOLD TRAUMA WITH CARE

1. Audre Lorde, *A Burst of Light: And Other Essays* (New York: Firebrand Books, 1988).

2. "Republic of Korea Prohibits All Corporal Punishment of Children," End Violence Against Children, March 25, 2021, www.end-violence.org/articles/republic-korea-prohibits-all-corporal-punishment-children#:~:text=No%2017095)%20and%20the%20repeal,the%20use%20of%20corporal%20punishment.

3. Katrin Marquez, "Is Violence Necessary to the Korean Education System?" *10 Magazine*, October 21, 2015, updated June 17, 2020, https://10mag.com/corporal-punishment-in-korea/.

4. Resmaa Menakem, *My Grandmother's Hands: Racialized Trauma and the Pathway to Mending Our Hearts and Bodies* (Las Vegas: Central Recovery Press, 2017).

5. Menakem, *My Grandmother's Hands*.

6. "Trauma," American Psychological Association, accessed May 17, 2021, www.apa.org/topics/trauma#:~:text=Trauma%20is%20an%20emotional%20response,symptoms%20like%20headaches%20or%20nausea.

7. Janet E. Helms, Guerda Nicolas, and Carlton E. Green, "Racism and Ethnoviolence as Trauma: Enhancing Professional Training," *Traumatology* 16, no. 4 (December 2010): 53–62, https://doi.org/10.1177/1534765610389595.

8. Koko Nishi, MA, "Mental Health Among Asian-Americans," American Psychological Association, 2012, www.apa.org/pi/oema/resources/ethnicity-health/asian-american/article-mental-health.

9. Staci K. Haines, *The Politics of Trauma: Somatics, Healing, and Social Justice* (Berkeley, CA: North Atlantic Books, 2019).

10. Maria Yellow Horse Brave Heart, "The Historical Trauma Response Among Natives and Its Relationship with Substance Abuse: A Lakota Illustration," *Journal of Psychoactive Drugs* 35, no. 1 (2003): 7–13, https://doi.org/10.1080/02791072.2003.10399988.

11. Maria Yellow Horse Brave Heart, "Wakiksuyapi: Carrying the Historical Trauma of the Lakota," *Tulane Studies in Social Welfare* 21 (January 2000): 245–266, https://citeseerx.ist.psu.edu/viewdoc/download?doi=10.1.1.452.6309&rep=rep1&type=pdf.

12. Brave Heart, "The Historical Trauma Response."

13. Haines, *The Politics of Trauma*.

14. Menakem, *My Grandmother's Hands*.

15. Audre Lorde, *Conversations with Audre Lorde*, ed. Joan Wylie Hall (Jackson: University Press of Mississippi, 2004), 16.

16. Martha Beck, "Quit Suffering from 'Dirty' Pain," CNN, January 15, 2008, www.cnn.com/2008/LIVING/personal/01/15/o.leash.on.life/index.html.

17. Menakem, *My Grandmother's Hands*.

18. Timur Kuran, "A Conspiracy of Silence," interview with Hidden Brain podcast, accessed May 18, 2021, https://hiddenbrain.org/podcast/a-conspiracy-of-silence/.

19. Menakem, *My Grandmother's Hands*.

20. Prentis Hemphill (@prentishemphill), "Healing makes room for us to fight in the places where it's necessary and love in the places we long to," Instagram post, January 8, 2021, www.instagram.com/p/CJy5nx5gOsR/?utm_source=ig_web_copy _link.

21. "What 'Holding Space' Means + 5 Tips to Practice," Gender & Sexuality Therapy Center, January 17, 2020, https://gstherapycenter.com/blog/2020/1/16/what -holding-space-means-5-tips-to-practice#:~:text=%E2%80%9CHolding%20space %E2%80%9D%20means%20being%20physically,judgment%20while%20you%20 are%20present.

22. Tessa Petak, "Tarana Burke Says Our Nation Has Been Traumatized—and We Need to Look to Survivors to Heal," *InStyle*, February 16, 2021, www.instyle.com /reviews-coverage/ladies-first-podcast-laura-brown/448.

23. Prentis Hemphill, "A reminder," Instagram post, April 5, 2021, https://www .instagram.com/p/CNSzFO1A21C/?utm_source=ig_web_copy_link.

24. Menakem, *My Grandmother's Hands*.

25. Brave Heart, "Wakiksuyapi."

26. Haines, *The Politics of Trauma*.

27. Chanel Miller, *Know My Name: A Memoir* (New York: Viking, 2019).

13. CREATING OUR OWN LIBERATORY TOOLS

1. Jaclyn Diaz and Vanessa Romo, "8 People, Many of Them Asian, Shot Dead at Atlanta-Area Spas; Man Arrested," NPR, March 17, 2021, www.npr.org /2021/03/16/978024380/8-women-shot-to-death-at-atlanta-massage-parlors-man -arrested.

2. United States Congress, "1875 Page Act," Asian American Digital History Archive, accessed May 18, 2021, https://aadha.binghamton.edu/items/show/212.

3. "Chinese Exclusion Act: Primary Documents in America History," Library of Congress, accessed May 18, 2021, https://guides.loc.gov/chinese-exclusion-act.

4. "8 Dead in Atlanta Spa Shootings, with Fears of Anti-Asian Bias," *New York Times*, March 26, 2021, www.nytimes.com/live/2021/03/17/us/shooting-atlanta -acworth.

5. Michelle Kim (@michellekimkim), "You would never," Instagram post, March 19, 2021, www.instagram.com/p/CMnGcQBLmNr/?igshid=1axfr5db4fv75.

6. "Frequently Asked Questions," Asian Americans Advancing Justice-Atlanta, accessed May 18, 2021, www.advancingjustice-atlanta.org/faqs.

7. Sex Workers & Allies Network, "Sex Work vs Trafficking: How They Are Different and Why It Matters," Yale Global Health Justice Partnership, June 2020, https://law.yale.edu/sites/default/files/area/center/ghjp/documents/issue_brief _sex_work_vs_trafficking_v2.pdf.

8. Tim Shorrock, "Welcome to the Monkey House," *New Republic*, December 2, 2019, https://newrepublic.com/article/155707/united-states-military-prostitution -south-korea-monkey-house.

9. Katharine H. S. Moon, "Military Prostitution and the U.S. Military in Asia," *Asia-Pacific Journal* 7, no. 3 (Jan 2009), https://apjjf.org/-Katharine-H-S--Moon /3019/article.pdf.

10. "Number of Military and DoD Appropriated Fund (APF) Civilian Personnel Permanently Assigned by Duty Location and Service/Component (as of March 31, 2021)," Defense Manpower Data Center, May 6, 2021.

11. "8 Dead in Atlanta Spa Shootings."

12. David Vine, "'My Body Was Not Mine, but the US Military's,'" Politico, November 3, 2015, www.politico.eu/article/my-body-was-not-mine-but-the-u-s -militarys/.

13. Audre Lorde, "Age, Race, Class, and Sex," in *Sister Outsider: Essays and Speeches* (Berkeley, CA: Crossing Press, 1984).

14. Eyewitness News, "NYPD Announces New Initiative to Combat Anti-Asian Hate Crimes in NYC," WABC, March 25, 2021, https://abc7ny.com/anti-asian-hate -crimes-nypd-initiative-bias-crime/10447140/.

15. Connie Wun, "Ignoring the History of Anti-Asian Racism Is Another Form of Violence," *Elle*, March 1, 2021, www.elle.com/culture/career-politics/a35635188 /anti-asian-racism-history-violence/.

16. Christine Willmsen, "'Bubbly Kid' Was Fatally Shot by King County Deputy Hours Before High-School Graduation," *Seattle Times*, June 28, 2017, www.seattle times.com/seattle-news/crime/bubbly-kid-was-fatally-shot-by-king-county-deputy -hours-before-high-school-graduation/.

17. "Justice for Christian Hall," accessed May 18, 2021, www.justiceforchristian hall.com/; and Jacey Fortin, "California Man Died After Police Knelt on Him for 5 Minutes, Family Says," *New York Times*, February 25, 2021, www.nytimes.com /2021/02/25/us/angelo-quinto-death-police-kneel.html.

18. Melissa Gira Grant and Emma Whitford, "Family, Former Attorney of Queens Woman Who Fell to Her Death in Vice Sting Say She Was Sexually As- saulted, Pressured to Become an Informant," The Appeal, December 15, 2017, https:// theappeal.org/family-former-attorney-of-queens-woman-who-fell-to-her-death-in -vice-sting-say-she-was-sexually-d67461a12f1/.

19. Red Canary Song, "Red Canary Song Response to 8 Lives Lost in Atlanta,"

Google doc, accessed May 18, 2021, https://docs.google.com/document/d/1_Qom FJnivTZL5fcCS7eUZn9EhOJ1XHtFBGOGqVaUY_8/edit.

20. Beenish Ahmed, "Atlanta Killings Revive Memory of Vincent Chin and Another Time of Anti-Asian Sentiment," Michigan Radio, April 5, 2021, www .michiganradio.org/post/atlanta-killings-revive-memory-vincent-chin-and -another-time-anti-asian-sentiment-1; and Renee Tajima-Peña, "The History of Anti-Asian-American Violence," New Yorker, March 25, 2021, www.newyorker.com/news /q-and-a/the-history-of-anti-asian-american-violence.

21. Tracy Wilkinson and Frank Clifford, "Korean Grocer Who Killed Black Teen Gets Probation," LA Times, November 16, 1991, www.latimes.com/archives/la-xpm -1991-11-16-mn-1402-story.html.

22. Christina Carrega, Aidan Mclaughlin, and Dareh Gregorian, "Former NYPD cop Peter Liang spared jail time in fatal shooting of Akai Gurley at Brooklyn housing project," New York Daily News, April 19, 2016, www.nydailynews.com/new-york /brooklyn/ex-nypd-peter-liang-spared-jail-death-akai-gurley-article-1.2607310.

23. Daniel Bird, "Atlanta Shooting Survivor Was 'Handcuffed for Two Hours' While Wife Lay Dying," Daily Mirror (London), March 20, 2021, www.mirror.co.uk /news/us-news/atlanta-shooting-survivor-handcuffed-two-23763025.

24. Kamila Daza, "En Exclusiva: Hispano que sobrevivió a la masacre en Atlanta relata cómo le mataron a su esposa," Mundo Hispánico, first published March 20, 2021, updated March 22, 2021, https://mundohispanico.com/hispano-sobrevive -masacre-atlanta-spa/2/; and Kim Bellware and Paulina Villegas, "An Atlanta Victim's Husband Survived the Attack, but Police Detained and Handcuffed Him for Hours," Washington Post, March 22, 2021, www.washingtonpost.com/nation/2021 /03/22/mario-gonzalez-atlanta-spa-shootings/.

25. Grace Lee Boggs and Angela Davis, "American Revolutionary: On Revolution at Berkeley," PBS video, June 29, 2014, www.pbs.org/video/pov-american -revolutionary-revolution-berkeley/.

26. Hyejin Shim, speech at the post-Atlanta shooting community vigil in San Francisco Chinatown, March 20, 2021.

27. Mia Mingus, "Transformative Justice: A Brief Description," Transform Harm, accessed May 17, 2021, https://transformharm.org/transformative-justice-a -brief-description/.

28. Mingus, "Transformative Justice: A Brief Description."

29. Ruth Wilson Gilmore, "Ruth Wilson Gilmore makes the case for abolition," interview with Intercept, June 10, 2020, https://theintercept.com/2020/06/10/ruth -wilson-gilmore-makes-the-case-for-abolition/.

30. John Grisham, "Why the Innocent End Up in Prison," Chicago Tribune, March 14, 2018, www.chicagotribune.com/opinion/commentary/ct-perspec-innocent -prisoners-innocence-project-death-row-dna-testing-prosecutors-0315-story .html.

31. "Highest to Lowest—Prison Population Total," World Prison Brief, www .prisonstudies.org/highest-to-lowest/prison-population-total.

32. Angela Y. Davis, "Why Arguments Against Abolition Inevitably Fail," Abolition for the People, October 6, 2020, https://level.medium.com/why-arguments -against-abolition-inevitably-fail-991342b8d042.

33. "M.H.First Oakland," Anti Police-Terror Project, accessed May 17, 2021, www.antipoliceterrorproject.org/mh-first-oakland.

34. "Don't Call the Police," accessed May 17, 2021, https://dontcallthepolice.com/.

35. Eda Yu, "Public Safety for Asian Americans Starts with Nurturing Our Communities," KQED, April 26, 2021, www.kqed.org/arts/13896306/public-safety -for-asian-americans-starts-with-nurturing-our-communities.

36. Stop AAPI Hate, accessed May 17, 2021, https://stopaapihate.org/.

37. Jenny Wang, PhD (@asiansformentalhealth), Instagram page, www.insta gram.com/asiansformentalhealth/.

38. Annie Sciacca, "Oakland Mayor's Proposed Budget Increases Police Spending," *East Bay Times* (Walnut Creek, CA), May 11, 2021, www.eastbaytimes.com /2021/05/11/oakland-mayors-proposed-budget-increases-police-spending/.

39. Katherine Fung, "Oakland Mayor Blames Crime Wave Against Asians on Defunded Police; Black and Asian Activists Disagree," *Newsweek*, February 11, 2021, www.newsweek.com/black-asian-communities-fed-being-pitted-against-each -other-city-officials-1568410.

40. Libby Schaaf (@LibbySchaaf), "The rise of anti-Asian violence is reprehensible," tweet and video, March 25, 2021, https://twitter.com/libbyschaaf/status/13751 61070126387202?lang=en.

41. Boggs and Davis, "American Revolutionary."

14. OWN YOUR SPACE

1. Mariame Kaba, "Capitalism Rations What We Most Need—Let's Demand Medicare for All: A Conversation with Mariame Kaba," interview with Truthout, January 13, 2017, https://truthout.org/articles/capitalism-rations-what-we-most -need-let-s-organize-for-universal-medicare-a-conversation-with-mariame-kaba/.

2. Audre Lorde, "The Master's Tools Will Never Dismantle the Master's House," in *Sister Outsider: Essays and Speeches* (Berkeley, CA: Crossing Press, 1984), 110–114.

3. Angela Davis, "Angela Davis talk at SIUC on Feb. 13, 2014," Southern Illinois University, YouTube video, 56:45, February 16, 2014, published by James Anderson, www.youtube.com/watch?v=6s8QCucFADc&t=2316s.

4. Project Implicit, Harvard University, accessed May 17, 2021, https://implicit .harvard.edu/implicit/.

5. Mason D. Burns, Margo Monteith, and Laura Parker, "Training Away Bias: The Differential Effects of Counterstereotype Training and Self-regulation on Ste-

reotype Activation and Application," *Journal of Experimental Social Psychology* 73 (November 2017): 97–110, https://doi.org/10.1016/j.jesp.2017.06.003.

6. Joan C. Williams and Marina Multhaup, "For Women and Minorities to Get Ahead, Managers Must Assign Work Fairly," March 5, 2018, https://hbr.org/2018/03 /for-women-and-minorities-to-get-ahead-managers-must-assign-work-fairly.

7. Lorde, "Learning from the 60s," in *Sister Outsider*, 134–144.

15. FIND JOY IN COMMUNITY

1. Janaya Khan, "From Homelessness & Obscurity to the Future's Brightest Light: Non-Binary Activist Janaya Khan," February 4, 2021, YouTube video, 15:25, published by StyleLikeU, www.youtube.com/watch?v=7vmpxcq_XZg.

2. Grace Lee Boggs, *The Next American Revolution* (Berkeley: University of California Press, 2012).

3. adrienne maree brown, *Emergent Strategy: Shaping Change, Changing Worlds* (Chico, CA: AK Press, 2017).

4. brown, *Emergent Strategy*.

5. Prentis Hemphill, accessed May 18, 2021, https://prentishemphill.com/.

6. Asian American Leaders Table, "AAPIs Rising," www.AAPIsRising.org, June 1, 2021, YouTube video, 5:23, https://youtu.be/_M5kzr4oUf8.

7. Angela Davis and Erika Huggins, "Teaching as a Tool for Change," Artspace New Haven, September 9, 2020, Facebook video, 57:40, www.facebook.com/art spacenh/videos/3565371523473184.

8. Audre Lorde, "Eye to Eye," in *Sister Outsider: Essays and Speeches* (Berkeley, CA: Crossing Press, 1984).

9. Ericka Huggins, 32nd Annual Empowering Womxn of Color Conference: Unbound and Unboxed, March 18, 2017, https://ewocc.files.wordpress.com/2017/03 /programme2017_v2_hq_final.pdf.

10. Ericka Huggins, "Spiritual Activism and Social Justice," Central Oregon Community College, April 9, 2020, YouTube video, 1:16:24, https://youtu.be/5wx -gh_Ektw.

INDEX

ABOUT THE AUTHOR

Andria Lo

Michelle MiJung Kim (she/her) is a queer immigrant Korean American woman writer, speaker, activist, and entrepreneur. She is CEO and cofounder of Awaken, a leading provider of interactive equity and inclusion education programs facilitated by majority people of color educators, where she has consulted hundreds of organizations and top executives across various industries, from technology to nonprofits to government agencies to universities. As a lifelong social justice advocate, Michelle has served on a variety of organizations such as the San Francisco LGBTQ Speakers Bureau, San Francisco Human Rights Commission's Advisory Committee, LYRIC nonprofit's Board of Directors, and Build Tech We Trust Coalition. Michelle currently serves on the board of Asian Americans for Civil Rights and Equality (AACRE). Her work has appeared on platforms such as *Harvard Business Review*, *Forbes*, the *New York Times*, and NPR, and she has been named Medium's Top Writer in Diversity three years in a row. Michelle lives in Oakland, California.